WESTERN PRIVILEGE

 WORLDING THE MIDDLE EAST

Western Privilege

WORK, INTIMACY, AND POSTCOLONIAL HIERARCHIES IN DUBAI

Amélie Le Renard

STANFORD UNIVERSITY PRESS

STANFORD, CALIFORNIA

STANFORD UNIVERSITY PRESS
Stanford, California

English translation of a revised edition © 2021 by the Board of Trustees of the Leland Stanford Junior University. All rights reserved.

A previous version of this work was published in French in 2019 under the title *Le privilège occidental: Travail, intimité et hiérarchies postcoloniales à Dubaï* [Western Privilege: Work, Intimacy, and Postcolonial Hierarchies in Dubai] © 2019, Presses de la Fondation nationale des sciences politiques.

No part of this book may be reproduced or transmitted in any form or by any means, electronic or mechanical, including photocopying and recording, or in any information storage or retrieval system without the prior written permission of Stanford University Press.

Printed in the United States of America on acid-free, archival-quality paper

Library of Congress Cataloging-in-Publication Data
Names: Le Renard, Amélie, author.
Title: Western privilege : work, intimacy and postcolonial hierarchies in Dubai / Amélie Le Renard.
Other titles: Privilège occidental. English | Worlding the Middle East.
Description: Stanford, California : Stanford University Press, 2021. | Series: Worlding the Middle East | "A previous version of this work was published in French in 2019 under the title Le privilège occidental : travail, intimité et hiérarchies postcoloniales à Dubaï." | Includes bibliographical references and index.
Identifiers: LCCN 2021018470 (print) | LCCN 2021018471 (ebook) |
    ISBN 9781503613843 (cloth) | ISBN 9781503629233 (paperback) |
    ISBN 9781503629240 (epub)
Subjects: LCSH: Foreign workers—United Arab Emirates—Dubayy (Emirate)—
    Social conditions—21st century. | Whites—United Arab Emirates—Dubayy
    (Emirate)—Social conditions—21st century. | Whites—Race identity—United
    Arab Emirates—Dubayy (Emirate) | Dubayy (United Arab Emirates : Emirate)—
    Emigration and immigration—Social aspects. | Dubayy (United Arab Emirates :
    Emirate)—Emigration and immigration—Economic aspects. | Dubayy (United
    Arab Emirates : Emirate)—Race relations.
Classification: LCC HD8666 . L4713 2021 (print) | LCC HD8666 (ebook) |
    DDC 331.6/2121095357—dc23
LC record available at https://lccn.loc.gov/2021018470
LC ebook record available at https://lccn.loc.gov/2021018471

Cover art and design: "The Greens," © Clare Napper | highlife-dubai.com
Text design: Kevin Barrett Kane
Typeset at Stanford University Press in 11/14 Arno Pro

Contents

Acknowledgments

First of all, may I thank all those who entrusted me with their personal stories or facilitated the work I did in Dubai. They confided episodes of their lives and engaged me in thought-provoking discussions. I hope to get the chance to interact together again around this book.

Deep gratitude also to Sylvie Tissot for overseeing the long process that eventually resulted in this book. I greatly benefitted from her constructive criticism and our inspiring conversations around the topics our work shares in common. Further thanks to Catherine Achin, Marylène Lieber, Catherine Marry, Patrick Simon, and Neha Vora for their participation at the public presentation for the "habilitation" and for their helpful comments on the early draft that greatly improved the final version. My ongoing exchanges with Ahmed Kanna and Neha Vora in view of our joint book project *Beyond Exception* (published in 2020) have provided much nourishment for the present work. This book owes much to our discussions and common elaborations! Thanks also to Laetitia Bucaille for her support of the initial book project and her enlightening feedback and to Paola Bacchetta for her invitation to Berkeley, which enabled me to delve more deeply into issues of gender, class, race, and sexuality.

Warm thanks to all those who read all or part of my draft at various stages of production and who encouraged me to persist in taking my research into somewhat uncustomary territory: Laure Bereni, Sébastien Chauvin, Claire Cosquer, Bintou Dembele, Karine Duplan, Abir Kréfa, Soline

Laplanche-Servigne, Nasima Moujoud, Myriam Paris, Sophie Pochic, Cha Prieur, Sertaç Sehlikoglu, and Mira Younes.

My incentive to pursue research and to write owes much to some formal and informal collectives. Thanks firstly to our research team Interlocked Social Hierarchies: Gender, Class, Race at the Centre Maurice Halbwachs (CMH). The Global Gender project also provided a stimulating space for sharing; special thanks to Ioana Cirstocea and Delphine Lacombe for this collaboration. I greatly benefitted from lively exchanges with Elisabeth Marteu, Alexandre Jaunait, Myriam Paris, and Lila Belkacem around the intersectionality of gender, sexuality, nation, and race. Thanks finally to the Gender and Neo-orientalism group, the editorial board of *Genre, Sexualité et Société*, the Collaborative Institute on Migration, and the teacher/student community of the Master's in Gender Studies at EHESS for so many stimulating and inspiring discussions.

Many thanks to all those who made my fieldwork possible via the Global Gender project, the TEPSIS Laboratory of Excellence, and the Centre Maurice Halbwachs, especially Patrick Michel for backing this project, as well as Solenne Bertrand, Arlette Mollet, and Isabelle Sylvestre for their collaboration in organizing the various trips that made my fieldwork possible. Thanks to Lucile Grüntz for time spent together on my first research trip to Dubai in 2012, and to A.M., L.A., R. A., and S. O. for great moments and precious conversations in Abu Dhabi. And thanks to Claire Beaugrand, Pascal Ménoret, and Roman Stadnicki for co-organizing the conference at New York University Abu Dhabi in 2012 that enabled me to begin my fieldwork.

The translation of the book into English has been a relatively fluid process, thanks to several people that made it possible. First, I would like to thank Kate Wahl for her enthusiasm for this project from its very beginning and for her responsiveness and highly valuable suggestions. Thanks a lot to reviewers who made very useful comments and suggested additional references, which helped me strengthen my argument in the English version of the book. Thanks to Pardis Mahdavi for being so enthusiastic. The translation would not have been possible without funding, and I thank the TEPSIS Laboratory of Excellence, again, for agreeing to finance translation. Jane Kuntz has been a wonderful translator, making the book possibly easier to read in English than in French; I am very grateful for her work. I also thank the Stanford University Press team for their work on my book in a very difficult period for all of us, and especially copyeditor Barbara Armentrout for explaining all of her edits, which made me learn a lot about English writing!

And finally, for countless inspiring conversations around the topics of this book, my deepest thanks to Bintou; and my deepest thanks also to my friends, especially Cha, Malo, Marie-Laure, Mira, Myriam, Nabou, and Yasmine, for being here in these challenging years.

This book is dedicated to N. L. D.

WESTERN PRIVILEGE

INTRODUCTION

EVERY YEAR IN DUBAI, the local French community holds a *dîner en blanc,*
a "white dinner," in a prestigious venue that is kept secret until the day before.
The guests must come dressed in white and bring white food to share. Although the idea for this white dinner came from a similar event held in Paris,
it takes on a special significance within the context of Dubai. Historically, the
white clothing worn by settlers in certain colonies served as a status marker
in that it distanced them from dirty work.[1] In the Emirates today, as in other
Gulf States, it is the male nationals who dress in white. At the Dubai white
dinner, most guests, though not all, are fair-skinned, and all belong to a hand-
picked elite. On this occasion, the sophistication so often ascribed to them is
on full display.

At the heart of major financial, commercial, and migratory networks, the
city-emirate of Dubai, 90 percent of whose inhabitants are not of Emirati nationality, is a strategic site of inquiry into reconfigurations of social hierarchy
at a global scale. Its labor laws are tailored to neoliberal ideology: the state has
deregulated trade and created free zones, while at the same time maintaining
control over the country's resources, population, and sovereignty.[2] My book
takes a close look at this hub city of postcolonial globalization, with a focus
on the transformations of Western hegemony and whiteness through the experiences and trajectories of residents holding so-called Western passports,
who typically occupy socially advantageous positions.

The expression *Western passport* might seem surprising. The West is not a country. And yet, having or not having a Western passport produces a clear split at the global level. It can take a variety of forms, which is why a scaled study of an urban society like Dubai is of such interest. People there use the term "Western passport" as a matter of course, for it refers to a difference in status. A Western passport allows access to considerable advantages. It facilitates passage across national borders and represents an important differentiator and ranking criterion within the globalized job market. Constructed by these advantages, the status of Westerner is also invested with meaning both by those who relate to it and by those who use the term to describe others. In Dubai, Westerners constitute a social group designated as such, whose members share the experience of being structurally privileged. Their advantageous position is often deemed legitimate not only by the group itself but also by some of those who are not included. The job market is heavily segmented among nationalities, often grouped into larger entities with fluid boundaries: people in Dubai routinely talk about "Westerners," "Arabs," and "Asians." *Western* thus constitutes a local category constructed by structural advantages and representations, but it is also an unstable one, in part because a portion of Dubai's upper-class inhabitants have two nationalities, one of which is Western.

In this book, I will be suggesting that we think about how Westerners are constructed as a dominant group in Dubai from a feminist postcolonial perspective that will attend to both professional practices and intimate settings. This approach allows me to highlight transformations and reproduction of hierarchies that interlock race, nationality, gender, and sexuality. Building on numerous works in the social sciences, I will be considering race as a social construct achieved through a process of categorization, ranking, and othering based on characteristics perceived as natural or inherited. This construct varies depending upon sociohistorical configurations, and it delineates categories and groups whose boundaries are unstable and blurred. The construct of Westerners in Dubai points to transformations of race, class, and nationality as social hierarchies that extend beyond the city. In the former British protectorate, now a "city-corporation,"[3] Westernness and whiteness have become selling points for the brand of Dubai as a crossroads of globalization. This configuration produces particular forms of racialization, involving both advantages and stereotypes with regard to persons perceived as white and/or Western.

A SOCIOLOGICAL PERSPECTIVE ON WESTERN HEGEMONY

The term *Western* continues to be used in some social science circles as a self-evident category. Countless studies speak of "Western democracies" or "Western societies" without questioning this partitioning of the world. Others demarcate the West as a very special zone about which one might easily generalize. However, the use of the term *Western* is by no means innocuous. The creation of the West as a thought category is linked to colonial history and to the determination of an Other, the East, or, more recently, the Third World.[4] The persistent, routine use of *the West* as a category indicates the power of a colonial worldview that occludes the analysis of social hierarchies on a transnational or global scale. As Stuart Hall has pointed out, *the West* is a fungible term: it designates a category of country, an imaginary, a standard, a criterion for evaluating other societies, and therefore, an ideology. For this author, "if we use the discourse of 'the *West and the Rest*,' we will necessarily find ourselves speaking from a position that holds that the West is a superior civilization."[5] In a historical essay published in 2003 dealing with the notion of the West, Sophie Bessis analyzes the way in which, over the past five centuries, the West has been fantasized as a distinct and superior civilization, whose lineage has been reconstructed as descending directly from Greek and Latin culture. This reading implies the foreclosure of non-Christian sources, eclipsing a whole history of circulation across the shores of the Mediterranean. This long history results in "a shared Western tradition of viewing the Other with a sense of superiority [that] seems to transcend the particular national heritages and specific colonial cultures," according to the introduction to a journal issue devoted to postcolonial approaches to expatriation.[6]

Although the notion of the West has been questioned by authors interested in its historic construction and its discursive dimension,[7] few sociological studies have contextualized its use.[8] It was after sketching out my thoughts on this subject in Saudi Arabia[9] that I traveled to Dubai for the first time in 2012. The word *Western*, in Riyadh as in Dubai, is used routinely and refers to a social group. Using the tools of sociology, my purpose here is to study the way this structurally privileged group has formed by analyzing which advantages and identifications have constructed the status of Westerner in a formerly colonized city and how this status intersects with positions of class, gender, race, and, in particular, whiteness.

I will approach the subject from a postcolonial perspective, in the sense of an epistemological break (not of periodization), as defined by Sara Ahmed[10]: it is about rethinking how colonialism, at various periods, permeated

> all aspects of social life, in the colonized and colonizing nations. It is hence about the complexity of the relationship between the past and present, between the histories of European colonization and contemporary forms of globalization. That complexity cannot be reduced by either a notion that the present has broken from the past (a narrative that assumes that decolonization meant the end of colonialism) or that the present is simply continuous with the past (a narrative that assumes colonialism is a trans-historical phenomenon that is not affected by local contexts or other forms of social change).

The Gulf countries have only recently been addressed from that angle: in that regard, this book falls within the scope of what might be termed a postcolonial turn in studies of the Arabian Peninsula. In the region, the issue of imperialism had for a long while been underestimated, even unaddressed.[11] Yet, some of the Gulf Cooperation Council countries were first of all British protectorates. The territories that today make up the United Arab Emirates (UAE), the federal state to which Dubai belongs, became independent only in 1971, making their colonial past a relatively recent one. Independence failed to bring about a change in leadership: the same ruling families remained in power, at the head of more or less repressive regimes, all allied with the former colonial power and, more broadly, with Europe and North America. For several decades, the Gulf has been a hub where goods, people, and capital circulate, and it represents a key for understanding the modalities of current economic globalization.[12] Rather than a phantasmagorical stage of hyper-capitalism, an embodiment of the worst possible future scenario,[13] urban Dubai society, singular but in no way exceptional, is shaped by non-egalitarian flows very much in step with today's globalized world. It represents a trade hub and production center where highly qualified personnel mingle with the far vaster numbers of those who serve them.[14] Dubai is perpetually under construction, a boom city that the soaring oil revenues of the 1970s in the region dramatically transformed. Since then, the government has adopted a strategy of economic diversification. The city has been built and expanded by hundreds of thousands of workers, notably from Nepal, Sri Lanka, Bangladesh, India, and Pakistan, a trend that continues to this day. The vast majority of the population is foreign, a result not only of migratory flows but also of the difficulty, or for some, the impossibility of obtaining Emirati nationality, including those who were born in Dubai and have lived there for their entire lives. In this context, the passport, beyond separating national from nonnational, plays a key role when it comes to social hierarchies and racialization. The social structure of Dubai cannot be understood unless one takes into account the hierarchy of passports and its link to coloniality, understood as the hierarchy among various zones in the world directly resulting from colonization.[15] The construction of skills as something typically Western has everything to do with coloniality.

Interesting in and of itself, the case of Dubai also serves as an eye-opening microcosm of the staggering inequality of work conditions across the globe. As I was able to observe throughout my investigation, it is a prime location for people to take stock of their place in society and the world: since the vast majority have to leave their home countries to come work in Dubai, they are likely to denature the social order of this high-turnover city, while at the same time seeking to differentiate themselves from it—I shall come back to that point. I am interested here not only in the advantageous construction of Western status but also in the way those who benefit from it experience the change of social status subsequent to their move to Dubai as compared with their previous position. I see this status as multidimensional: the issue of class overlaps with nation and race in a world marked by coloniality, as well as with gender in a world where distinction and hierarchy among men and women are so pervasive. The adjective *social* refers here to the entanglement of all these dimensions and cannot be reduced to class alone.

SHARED STRUCTURAL ADVANTAGES

Western passport holders share certain structural advantages. Beyond the mere label, the term *Western* refers to a social hierarchy. Building on studies dealing with masculinity[16] and with race and whiteness,[17] my study looks at the way these structural advantages create the social group of Westerners. The term *structural advantage* allows me to analyze what affordances this passport provides to this group, promoting them, almost at the outset, to the middle and upper classes within this urban society, regardless of their initial class belonging.

Those who obtain this passport as a matter of course have something in common, what might be called "existential luck,"[18] as compared to others. The structural advantages it affords come with positive stereotypes that tend to legitimize this hierarchy. These stereotypes might be about Westerners in general or some specific nationality. In fact, the Westerner category, a kind of pan-national label, is deployed in Dubai as nonexclusive, alongside other categories—notably that of nationality. Because certain stereotypes attribute qualities to a set of persons defined by their assumed common provenance, in this case national or pan-national, they can produce a form of racialization in favor of the relevant persons. To understand how this advantageous status has been constructed, it matters that we understand the material underpinnings on which these representations are based. In Dubai, as in other contexts, nationalities have been historically racialized. Under the British protectorate, the authorities of the city-states that made up the "Trucial Coast" gradually came to endorse a non-inclusive definition of citizenship, strongly associated with Arabness. Concurrently, a number of oil companies brought over experts, mostly British or American nationals, to take the highest positions. Still, this process was limited and came late to Dubai, where fewer than four hundred British nationals were counted in 1968, a figure that has increased continuously, starting in the 1970s with the construction of infrastructure intended to make Dubai a key trade nexus.[19] The linkage between expertise, Westernness, and whiteness is revived and reinvented today through the hierarchies that structure the Dubai professional scene.

In majority white societies, white people tend to not perceive themselves as members of a specific racial group. Whiteness gets defined as the norm, an unnamed status, unmarked as such,[20] though such perception is limited to white people: nonwhite people do notice the whiteness of white people.[21] The status of Westerner, numerically in the minority in Dubai, differs greatly from whiteness in majority-white societies: first of all, Western passport owners do not see this status as neutral but name it explicitly, identify with it, and often associate it with a particular cultural content. This status overlaps with whiteness without being its exact equivalent. How do people with such a diverse range of trajectories inhabit such a privileged status? This process, as we shall see, implies class mobility, changes in affective and domestic life, and forms of racial reframing. The Western subjectivities such as they get constructed in Dubai via this process seem to me to "function as anchors and relay points for the exercise of ... power."[22]

The group of Westerners is bound together by their shared advantages while riven by hierarchies involving whiteness, class, gender, and sexuality. As my work in Dubai progressed, I found the intersection between Westernness and whiteness less obvious than I had imagined at the outset: these two statuses only partially overlap. In other words, Western is not necessarily synonymous with white in Westerners' imaginations nor in that of the people they come into contact with. The boundaries of Westernness as a status are blurry, porous, and shifting. The field of study that deals with expatriation and privileged migration, with a focus on the migration of persons coming from so-called Western countries, has shed invaluable light on whiteness.[23] Some of the results presented here resonate with previous works on white residents in Dubai and in other global cities (and former British colonies), such as Singapore and Hong Kong.[24] While building on this foundation, the originality of my work consists in comparing the experiences, practices, and discourses of white and nonwhite Western passport holders residing in Dubai, where previous studies of privileged migrations have most often focused on whites.[25] By systematically contrasting the experiences of white and nonwhite Western passport holders, I was able to identify the specificity of whiteness as a privileged status among Western passport holders and to make visible the trajectories of nonwhite Western passport holders who benefit, to a lesser extent, from Western privilege while also facing forms of stigmatization and marginalization. Beyond this, the similarities and contrasts between the two groups reveal how Dubai's neoliberal discourse on multiculturalism, combined with the use of whiteness in the city's branding, impacts racial categories and produces conditional and limited inclusions. Such reflection echoes works on neoliberalism, multiculturalism, and selective inclusions in other contexts, especially the United States and some European countries.[26]

Beyond white subjectivities in a migration setting, a topic dealt with by various studies on expatriation—which only scarcely analyze what white positions reveal about the context of the relocation—this book aims to shed light on how Westerners have participated in Dubai's social order as residents who make up a portion of its middle and upper classes. Countering the notion that these people are just passing through, living temporarily in transnational spaces,[27] my study demonstrates that, despite their migrant status and their unfamiliarity with Dubai society, some of these persons quickly move into dominant positions through which they contribute to shaping local social hierarchies. In other words, they are stakeholders in Dubai's social order: I deconstruct the discourse presenting Westerners in the Arabian Peninsula as outsiders, having no role in the perpetuation of inequality. This belief is central, I argue, to the construction of their privileged subjectivities.

Studying how Westerners have coalesced into a dominant group prompts us to rethink certain reconfigurations of class and race in a world marked by coloniality and neoliberalism, thereby refreshing the way we look at social hierarchies generally approached from different angles. Until very recently, studies carried out on the Gulf nations, by focusing mostly on subaltern groups, have tended to render invisible the position of Westerners in these societies.[28] By analyzing how the social group of these privileged individuals comes into being, my book sheds new light on the urban societies of the Gulf and also examines the transnational transformations of social hierarchies.

LABOR DIVISION, INTIMACY, AND THE CONSTRUCTION OF WESTERNNESS

Both their positions within the job market and their personal lifestyle patterns have tended to construct Westerners as a distinct group. The advantages they enjoy in the job market constitute a central component in the construction of their social position. But the legal dependence of some persons with regard to others, as wives most notably, has proven to be an equally structuring aspect; it shapes a vision of intimacy vested as a source of distinction. In this book, I analyze how the group gets constructed in professional spaces as well as in domestic and leisure settings and through a particular overlapping of gender, class, race, nationality, and sexuality. Job market and private life are merged by an empirical approach that links the material and subjective dimensions to better highlight the overlapping social hierarchies.

This approach draws inspiration from various feminist works. The choice to link labor and intimacy has long been at the core of intersectional approaches that have sought to interconnect gender, class, and race, as well as transnational feminism, which prompts us to think of social hierarchies outside the confines of national borders.[29] Work, whether paid or unpaid, has historically been a locus for constructing social hierarchies of gender, class, and race for workers at the lowest rung of the social ladder as well as for those at the top. Whiteness in particular has been constructed through division of labor, shaped by slavery and various phases of colonization, and gets recast today via the hierarchies that structure the way work is organized.[30] Yet, it is rarely addressed by studies devoted to professional transnational mobility.

Work organizations construct the status of Westerner through such components as salaries, contracts, careers, management styles, and job segmentation. Intersectional approaches in the sociology of organizations deployed by Joan Acker[31] and Evangelina Holvino[32] have analyzed the way work organizations contribute to constructing hierarchies of gender, class, and race by placing demands on salaried personnel, easier for some to meet than for others, or through hiring and promotion mechanisms, or salary differentials, to name just a few examples. Holvino[33] suggests spotlighting the role of organizations in the production of hierarchies among nationalities and sexualities. Building on this work, my book analyzes the way work organizations construct the status of Westerner by asking the following questions: What are the structural advantages afforded to Western passport holders and how are these advantages modulated according to their position in gender, class, and racial hierarchies? What does this status involve in terms of embodiment and self-presentation? How does this distinctive construct of Westernness shape hierarchies beyond the professional sphere? When it comes to people in high-ranking jobs, such issues have not been widely developed by the sociology of work and organizations. For instance, discussions about qualifications and skill levels have rarely linked the ranking of diplomas to the place where they were obtained or to the presumption of skill sets among people of a certain national origin, real or assumed, apart from the countless studies of the ethnicization of labor, which deal mainly with categories of low-paid jobs.

By approaching the professional world of Dubai from this perspective, I was faced with dividing lines of inclusion and exclusion that did not always match up, or at least not automatically, with the border between whiteness and nonwhiteness. In this regard, my thought process was sparked by analyses of the ways in which race and class hierarchies have been rearranged by neoliberalism. According to Aihwa Ong,[34] based on various cases in East Asia, neoliberalism favors graduates of American universities, "educated, multilingual and self-reflexive," or what she terms "flexible citizens."[35] Jodi

Melamed claims that neoliberal multiculturalism in the United States transformed the process of racialization throughout the 2000s: neoliberalism, she believes, has given rise to a distinction among worthy multicultural citizens and the unworthy, excludable on the basis of their monoculturalism, inflexibility, deviance, or criminality.[36] In other words, a boundary separates those who claim a hybrid binational, bicultural identity and who, under certain conditions, could be included in the middle and upper classes from those cast into a single subaltern status and whose exclusion from advantageous positions will persist.

These analyses, carried out in a variety of contexts, resonate with my own investigation in Dubai, a country often seen as one of the world capitals of neoliberalism and marked by a recent colonial past. While whiteness is a distinctive status there, Westernness as a privileged status tends to match, without totally overlapping. In Dubai, nonwhite Western passport holders do benefit from structural advantages and can be included in a hegemonic group. Still, in certain circumstances, they are relegated to their nonwhiteness and hence excluded from certain places, milieus, or professional positions. Their membership in an advantaged group, therefore, is never absolute and can be considered as much a promise as a reality.[37] Admittedly, forms of hybridity and diversity are celebrated in Dubai, as proclaimed on the city's official website: "Dubai is a melting pot of East and West. The city boasts influences from all corners of the globe, thereby offering its residents a glimpse of nearly all cultures via its restaurants and shops, and through its daily living." This celebration of a peaceful melting pot, happy and consumer-oriented, coexists nevertheless with a valuing of whiteness and the corresponding devaluing of other racial positions. The aim therefore is to scrutinize the unstable boundaries of racial categorizations prevalent in Dubai and how they overlap with class, while casting a critical eye on the "promises of inclusion," their counterparts and their corollaries in terms of exclusion.[38] This approach makes it possible to analyze the reconfigurations at work without idealizing the forms of inclusion that remain circumscribed, selective, and precarious.

Race historically has been constructed as much by work as by forms of hierarchy in the intimate sphere, in matters of family and reproduction, which are in fact inseparable dimensions.[39] The notion of intimacy refers to physical proximity, domestic arrangements, and affective economies that go beyond the notion of sexuality. It allows for an approach to various aspects of affective and/or domestic life: the kinds of relationships that one enters into—notably, matrimonial, sexual, or friendship-based; the people one lives with; the way one raises children.[40] Whether or not one identifies with a model of heterosexuality or lives in a couple or alone; in a rent-sharing arrangement, a dormitory, or a workers' camp; with a live-in maid or at the home of one's employer; with or without children—whether or not one is recognized as their parent—these are all structuring dimensions of intimacy that social norms valorize or devalue. The term *intimacy* also refers to a range of affects.[41] The way people cultivate forms of affective proximity or distance with others is of particular interest in my inquiry, inspired by certain queer postcolonial approaches, and has informed this book.[42]

The questions I ask are therefore the following: Who lives with whom? Who interacts with whom? Who arouses mistrust or aversion? How does affective distance get created despite spatial proximity? And conversely, which affective proximities are considered desirable, respectable? These questions are essential when it comes to establishing social boundaries, questions that combine class, race, and gender dimensions. Such understandings of sexuality and intimacy highlight Westerners' distinctive heteronormativity, which is involved in how they form as a group and distance themselves from those they consider radically other and categorize as deviant. Paradoxically, although heteronormativity is based on the centrality of the heterosexual couple with its strict differentiation and division of men's and women's roles and, more generally, its binary, hierarchical vision of the male/female divide, we shall see that this view goes hand in hand with discourses associating the West with egalitarian relations.

Even though professional work and intimacy are generally treated separately in the interest of clarity, these two dimensions are always linked. For instance, the life of Western residents outside the professional world is a core concern for the work of non-Western residents, such as nannies and maids, who live in their employers' homes. Work status impacts the forms of intimacy to be adopted, since only a salary beyond a certain threshold gives the right to sponsor "dependents" (possibly spouse, children). Beyond the issue of sponsorship, the close control of low-paid workers, their housing conditions, and the absence of public goods for foreign children (especially schools and healthcare) make it almost impossible for them to bring up children in Dubai. On the other hand, certain forms of intimate life affect the professional position: a married woman raising children frequently meets discrimination in the job market. Throughout my discussion, I will also be dealing with forms of emotional, corporeal, and moral work that are involved in both professional relations and intimacy.

The connection between professional work and intimacy in the Arabian Peninsula is grounded in the history of industrial imperialism. Apart from unequivocal vertical job partitioning, industrial imperialism also affected hierarchies within the private sphere: in Saudi Arabia, only the American employees of Aramco, then a US oil company, upon completion of a certain period with the company, had the right to "bring over" a spouse and live "as a family" in one of the large air-conditioned villas set aside for them, unlike Saudi workers, who were housed as "single men" in dormitories with metal roofs, crushed by the heat.[43] There is no equivalent study for the British companies on the Gulf coast, which notably leaned toward employing the Indian subjects of the British Empire. However, reports from the Kuwait Oil Company pointed out that most Indian workers lived in prefab housing that lacked proper facilities for washing or cooking, fourteen men occupying a space intended for ten.[44] In other words, the right to (heteronormative) family life was used as a tool for differentiating among salaried employees. Though this history of the oil industry does not directly concern Dubai, the link between professional, national, and racial hierarchies and the differentiation of intimacies does structure the current neoliberal biopolitics. With regard to foreign residents, as we shall see in chapter 4, this biopolitics does not aim to encourage reproduction and demographic growth but to maximize profit to be made from these lives. To achieve this, a hierarchy of intimacies is established. This would explain why the city is perceived as particularly family-friendly by many Westerners, while everything is done to dissuade people with low-paid jobs and no Western passport from having children in Dubai.

FIELD RESEARCH IN A CORPORATE CITY

My fieldwork was conducted mainly during three one-month stays, between which I also did some interviews in France, in person or over Skype, and followed French-language groups on Facebook. The interviews, conducted mostly with Western passport holders, lasted from one to three hours and covered their professional work experiences, affective relations, leisure, and home life in Dubai. They did not bear on identity as such, which would have led to asking overt questions about what it means to be Western in Dubai. They are narratives about what it's like to move abroad and live in a new place, stories that reveal how these individuals position themselves in the Dubai social order and legitimize or question the advantages they enjoy.

I took on Dubai at a particular moment in my research itinerary. After a doctoral dissertation devoted to the lifestyles of young Saudi women in Riyadh, work that drew on feminist postcolonial approaches to gender in the Middle East,[45] I analyzed the discourses of some Western male managers that I had met in Riyadh and how they impacted the hierarchies of gender, class, and nationality at a multinational bank,[46] before I switched fieldwork sites. In the first place, my interest in Western residents in the Arabian Peninsula resulted from both a willingness to analyze their roles and the impacts of their stereotypical discourses, following my disconcerting encounters with them in Riyadh, and a need to question my own position as a white researcher and part-time resident there, trained to be an "expert" about the region.[47] The heterogeneous nature of the population I encountered in Dubai during my first visit convinced me that this would be an interesting place to study how Westernness and whiteness get recombined, despite certain obstacles: an extremely high cost of living, difficulties in penetrating the corporate world, and my unease in spaces intended for and frequented by Western residents—an unease that hindered a long-term ethnography but that I leverage in my analysis.

In the course of these stays, I came up against problems I had not anticipated. For instance, my interviewees proved unfamiliar with social science, and the fact that I was not selling anything sometimes led to misapprehensions. Another obstacle involved the mode of relating to the middle and upper classes in this neoliberal corporate city, which shapes one's self-presentation to others. It proved at times difficult to get beyond a too-smooth register: certain interlocutors unconsciously adopted an attitude typically expected during a job interview, which consists of presenting one's choices in a positive manner, putting one's best foot forward. In most exchanges, however, I was able to set a more sincere self-narrative register. Many said they were tired of Dubai, frequently complaining about the alleged "superficiality" of its inhabitants, a critique that sets them apart.

A problem of a different order was the reluctance of management-level employees to open their organization's doors to me. It was only after many fruitless attempts and by dint of sheer persistence that I managed to gain access to two companies, which I call here Hotel A and Startup Z. For that, I got the consent of individuals who had nothing at risk since they were the owners or co-owners of the company. All my other attempts with people who were senior-level but not at the very top proved unsuccessful.

During my first two stays (2012–2013), I conducted fifty-three interviews, mostly with individuals in jobs considered as high-skill, whom I was able to meet through my intermediary contacts. Given my research objective, I gave priority to residents holding Western passports (or two passports) and met residents with British, French, German, Belgian, US American, Canadian, Norwegian, Swiss, Italian, Austrian, and Australian nationalities. But I also interviewed Emirati citizens, male and female, as well as passport holders from other countries, such as India, Iran, Tunisia, Lebanon, the Philippines, Pakistan, Sudan, and Saudi Arabia, some of whom had spent most of their lives in the UAE. This enabled me to grasp the experiences specific to Western passport holders and to understand the way those who do not benefit from such a passport perceive the advantages of having one, an often critical stance suggesting that this privileged status is contested. Because the aim of this book is to center Western privilege, non-Western middle- and upper-class inhabitants' experiences are evoked but cannot be developed.[48]

Upon returning from my second stay, I decided to pursue my inquiry in France. So, I issued a first call for interviews on some Facebook groups that bring together French people living in Dubai, specifying that I wished to meet individuals who had lived for several years in that city. I conducted eight interviews with individuals recently returned from Dubai, either temporarily or permanently, and found some of them captivating. These people had achieved a greater distance in their assessment of life in Dubai and were more self-reflective when it came to their own career paths: I felt I had entered into the complexity of their life choices. I decided that, for the remainder of my fieldwork, I would focus on French nationals living in Dubai, with emphasis on the core issue of reconfigurations of class and race.

A few months later, I issued another call among the same Facebook groups to meet with French residents during my upcoming, and final, stay in Dubai, in early 2015. In five years, their numbers had doubled, and one hundred new French nationals were registering every month at the consulate. In the Emirates overall, the French numbered around 25,000 in 2015, the second largest European nationality after the British (120,000);[49] in Dubai, they numbered between 15,000 and 20,000, 75 percent of whom were under the age of 40.[50] My call for interviews received numerous responses, fortunately for me, from people of widely varying backgrounds, who held jobs in various fields and at all hierarchical levels in France before they came to Dubai. Compared with other Western passport holders in Dubai, the French are distinct in two noteworthy respects. On the one hand, these individuals have left behind the comfort of a state where they benefitted from considerable (though underfinanced and deteriorated) public infrastructure, such as low-cost social security, subsidized daycare, and cost-free schools, for a city shaped by neoliberal ideology, where public services are partly reserved for nationals only. This experience differs from the experience of US American nationals, for instance. On the other hand, the French nationals are introduced into a context where the impact of nationality on salary levels is accepted as a given and where simply being French carries a number of stereotypes with advantageous consequences, even though they have been socialized in a country that prides itself on an ideology of color blindness. In France, as in some other European societies (Germany, for instance), color blindness is matched by the shared belief that nonwhiteness means non-European. Nonwhiteness amounts to otherness and foreignness, while whiteness is considered the norm.[51] Put another way, a universalizing discourse that denies structural racism coexists with forms of discrimination and condescension toward people of color.[52] The French term *personnes racisées*, here translated as "people of color," refers to the experience of constantly being reminded of and reduced to one's supposedly pre-French "origins," with all the accompanying forms of discrimination and oppression. Unlike social contexts where the use of ethno-racial categories is welcome in the public sphere—in the United States, for example, where it gets declared in the national census, or in the United Kingdom—there is no agreement in France as to how to describe the various positions with regard to race.[53] This also influenced word choice during my interviews, as we shall see. Beyond these two characteristics of France, interviews with non-French Western passport holders led me to think that other nationalities' experiences are comparable, even if conducting a systematic comparison between two nationalities was beyond my possibilities.

In total, I interviewed 98 persons: 55 women and 43 men, 58 of them French nationals[54] and 40 of other nationalities, 19 of whom had a Western passport (5 of these in addition to another passport). In the course of my different stays, I was housed in studio apartments, hotels, and rooms rented from residents, which allowed me to share in the daily life, if only for a few days each, of an Indian family, a Libyan woman, two co-tenants—one Russian, the other Ukrainian—and finally, a French expat contract worker.

In 2019, I tried to find out what happened to the 58 French people that I had interviewed in Dubai between 2012 and 2015. I was able to speak to 17 of them (on the phone, for most of them) and found information regarding 28 more either from professional network websites, through mutual contacts, or by exchanging messages.[55] Out of the 45 individuals I was able to track down by 2019, 25 were still living in Dubai or the UAE, 11 had gone back to France, and 9 had moved to a different location (London, Casablanca, Tunis, Berlin, Montreal), two of whom moved after stopping over in Paris for professional training. In the meantime, the economic situation had deteriorated in Dubai, notably due to the fall in oil prices, and this had had an impact on nearly all the people I interviewed, mostly negative, except for three of them, whose companies and jobs were unaffected and who had taken advantage of lower real estate rates to move into spacious villas. The results of this particular set of interviews, which did not make it into the French version of this book, are developed here in chapter 7.

DIVERSE TRAJECTORIES

As studies on privileged migration have shown, migrants holding Western passports present a wide variety of profiles, life trajectories, career paths, and education,[56] and this holds true for the individuals I interviewed in Dubai. Two profile types stand out, however, among the Western passport holders who were raised in Western countries, and these persons are at the core of my study. These profiles differ from each other by virtue of both their professional positions and their lifestyles, though they do not represent the full picture of the lives observed, which are always more complex. I call the first profile "guest families," in the sense that these individuals fit the model family life made available to the well-to-do foreign residents of Dubai.[57] In this model, the man is under expatriate contract and therefore is not subject to Dubai's labor laws. Some of these men work for firms that organize the way their personnel move among the various subsidiaries of multinational corporations—petroleum, tobacco, or insurance, for example. Their job will often involve visits to a series of other countries. Others are sent by their company to Dubai to monitor operations there or to act as a bridge with corporate headquarters, notably in sectors such as information technology, logistics, and transport; in this case, it is often their first posting abroad. This expat contract impacts several other people: the spouse and children obtain visas as the man's dependents, which is not peculiar to Dubai. The contract comes with considerable material advantages that enable the family to adopt a lifestyle commensurate with that of the upper class. Among my sample, persons corresponding to this model or something approaching it were mainly white, coming from middle and upper classes. Among all these couples except one, it was the man who had the expatriate contract or a local contract whose advantages were modelled on an expatriate contract. These individuals were planning to stay in Dubai for only a few years, although some ended up living there for the long term.

The second profile, which one might sum up as "singles with local careers," is made up of younger individuals who set out on their own, with "single" migrant status, often right after graduating from university, coming mostly from working-class backgrounds, seeking professional success and upward social mobility. As these persons generally arrive in Dubai without jobs, they are looking for local contracts on site and are therefore unseen when it comes to studies on professional mobility—French studies in particular, which often focus on salaried personnel who accept an offer from their company to work in a foreign country. Most have university degrees, often in international business, marketing, finance, or communication. Many have never lived abroad. By pursuing careers locally or, more precisely, by working their way through various companies on local contracts, some of these individuals manage to rise quickly through the ranks. After their first year of jet-set clubbing and restaurant hopping, many complain about the superficiality of their relationships in the city.

For both profiles, the lifestyle in Dubai differs from how they lived back home, but the change is more pronounced, sometimes radically so, for those in the second category. The disparate situations brought to light by the interviews suggest that we might deconstruct a few popular misconceptions about migration, notably the oft-cited opposition between "migrant" and "expatriate." Not all persons coming from hegemonic countries to live and work in non-hegemonic countries belong to an elite, nor do they necessarily possess "international capital"—that is, speak English fluently, belong to transnational networks, frequently travel to various countries.[58] Among the persons I came across in Dubai, those who had arrived legally with an expatriate contract were in the minority. Most did not belong to the upper class and, depending on the case, had come to Dubai to look for work, to launch or speed up their careers, and to make some money, which they succeeded in doing to varying degrees. Their English skills were not always good when they first arrived, and several had to make a considerable effort to attain a satisfactory professional level in that language, the most widely used in the Dubai work world. In this group, among the French, many came from working-class backgrounds. The parents of several of them were born in Tunisia, Algeria, or Morocco and had been living for decades in various cities throughout France, where the father spent his whole life as a factory worker and the mother either also worked in a factory or in the childcare sector or just raised her own children. A few had parents from the Middle East, the Indian subcontinent, the Antilles, or sub-Saharan Africa. Some had one white parent and one nonwhite but were still constantly assumed to have non-French "origins" and experienced structural discrimination.

These two profiles partially correspond to certain concepts developed by privileged migration studies. Some research work speaks of expatriates. However, this term, in common parlance, contributes to the persistence of a dichotomy between "expatriates" (coming from the rich countries of the "North") and "migrants" (from countries in the "South"), which makes the use of such a term problematic for the social sciences. The term tends to naturalize Western and white privileges by making them invisible and presupposes a homogenous perception of "migrants" as opposed to "expatriates." For Catrin Lundström,[59] using the term *migrant* to refer to persons outside the stereotype (poor, coming from the South) makes it possible to rethink this stereotype more critically.[60] In research focused on labor migration, the choice of concepts is based on the professions of the subjects under consideration: the males of the "guest families" are said to correspond to "highly skilled migrants," whereas the single males belong to the "middling transnationals" category.[61] Still, the first category tends to obscure both college graduates from countries in the South working at jobs far beneath their qualifications and highly qualified women for whom migration means leaving behind a career in order to accommodate that of their husband.[62] My approach, which takes account of both intimacy and work, considers that these categories fall short. A critical approach to the opposition between skilled and unskilled jobs and individuals is developed throughout the book, since postcolonial hierarchies of countries and universities combined with gender, class, and race hierarchies define what is valued as "skills" on job markets all over the world. And finally, none of these individuals came under the category of life-style migrants (mostly retirees) who relocate in the hope of improving their quality of life rather than for professional reasons.[63] Above all else, they were "migrant workers," and, without a job, they would lose their residency card. Their professional and financial aspirations, however, do not account for all dimensions of their life choice: if these people remain in Dubai, it is also for the "quality of life" and the "sense of success" that the city offers, a reflection of their enhanced rank on the social ladder. Since I am particularly interested in Westerners as inhabitants of Dubai and their positions in the local job market and in this urban society, I will more often refer to them as residents. As other specialists of the Gulf region have shown,[64] the term *resident* rather than *migrant* helps us move beyond the ideology of these countries' governing officials, which considers all foreigners as "temporary workers," even though some were born and have spent their entire lives in the Emirates without obtaining nationality, the passport not necessarily corresponding to the place of birth. With regard to Westerners, the term *resident* also emphasizes the fact that these people are not merely passing through with no impact on the social order, but rather, that they do indeed occupy dominant positions.

AN EPISTEMOLOGY OF UNEASE

As noted by Catrin Lundström,[65] in order to study middle- and upper-class whites, it helps considerably to identify as a white woman and have the social status of an academic. The sociologist tells of her effort to *pass* among groups of heterosexual Swedish women who had moved to the United States by means of practices that incorporated respectable heterosexual femininity, shaped by gender subordination, structural advantages of being white, and membership in the middle or upper class. This effort included both body image practices, such as letting her hair grow longer, and behaviors, such as remaining silent when she completely disagreed with a statement someone had just made.

Lundström's analysis could in large part apply to certain elements of my experience with middle- and upper-class whites living in Dubai as couples with children. I tried to project a self-image as a respectable white woman, foregrounding my professional status, paying special attention to how I dressed and wore my hair. I also attempted somewhat successfully to revisit the rules of relaxed politeness, acquiescence, and silent listening that I had learned during my early upbringing as a girl from a white, bourgeois family in a mid-sized French town. And yet, although I refrained from any form of judgment, the mere fact of my asking questions may have led my interlocutors to reflect upon their own situation and position. This was sometimes the case when I would ask how much they earned, which I did systematically. Still, nothing I did could prevent my feeling out of place in the various environments I encountered: many of the situations I experienced throughout this study left me with an overwhelmingly persistent sense of unease.

I benefitted from my passport, which first of all allowed me to stay in the Emirates on a tourist visa delivered free of charge upon my arrival at the airport. Thereafter, being French proved to be an asset, both among other French residents and with regard to the social status that the latter enjoy in Dubai. The fact that I was perceived as French, Western, and French-speaking but also a specialist on matters concerning the Arabian Peninsula, having published two books on Saudi Arabia, earned me, by turns, the status of sharing something with the people I encountered and an enhanced credibility in their eyes. My having made the same trip they had was also a confidence-builder, even though I did observe a certain wariness in the statements made by many French nonwhite interviewees when it came to racism in France, a wariness that might stem both from my own position in the race spectrum and from the possible sociopolitical delegitimizing of such an interpretive framework in the French context.

Throughout the vast majority of the interviews, I got the feeling that the people had shared with me the salient features of their life choices, as well as their doubts and misgivings. Some divulged their stories with a kind of sincerity and/or self-reflectiveness about their itinerary that I found captivating and at times touching. But the interview format rarely moved toward a more informal interchange. The characteristics of this group of Westerners, to be analyzed in subsequent chapters, supply some clues as to why: the overriding utilitarian nature of social relations, the trouble I had fitting in since I did not belong to any company, my trouble conforming to the gender norms of the "proper appearance" that shape the boundaries of Westernness and whiteness, and my rather fleeting presence in a city where everything seemed to be all too ephemeral. I was rarely invited to take part in activities beyond the interviews, which I registered as a form of rejection. My nonconformity to the norms of these social settings made me an ideal confidant but not a worthwhile acquaintance to be introduced to a group of peers. The scarce times I was invited to have drinks in fancy bars, I felt out of sync, which is why my analysis of nightlife is mainly based on interviews, not on a rich ethnography: as an outsider to heterosexual dating, I was not the right person to conduct it.

If my moderately open-armed acceptance among the Western residents of Dubai was based partly upon my ability to deploy resources linked to my early upbringing and upon my professional status, this role did not square with my political convictions or my current way of life, which created a certain sense of unease. It took constant work to overcome this feeling, the kind of emotional labor that differs from the empathy required to conduct field research among individuals in difficult situations, a work modality in the social sciences that has received far more attention. Not only did I have to manage various degrees of animosity,[66] but I also had to deal with certain behavioral constraints required by my study.[67] Although, thanks to my upbringing and position on the race and gender spectrum, I was never to meet with the kind of rejection that others might have experienced, notably among middle- and upper-class whites,[68] my attempts at integrating the social scene of Westerners in Dubai were never devoid of a certain discomfort: I constantly felt I did not belong, that I was playing a role, except at certain relatively rare moments where I sensed a genuine exchange was taking place. Having little in common with the interviewees, not belonging to their bracket of Western middle and upper classes in Dubai, proved a useful leveraging factor for certain aspects of my analysis, such as the role of heteronormativity in constructing class and race boundaries.[69] But studying individuals in a face-to-face setting, from a minority position in certain respects, can be a lot to handle and requires a serious effort to reassure and to fight against negative feelings, extra labor added to the fatigue involved in any study, between negotiating the interviews in the first place and listening to extensive life narratives.

STEPPING BACK FROM EXCEPTIONALISM

At the time of writing, I was faced with another challenge: to resist the temptation to judge Dubai as being better or worse than any other city. The remarks I collected contain numerous value judgments about the city and its inhabitants but also various justifications for moving there. To the extent possible, I tried to treat these assessments and justifications as material to analyze without being swayed by them. This is all the more challenging in that the Gulf States are generally represented as somehow exceptional, whether by the people living there, through some academic work, or via media messaging. These representations depict them as immensely wealthy countries, ruled by emirs described as anything from uneducated latter-day slaveholders to visionary enlightened despots compared to their backward, conservative societies. While some of these representations conspicuously resonate with nineteenth-century orientalism, others update it for the present—for example, whenever the cities of the Gulf are seen as futuristic or viewed through the exceptionalist prism of Wahhabism or as annuitant oil states. In fact, the notion of exceptionalism encompasses all these contemporary representations whose common feature is to situate the Gulf countries in an absolute otherness, as we developed in a cowritten book with anthropologists Ahmed Kanna and Neha Vora.[70]

Discourses on Dubai as a "stage of capitalism" are also tinged with a moralism that depicts the city as a place somehow worse than elsewhere. Neha Vora writes, "The implicit message that migrants are treated worse in the Gulf reproduces a civilizational narrative about the Middle East while erasing the hardships many migrants face in Western countries,"[71] notably in light of anti-immigration policies. My point here is not to compare regimes, since each has its own logic and exclusion mechanisms while still mutually influencing each other. The postcolonial hierarchies highlighted in this work, such as the valorizing of whiteness in the job market or the low wages of domestic employees, are embedded in inequalities at the global scale, far surpassing Dubai.[72] Certain specificities, such as the absence of a minimum wage, render them particularly salient but not completely different from what happens in other contexts, especially given current neoliberal and anti-migration policies all over the world. In Dubai, Western passport holders constantly come into contact with people whose salaries are ten, twenty, or fifty times lower than theirs and who work in exhausting and precarious conditions. Some are paid to serve them. My research shows the various ways in which those Westerners respond to this reality, particularly by erecting forms of affective distance and distinction through various means, and the ways in which they seek to perpetuate, justify, and protect the structural advantages that shape their

CHAPTER 1

THE CONSTRUCTION OF SKILLS

"As for myself, I have always . . . been motivated by an expat situation. That undoubtedly has something to do with my roots; I'm the great-great-grandson, great-grandson, and grandson of pieds noirs [people of European ancestry who lived in Algeria when it was a French colony]. . . . So they were people who already had a colonizing impulse in the family, to not stay put . . . in one place. So, it's always been a dream for me."

DURING MY INTERVIEW WITH LOUIS, an expatriate contract worker in his 50s, this is how he expressed his aspiration to leave France. This way of inserting expatriation into the continuity of colonization is exceptional as compared with my other interviews. No other interviewee so explicitly established such a clear link between expatriates and colonists. Although some did see themselves walking in their parents' footsteps, their parents had migrated from the former colonies to France in search of a better life. At a more general level, there are some similarities between the status of Westerners in Dubai and that of colonists, but the connection between the two statuses, each of which covers a wide variety of situations, is far less straightforward and obvious than Louis's statement would suggest.

This chapter analyzes the image of professional skill sets associated with Westerners. This image stems from a global hierarchy of knowledge rooted in long history. The presence of Westerners and the structural advantages they enjoy fit patterns established during the British protectorate, although current modalities do not reflect a mere continuity with the past. The number of residents in Dubai with Western passports has increased considerably throughout the 2000s, a time of economic boom for the city linked to a policy of diversification that aims to reduce the country's dependence on oil. Certain trends in the Dubai government's migration policies, in conjunction with strategies of semipublic and private organizations, can explain this influx. This chapter sheds light on these trends, which have forged a status characterized by its ambivalence, combining structural advantages and a relative unpredictability when it comes to employment and residency rights. The experiences of Western residents in Dubai are shaped by both the postcolonial construction of skills as Western and the state's construction of foreign "temporary workers." It is important to closely examine the complex status of Western passport holders in Dubai, to consider them as structurally advantaged migrants, and to scrutinize the nature of the advantages that construct their status.

To illuminate this particular status, I draw on the notion of the coloniality of power in the construction of knowledge,[1] according to which "the colonial difference, from the 16th to the 21st century, has been the mechanism whereby non-Western knowledge is subalternized."[2] This notion makes it possible to understand how, beyond the history of the British protectorate, a particular construction of knowledge marked by coloniality tends to shape Dubai's job market. Or more to the point, the construction of skill sets as something Western, in the Arabian Peninsula as in many other places, has direct consequences on the status of people living there.

RACIALIZATION UNDER THE PROTECTORATE

Dubai is a city-emirate that belongs to a federation of seven emirates called the United Arab Emirates (UAE), whose political capital is Abu Dhabi. Contrary to the emirate's official self-representation, often relayed by international media, Dubai was not, a few decades ago, a tiny Arab village cut off from the world. Rather, it has a long history as a hub city where merchants have worked and lived—not only "Arabs" but also "Iranians" and "Indians," according to the categories used in historical works.[3] Like the region as a whole, it has a recent slave-trading past underrepresented in the social science literature. Slaves worked notably as pearl divers in the early twentieth century.

In his study of Dubai,[4] which he calls a corporate city, Ahmed Kanna focuses on the shift from a mode of governance marked by "ethnic pluralism" in the nineteenth century to what he characterizes as an "Arab ethnocracy" in the twentieth century, a concept he borrows from Anh Nga Longva (1997). According to Kanna, an ethnocracy amounts to a powerful "instrument of political domination by the state and its privileged allies in the multinational capitalist class."[5] The construction of an advantaged and racially exclusive Emirati national identity is inseparable from the history of the British protectorate. In other words, the structural advantages of being an Emirati national and the privileged status of Westerners were historically co-constructed under the British protectorate and beyond.

Starting in the 1820s, when the British government asserted its domination over this shore of the Gulf, its purpose was to secure access to India in response to competition from other colonial powers. In the territory that would later become the UAE, two major families dominated: the Qawasim and the Bani Yas. The British viewed these families' powerful flotillas as a threat and henceforth accused them of piracy. Throughout the entire nineteenth century, Great Britain imposed restrictive treaties on the emirates and *sheykhats* of the region, whereby no foreign relations could be established without the prior accord of Great Britain—as the British put it, the Pirate Coast thus became the Trucial Coast. In order to oversee the region, the British chose a few local chiefs, to whom they guaranteed "protection," and turned them into absolute, hereditary rulers over well-circumscribed territories where the borders had once been much more fluid.[6] The British colonizers believed the populations living in these territories were primitive and kept them uneducated.[7] They also sought to increase the Gulf population's economic dependence on British colonial India and then on Britain itself.[8]

In Dubai, the new reigning dynasty of the Al Maktoum succeeded in securing the territory for commercial trade. Although maritime traffic between Gulf ports and the Indian Ocean was long-standing, British colonization amplified the presence of Indian merchants along the "Trucial Coast" ports. More broadly, the British administration in the Gulf favored the importation of labor coming from other colonies or from Britain itself, though these workers were discouraged from mixing with local communities. Rather, they were deployed to discipline the population and keep it in check, notably through administration and security measures.[9] In Dubai, however, most of the Indians who settled there were merchants. Already in 1865, they accounted for the second largest "business community" of the city,[10] where, as British subjects, they conducted their trade under the protection of the British Empire. In the early twentieth century, traders from Persian shores, often Sunnis and members of Arab families, were induced to settle in Dubai, and the port gained prominence in regional trade.[11] By 1939, Dubai was the most populous city of the coast, numbering around 20,000 inhabitants, a quarter of whom were foreign, mainly Persian, Indian, and Baluchi.[12] British policy tended to differentiate among the trader communities by assigning them distinct statuses, which served to fuel tensions among those who had lived longest in the region, notably with regard to the Indian merchants protected by the empire.[13]

By the 1930s, the British protectorate felt the effects of a clash between the ruling family, backed by the colonizer, and reformist movements. This growing dissent should be placed within the larger contexts of anti-colonial political activism in the societies of the region and of the gradual emergence of a pan-Arab identity. The reformist movements in Dubai at that time were critical of their ruler's dependence on the British and called for the ruling family to share its power and oil income. The suppression of these protests was bloody, particularly in 1939.[14] Still, demand for reform continued and radicalized. During the 1950s, challenges to dependence on the British assumed the form of an Arab nationalist discourse calling for independence, inspired notably by Nasserism.[15]

Beyond repression, it was the region's considerable enrichment during the 1950s, the early years of oil drilling, that enabled the rulers to contain calls for independence by redistributing part of the oil income to the national population and to promote a consumerist, development-oriented ideology. Oil exploration and drilling completed the state power's territorializing through its appropriation of territories once thought of as this or that group's zone of influence. The protectorates, peripheries of the British Empire, were now specializing in the production and export of petroleum to the central capitalist countries while importing manufactured goods.[16] This dependence proved beneficial for three social groups: the ruling families, the local elite among the merchant class who obtained royal concessions, and a class of local company executives, largely Western, who benefitted from preferential treatment in the job market.[17] Out of this drive for reform, only the idea of Arab nationalism has survived, though somewhat distorted, providing the basis of today's state definition of citizenship, the Arabness principle of the emirates. Even though the nationality laws and their differing applications, depending on which emirate and during which period, have given rise to more diverse ancestries than the official position would suggest,[18] many people of Indian ancestry have been deprived of nationality by the formation of the nation-state.[19] As for those coming from the other shore of the Gulf (today's Iran), they are divided between those who have Emirati nationality within the contemporary nation-state and those who do not.[20] It was the British colonialists who laid the groundwork for this outcome by territorializing power, by founding a nation-state under protectorate, by seeking the support of the so-called modernist elites, and by stigmatizing a population deemed backward and traditionalist.[21]

In this respect, the independence of the Emirates in 1971 did not represent a break. The dynasties in place have remained, having allied to form a federal state backed by the former colonial power, which retains the role of "protector" when it comes to securing the state against the regional giants, Iran and Saudi Arabia. The ruling dynasties have continued to manipulate national ideologies and the rapport between the governors and the governed elaborated and endorsed during the colonial period, such as the notion of protection and a racially exclusive nationalism. However, if independence for the Emirates came without major upheaval or disruption, it was in no way due to a supposed apathy on the part of the populations in question. The reform movements that contested the colonial ideology of protection were suppressed, and only one aspect of their demands—Arab nationalism—was appropriated and transformed by the leaders.[22]

The rift between the modernist elites allied with the colonists and the population stigmatized as backward permeates the Emirati society's imaginary, produced and relayed by the international media and by the society itself. Among the Emiratis, the only rationale critical of Dubai's politics that is able to speak out in the open is that of the "neoorthodox,"[23] who contest the foreign presence, the headlong rush into modernity, and the transformations to their way of life, while projecting an imaginary vision of Arab purity on shores whose population has always been a mix. Adopting an opposite stance, the "flexible citizens," the embodiment of Dubai's neoliberal program, claim to be modern, cosmopolitan, and exceptional compared to the rest of Emirati society.[24] These are often the persons to whom the neoorthodox discourse leaves few options—notably, the women.[25] State ideology, both racially exclusivist and geared toward neoliberal development, equivocated when it came to Emirati women's status and lifestyle, caught between a natalist model and a national drive to promote women in the professions.

Neoliberal ideology is at the core of Dubai's construction as a corporate city. Over several decades, the different emirates have adopted economic strategies that vary significantly. Where Abu Dhabi has built its wealth on petroleum exploitation, Dubai has benefitted only indirectly from its oil operations, seeking rather to make the city an essential nexus of world business, far beyond its role in trade across the Gulf and the Indian Ocean. To this end, it strengthened its ties with the former colonial power: British companies were granted numerous contracts, notably for some of the city's most iconic megaprojects. But it also diversified its partnerships beyond the former colonizer. Companies whose executives hail from a variety of countries have shaped the city, and a large number of nationalities live and work there side by side.

More broadly, the federation of the United Arab Emirates has established itself as an economic, political, and military ally to several European countries and the United States. For instance, in Abu Dhabi, a French military base was set up in 2009 and by 2014 was used most visibly to carry out operations into Iraq. Emirati intelligence services, among the most technologically advanced and powerful in the world, have actively collaborated with those of so-called Western countries. The UAE thus enjoys special ties with various Western governments, reinforced by intensive commercial trade and military interchange.[26]

THE COLONIALITY OF SKILLS

By the 1950s, with oil drilling and commercialization well underway in the region, development policies brought about a steep increase in the flow of migrants to the countries of the Gulf Cooperation Council, a phenomenon that intensified in the 1970s, a period marked by both national independence and the arrival in large numbers of British citizens to the Emirates.[27] In Dubai, the economic diversification boom of the 2000s (nowhere near equally shared by all the emirates) came along with the arrival of an ever-increasing number of nationals from other Western countries.[28] In the same way that Dubai has become an international airline hub, companies from any and all sectors have been encouraged to set up corporate headquarters in Dubai thanks to the low tax rates and the availability of free zones where national duties do not apply.[29] The governor of Dubai asserted his strategy in 2014: "By attracting the best talent from around the world, we can create a vibrant and diverse society that fuels innovation and prosperity—which in turn attracts still more talent."[30]

The search to "attract the best talent" amounts to a two-pronged economic strategy on the government's part: on the one hand, to emerge as a durable hub of the global economy and, on the other, to leverage the consumer needs of a well-to-do population, attracted notably by the tourism infrastructure developed during the 1980s in a city that had been able to boast only one hotel in 1950.[31] Despite the statements by the governor of Dubai suggesting a somewhat neutral and disembodied notion of "talent," Dubai's minister of labor is not insensitive to the issue of people's nationality nor the country where they earned their degrees, as demonstrated by approvals and refusals of work visas. I would like now to take a closer look at how this hierarchy among foreign nationals has been historically constructed.

In the last decades, migration policies have featured two figures: the temporary or "guest" worker (in Arabic, the "delegated" worker), who comes to Dubai with a work contract and whose visa expires with the termination of the contract, and the dependent who accompanies him or her under certain restrictive conditions. These two figures are gendered, and I explore throughout this book all the issues that entails. For the moment, let us have a look at the first. Persons authorized to come to Dubai within this framework are selected according to their nationality, in particular by means of the Emirati authorities' acceptance or refusal of their application for a residency visa. Although the criteria that determine these choices are never made explicit, several seem to influence which nationalities are selected: language, the supposed quality of training, and the labor "cost" (this can be negotiated in a bipartite manner between the two countries, as is the case for domestic employees). Equally important is the political position of the country of nationality, since the management of migration flows can often be deployed as diplomatic leverage.[32] And finally, the supposed propensity of persons of a given nationality for political mobilization.

Numerous studies of the Gulf have identified two distinct periods. The first, at the time when policies of pan-Arab regional integration were being enacted, was characterized by massive migrations from the occupied Palestinian territories and from Egypt and Syria, among others. People from Arabic-speaking societies represented around a quarter of foreign residents in the UAE in 1975.[33] By the 1980s, recruitment gave precedence to nationals from Southeast Asia and the Indian subcontinent for economic and political reasons;[34] running counter to the stereotype of political apathy, however, strikes by construction workers from the Indian subcontinent have been massive and numerous, even if they tend to go unreported both inside the country and outside.[35] During the 2010s, according to testimony I gathered, the "nationals of the Arab Springs," to borrow the evocative expression of one Tunisian interviewee, as well as holders of Iraqi and Iranian passports were especially targeted when it came to refusal to issue or renew visas. These periods fit into the history of exclusion of citizens from the surrounding region enacted by politically repressive Gulf regimes over several decades now.

For a long time, studies of migration to the Gulf have paid scant attention to the policies aimed at the citizens of Western countries.[36] Many researchers having Western passports benefitted from the advantageous conditions provided by these master-key passports without analyzing them. Yet, their migrant status in the UAE differs from that of persons not holding such a passport—not to mention the advantages that it brings to the job market. Western passport holders are first of all legally structurally advantaged, since they are entitled to a month-long stay without a visa, renewable by simply exiting and reentering the country, a right that was extended to three months but with more stringent conditions for renewal.[37] This offer extended to citizens of certain countries to come to the Emirates to seek employment on the spot constitutes a direct inducement to relocate, as compared to others who face difficulties getting a visa, often a costly proposition, unless they already have a signed work contract. An increasing number of citizens of Western countries settled in Dubai during the decade 2000 to 2010, and among those I interviewed, few were ever denied a residence permit. Their professional relocation is geared toward particular job descriptions: statistics published by the Dubai government reveal that "Europeans" and "North Americans," to an overwhelming extent,[38] occupy the most highly qualified professions, while "non-Arab Asians," for example, are distributed over the full range of professions, from high-ranking jobs to the lowest levels of organizations. The state appears to intervene directly in the construction of this distribution: according to an association that prepares French nationals for "expatriate life in the Emirates," certain work visas can be denied on the implicit grounds that the position or salary would not correspond to the status expected for a person of French nationality, for instance. This orientation, which tends to reserve the highest positions on the job market for citizens of Western countries, fits into the broader strategy that aims to attract skills that are stereotypically associated with Westerners.

In this regard, beyond the key position held by British companies in the business world and the direct legacy of the protectorate, coloniality shapes the notion of skills. In Dubai, as in many other contexts,[39] skill has been constructed as Western, and Westerners as the ones who know. The figure of the Western expert, historically male, even though the expert can be female under certain conditions, was deeply ingrained in the Gulf region during the twentieth century, in the wake of the early days of oil drilling, which led to numerous social upheavals described in novel form by the writer Abdul Rahman Munif.[40] Once British oil companies had moved into the coastal emirates, and American ones into Saudi Arabia, the local job markets were deeply and lastingly affected by "industrial imperialism."[41] These companies established a national and racial segregation of jobs and housing that was reshaped over time, though it never disappeared. By the 1930s, in the British protectorates of the Gulf region, the oil concessions were granted to companies on the condition that they preferably hire personnel living under British sovereignty or coming from Great Britain or the Indian subcontinent: the contracts included nationality clauses heatedly negotiated between the companies and the British authorities.[42] Only the jobs considered as unskilled were allocated to the local population, who were extremely impoverished at that time.[43] Organizations further reinforced this segregation of labor by, for example, supplying different drinking fountains for the British, Indians, and Bahrainis in Bahrain.[44] Desalinated, refrigerated water for some; brackish, ambient-temperature water for the others. In Bahrain, once again, numerous strikes broke out between 1938 and 1965 in favor of obtaining equal pay for Bahrainis and foreigners. Indian wage earners also mobilized during the 1930s and 1940s to protest harsh working and living conditions imposed on them by the oil companies in the region.[45]

In the emirates of the Trucial Coast (including Dubai and Abu Dhabi), oil exploration was nevertheless late in coming and slow to develop: it was only in 1959–60 that wells with enough commercially exploitable oil were first drilled in Abu Dhabi.[46] Oil was first exported in the early 1960s. Still, Dubai was the staging ground for the oil companies, starting in the early days of exploration.[47] If the phenomena characteristic of the oil industry under the British protectorate were late to impact the emirate of Abu Dhabi and, marginally, that of Dubai, the construction throughout the twentieth century of Gulf nationals as incompetent, along with their location at the bottom of professional hierarchies in the region-wide oil industry, permeates the collective, racialized imaginary, where "locals," "Indians," and "Westerners" remain separate entities.

In the interviews, the notion of the more highly skilled Westerner was often stated as a foregone conclusion:

> "It has to be . . . very high quality. That's one of the reasons why for key management and key positions, we are mostly looking to recruit Westerners." [Dieter, human resources manager, German national]

> "As Europeans, we've got the credentials. For any job that requires a certain intellectual level, we're uniquely positioned." [Kamel, on the job market, French national]

> "In Europe, firms are highly structured. Here, not so much. There's a learning curve you have to follow, you can't just rise diagonally straight up." [Juan, manager in luxury goods, French national]

In the job market, the belief in the superiority of training and university degrees obtained in Western countries is reflected in the structural advantages afforded to the beneficiaries as well as in the reliance on Westerners to construct an image of expertise.[48]

By the late 1980s, the government of the Gulf Cooperation Council advocated for the nationalization of jobs—that is, the partial replacement of the foreign workforce. In the UAE, however, these policies were carried out less stringently and later than in the neighboring countries, given the small proportion of nationals in the job market: in Dubai, Emiratis represent 4 percent of the labor force[49] and work mostly in state-run or partially state-run enterprises or are involved in private ventures, often as investors, rarely present in the day-to-day running of companies. Certain Westerners, however, are hired for the purpose of "skills transfer" to young Emiratis, notably in the education sector.[50] Joan, a Canadian entrepreneur who has been living in the region for some ten years, told me that she first came to work in a new public university for female Emirati students, where only Western female professors were employed. When I asked her about this recruitment policy, she replied: "For the quality of the education. They wanted to be westernized." The notion of expertise transfer perpetuates a relationship of coloniality whereby there are believed to be more advanced countries—and therefore persons—and less advanced ones, both countries and people.

ATTRACTING "WESTERNERS"

In 2014, the governor of Dubai declared: "A generation ago, many talented individuals would consider working outside the West a 'hardship posting.' Today, standards of living in the UAE, for example, are among the highest in the world. We have shown that the business of reversing brain drain is also the business of creating a better life for citizens and residents. Building happiness is, after all, the primary business of good government everywhere."[51]

This declaration pertains to an ideology of happiness associated with certain living conditions: for the governor of Dubai, happiness relates to a high "quality of life" and "standards of living." Implying a certain opulence, it would thus be reserved for the relatively well-to-do, a selectivity further reinforced by the way the governor delineates the target of this governmental action consisting of "creating happiness": if a "better life" is to be created for "citizens" and "residents," the second term would seem aimed specifically at "skilled individuals" defined as working or having worked in "the West"—who, incidentally, were asked to rate their "happiness level."[52] This ideology of happiness gave rise to the appointment in February 2016 of a minister of happiness, Ohood Al Roumi. Though this governmental foregrounding of happiness is hardly unique to Dubai,[53] it puts into words an agenda implemented over the past few decades that targets the more affluent residents, and it resonates with statements made by many of the persons I interviewed.

Once they had settled in, despite some early misgivings, the persons I interviewed often enjoyed their life in the city, at least the first years. Some of their words echoed the government's discourse on happiness. Having assumed they would be staying in Dubai only one or two years, many found it hard to leave this "quality of life" they so enjoyed, a term that showed up everywhere in the interviews. They habituated very quickly to what the city has to offer in terms of lifestyle, leisure, and consumer options. Living in Dubai has prompted many Western residents to increasingly aspire to a comfortable, even luxurious, mode of living. Though they admit that they work a lot, once work is finished, they feel like they are on vacation: the most recently

built neighborhoods reserved for well-to-do residents feature a concentration of company offices, restaurants, bars, clubs, walkways, fitness centers,
spas, and for some, beaches. Tourist infrastructure is intended for both tourists and these wealthy residents, and the persons I interviewed regularly
patronized Dubai's hotels: their bars and restaurants, their spas and swimming pools. Everything is arranged so that the workforce coming from rich
countries will feel they are on vacation for a few hours every week, without
wasting time on a daily commute or on domestic chores. In fact, several persons emphasized how important it was to them to adopt the kind of lifestyle
and leisure activities—going out to luxury establishments, for example—to
which they would never have had access in their home countries: in Dubai,
inclusion in a privileged set and adopting consumer practices and leisure activities typical of upper-middle and upper classes all became possible. One
interviewee, in that regard, spoke of a sort of "hotel lifestyle." Outside work,
Dubai resembles "a giant spa," said another interviewee—that is, a space entirely devoted to relaxation and wellness. This balance between professional
work and luxury leisure stands in sharp contrast with the lifestyles of many
of the residents working at so-called unqualified jobs; they generally work six
days a week and spend long hours on their commute—a trip on the subway
or bus often taking over an hour—without ever enjoying what the city has to
offer in terms of leisure amenities. Of course, a number of intermediary situations exist between these two extremes. Several persons holding a skilled
position but not a Western passport considered Dubai as a "waiting room"
before they emigrated elsewhere, as one accountant who self-described as
Kurdish-Iranian expressed it—which was also the case of many people holding low-paid jobs.[54] Similarly, Sami, an urban planner born in Dubai and of
Lebanese nationality, described Dubai as "the heaven nobody can belong to"
and hoped to soon move to Australia or Canada.

One of the city's branding rationales aimed at potential candidates for
jobs in Dubai, but also at investors, is the idea of security, in what is commonly perceived as an insecure region. According to their narrative, Dubai
offers an image of a smoothly run, thriving, forward-looking place in a vexed
and war-torn region. Dubai has become the staging ground for companies
working in various countries at war—Iraq and Afghanistan most notably—or
countries seen as inhospitable, such as Saudi Arabia. Dubai's security policy
does not involve any conspicuous militarization of public space that would

feature checkpoints and armed guards. The police keep a low profile, as if everything were being done to preserve the well-being of the most affluent inhabitants. The belief in a reliable security system is based on surveillance, not only institutional but also delegated to the inhabitants, in favor of the middle and upper classes.[55] It also involves a ban on street harassment and a more broad-based policing of public space. Several of my interviewees, particularly two persons of Pakistani and Lebanese nationality, consider security in Dubai through the prism of instability or even the war situations that have characterized their home country or region. Apart from people who hold two different passports, having grown up in the region, and a few American ex-military personnel formerly mobilized in Iraq and currently stationed in Dubai, the Western residents, generally speaking, have not experienced war situations, even if their home countries have been involved in armed conflict. Although they themselves do not use the rationale of peace, their emphasis on well-being and quality of life echoes the image of the city as a "bubble" connected to the world but cut off from the "problems" of the Middle East. This argument tends to make Dubai a solely economic city, located on the political fringe. Politics as a subject of conversation was absent in my interviews with Westerners, whether out of disinterest on their part or whether they considered it a taboo topic not to be raised for fear of repression. This is not the case among other residents, as pointed out by Kanna with regard to Iraqis.[56] The city has experienced several construction worker strikes, despite the absence of trade unions and the ban on any sort of activism.

Most of the residents socialized in Western countries that I met seemed to accommodate the multifarious repression of political activity. Complacency, or even collusion with the authoritarian governments is in fact a characteristic attributed to "expats" by a man of Lebanese descent, who stated, somewhat bitterly, in an interview: "Many people come here because it's easy and stay because it's easy. They don't want to make life more complicated than it is. Ninety-five percent of expats don't give a damn about Arab political life in the region. They couldn't care less about the Arab Spring. They are completely detached." This interview took place in late 2012—that is, at a time when several societies in the region were experiencing large-scale protest movements, repressed with greater or lesser degrees of violence.

Of the persons socialized in Western countries, especially whites, most showed a relatively limited interest in the ongoing political dynamics of the countries in the region. They saw the "Middle East," or MENA (Middle East and North Africa), to borrow the acronym in common use, as more of an economic region, depending on which companies or sectors were at issue, a set of markets whose hub is Dubai. I noted at times how little they knew about the history of Israel and the occupied Palestinian territories, despite widespread coverage of the issues over many decades, not to mention political movements in neighboring Arab countries. Once, a guest at a dinner expressed surprise, for instance, at a Palestinian work colleague's use of the word *Palestine*, considering it almost offensive ("as if Israel didn't exist!"). Aside from this sort of remark or other broad assertions about the political regime of the Emirates, politics did not appear to be a central conversation topic for these individuals. Their mode of comprehending the region leaned more toward economics and tourist activities. Given Dubai's position as airline hub, many took advantage of their weekends and time off to take short getaway vacations to India, Sri Lanka, Kenya, and sometimes Jordan. At most, some expressed regret that they could not tour neighboring countries due to an unstable political situation or civil war, thus constructing the region as a land of exploration that they were being denied. Their obvious disinterest in regional politics tended to reinforce their exceptionalist construction of Dubai as a bubble, a staging ground, and a hub.

In the final chapter of this book, I return to this ideology of "quality of life" and security and to some situated experiences of happiness in Dubai that various people have had, depending on their gender, class, and race positions.

"TEMPORARY WORKERS"?

The construction of skills as Western and the wish to attract these skills fit into a long history that results today in status boundaries among different groups of residents in the Emirates, boundaries that tend to prevent any identification or solidarity among members of distinct groups. Yet, in some respects, Western residents are "temporary workers"—or their dependents—from the standpoint of Emirati law.[57]

If the persons I interviewed were attracted to Dubai for jobs, high salaries, or the tax-free status, they also had other more complex and varied motivations. Several, some of whom were Western passport holders, had been living in the city for a decade and had even done part of their schooling there. Still, this study focuses mainly on persons who did not grow up in Dubai and who arrived there as adults. Among the persons I interviewed, just under half arrived in Dubai as the result of a job offer for them or their spouse, sometimes by way of a headhunter; it would never have occurred to them to move to this city without that initial professional opportunity that they deemed advantageous, for both the position and the salary being offered. Some, like John, a white male divorcee from California, first came for a contract in another country on the Arabian Peninsula and later explored the possibility of moving to Dubai because he deemed the quality of life superior to that of Saudi Arabia, for instance. Others, like Louis, quoted in the epigraph to this chapter, worked for the same group back home before migration. They were under expatriation contracts, registered in the labor legislation of the particular country,[58] or under a secondment contract—that is, a local contract for a predetermined period, which comes with a guarantee that the person will be given a job elsewhere in the home company once that period has elapsed. Eight women were present as spouses to men under expatriate contracts, and one man as spouse of a woman under such a contract. Among these nine (eight women and one man), seven had a professional activity or were actively seeking one, and two were stay-at-home wives with no professional activity. The women self-described as having "followed" their husbands and had not chosen Dubai as destination.[59]

The majority of the Western passport holders that I interviewed, however, came on their own initiative. By leaving home to live and work "abroad," although most emphasized their desire for an "international experience," many explained that they were also fleeing various difficulties. The most salient difficulty mentioned during the interviews was unemployment or what they felt was a bleak job market with few lucrative prospects; the second most-often mentioned was different forms of racism or discrimination; and third was a host of other problems, ranging from conflicts with family members to harassment in the professional or personal sphere. They chose Dubai for the possibilities the city offered in terms of career and salary or because they knew one or two people who would serve as a base or would even house them until they found a job.

Whatever the reasons, always diverse and complex, that drove these "temporary workers" to make the move, the government that oversees them strives to make these foreign residents profitable not only for the companies that employ them but also for the corporate city, by their work and their consumption. The term *temporary worker* does not encompass the different aspects of these men's and women's experience, since its provisional and temporary nature is so illusory,[60] and since these individuals developed varied and inventive modes of belonging that reached far beyond the work setting.[61] The status of temporary worker needs to be taken seriously, however, for what it implies about professional relations, on the one hand, and about the precariousness of residency, on the other. Close scrutiny of these implications challenges the oft-accepted dichotomy between "migrant workers," thought of as very constrained, and "mobile professionals," thought of as free to cross boundaries and stay wherever they want to. Residents of different nationalities under work contracts in the Emirates share certain elements of this temporary worker status, while others differentiate them.

From the standpoint of work, as Neha Vora has observed for Qatar,[62] the professional experience of many Westerners indeed corresponds to the model of temporary worker that prevails in a number of contexts, not just in the Emirates. In Dubai, this model applies to the so-called skilled professions: only a work contract allows for residency rights, which are suspended in case of dismissal or resignation. A status such as this one shapes people's relationship to work. Most of the persons I encountered came to Dubai, above all else, for professional reasons, directly or indirectly (to accompany a husband or, very rarely, a wife). In Dubai, the workweek is officially forty-five hours, which is supposed to enable the employer to leverage the visa fees. Still, although most of my interviewees admitted that they worked a lot, few challenged the legitimacy of the work-leisure balance that this schedule imposes. Several interviewees put into words the sort of subjectivities modeled by a neoliberal ideology that celebrates flexibility and mobility.[63] Here are two examples of such discourse:

> "I think it's great to really have my shoulder to the wheel, to be learning so much, and so early in my career, after all. Afterward, I have to admit that what I experienced in France, well, I didn't really learn much . . . it wasn't very advanced." [Devi, 30, French, master's degree, working in finance]

> "I get the impression, compared to our co-workers in France, that we know we're in an ejection seat, and at 6 or 7 p.m., we're still on the job if there's still work to get done. In France, when we try to call them on long weekends . . .

actually, almost nobody has their cell number, or they only answer half the time. . . . Then, there's the other thing: you're not supposed to call between noon and 2:00, you're not supposed to call before 9:00, you're not supposed to call after 6:30 p.m."

"But what about here?"

"Here's my work phone right here, I'm always on call. [*This interview is taking place on a weekend, late morning.*] I don't feel like I have to, but for me it's obvious . . . 24 hours a day. It might cause us to lose money if we aren't responsive. That's not exactly the mentality they have in France. Even on vacation, we have to be available. In France, someone at my job level wouldn't have to be, not all the time. . . . Because I get the feeling that everything here is moving so fast that whatever doesn't get done today, and we do it tomorrow, there are going to be consequences. . . . But anyway, we have such a nice living environment here, I really can't complain, so I guess it doesn't bother me to have to give so much at work. Because we have super evenings out, and great weekends, and because we get to travel so much." [Linda, 30, French, master's in international trade, working in logistics]

The way the French residents speak about their work in Dubai is often constructed in opposition to the professional world back home, whether perceived as a supposed lack of commitment, as mentioned by Linda, or difficulties involved in moving up the ladder, alluded to by Devi. This also refers to French labor law, more advantageous when it comes to paid leave and work hours than Emirati labor law—or American labor standards, for that matter. If such discourse recalls that of management-level employees in France's private sector or in other national contexts, here it is territory-specific: professional vitality was pegged not only to the private sector but to Dubai as a city and a society, as opposed to that of the home country. The omnipresence of work in their lives—we work all the time, we are never not on the job—was mostly presented as something positive: it's all worth it, it's even rewarding. This is how Jenny replied, a 30-year-old Australian resident working in franchise sales at Startup Z, when I asked her how she felt at her company, whether she enjoyed her work:

"Here, they encourage you to be someone who takes charge of business, not just a salaried employee. No one leaves the office at 6:00. Everyone is very involved. Over the weekend, we continue sending messages. It's constant. I never decline a call just because it's outside work hours. And with the time difference, I sometimes get work calls in the middle of the night. . . . So I work from home. But I do take a real interest in this work."

Dubai is described by some as a "lifestyle": to be able to see the beach from one's office on the twenty-fourth floor of a skyscraper, to answer your job-related emails over the weekend while lounging by a swimming pool, not tabulating your hours, considering your job as a fun hobby and your colleagues as family, working flat out for the success of the company and, by extension, the good of the corporate city. The salaried employees I encountered often presented themselves as busy and in a rush, which confirms how much work is valorized. From what I observed, they tend to claim they work more hours than they actually do—twelve to thirteen hours rather than ten, for example—as if they were trying to show me how important work was to them.

Only a few people criticized the all-important role of work. Cindy, an American, also in franchise sales at Startup Z, pointed out that companies were looking to "take advantage of employees" and she didn't feel she was being compensated for the "twelve to fifteen hours a day" that she worked. Several other interviewees complained that they worked too much. Certain work contracts in Dubai—notably, but not only for jobs considered as unskilled—require the employee to work six days a week. One French woman that I met up with in Paris told me she left Dubai for that reason. This intensive work pace was put forward by some to demonstrate the converging status of salaried foreigners, no matter what their nationality may be.

Western salaried workers under local contracts complained in particular about the uncertainty of their residency status due to their status as temporary workers. Dubai law does make dismissal easy, with no possibility of unemployment benefits. And since the residency permit is strictly tied to a job, a dismissed employee is required to leave the territory within thirty days unless he or she can find another job in the interim, which, as it turns out, is often the case. This tenuous residency situation has proven to be an important source of stress. Fear of being fired is particularly strong early in a worker's stay or even during a trial period, due to the huge costs involved in moving to Dubai: renting accommodations, which usually means paying a year's rent in advance; buying a car; and paying for school if the worker has children. The desire to at least break even prompts some, even those who are disappointed by their new living conditions, to remain in Dubai. Subsequently, the fear of dismissal does not necessarily diminish. Over the years, people lose their professional network back home, and although they can usually find another job in Dubai in case of dismissal, they must be extra careful not to be "banished," something that an employer can request in case of a dispute. The uncertainty awaiting them back in their home countries is greater for those who left for Dubai on their own initiative, with no safety net or backup plan, and who work under a local contract—which was the case for the majority of the persons I interviewed. Unpredictability is a mode of governing foreign residents, to the extent that it often discourages any protesting or complaining about an employer when a problem arises—such as unpaid wages or harassment.

This fear might seem surprising, given the advantages that most Western residents enjoy in Dubai. One of my interviewees most affected by fear of dismissal was Marie, a stay-at-home mother in her 40s, who had lived in Dubai for a number of years with her husband, a company executive and British national. The couple had moved to Dubai for the husband's job, but later he resigned from his company and was rehired on a "local contract." Since he and his wife both wished to remain in the country, he found a job and a salary that felt like the turning point they had desired for his career. Shortly thereafter, however, he was let go all of a sudden. Marie explained that this incident instilled a certain wariness in this couple who had been living the high life. This sudden and wholly unexpected dismissal made her realize that in Emirati companies, "they take, they throw out," regardless of the level of responsibility. Yet, without the income this job provided, the couple could not meet their current expenses (such as high rent and costly schooling for the children).

Several individuals, particularly those who have gotten used to spending a lot, said they feel like there is no safety net and dread the consequences of an eventual dismissal. This fear revealed a certain sociological contradiction: these persons were living an upper-class life, but their residency was justified in the eyes of the law by their status as "temporary worker." One might posit that it is this very contradiction—to be treated legally like everybody else while at the same time enjoying a privileged status—that aroused such anxiety among persons who in theory should have all the resources to get by in case of unforeseen circumstances.

EXPAT CONTRACT VERSUS LOCAL CONTRACT

Certain work contracts are governed not by Dubai labor law but, at least in part, by the law of another country: these are what is commonly referred to as expatriate contracts. Among the individuals of French nationality whom I interviewed, the expatriate contracts were held by white males; out of the thirteen cases, only one woman held such a contract. Most of them came from middle- and upper-class backgrounds and had earned graduate degrees, but two came from the working class and had done only two years of higher education after earning a vocational *baccalauréat*. Expatriate contracts create a hierarchy insofar as they confer numerous advantages: Firstly, they shelter employees from the unpredictability that "temporary workers" have to face. Further advantages include higher salaries, a company car, paid housing, schooling for children, an annual round-trip ticket to the country of origin for the whole family, and a service for moving and settling in. Such perquisites are nearly always included in the expatriate contracts, in which "the base salary goes straight to savings" in many cases, according to a man in this situation, whereas any benefits in local contracts have to be negotiated and are far rarer. Finally, when an expatriate contract does expire, the contract holder will often return to a job at the home company headquarters or move on to another expatriate job, whereas local contracts do not necessarily lead to a career outside the region.

Because expatriate contracts are extremely lucrative and are given mainly to white males, they contribute to producing the overlapping hierarchies of nationality, race, class, and gender in Dubai. They shape a specific model of heterosexuality, because these contracts, through various allowances and other measures, take into account the nuclear family—wife and children—who "accompany" the husband wherever his expatriate contracts take him. Most of the time, this model compels wives to abandon their careers in favor of organizing the family's life or taking part in paid or volunteer activities, which these women, during the interviews, always presented as secondary to their spouse's career. The husband earns enough to cover all the family's expenses, including the wife's, whose dependence is thus materially and legally established. It is foreign organizations that produce this type of hierarchy within Dubai society by taking advantage of differences between national laws.

"Secondment" contracts constitute intermediary situations between expatriate contracts and local contracts. People under secondment contracts do not have the social characteristics of the expatriates. All those I interviewed who were under such contracts were under 40 years of age, most did not have children, and several were women. Two of them said they applied for a job of this type within their company because they had been experiencing burnout. Their salaries were not very different from what they had been in their home country, but their expenses had risen significantly.

Certain secondment contracts, however, can prove quite advantageous: these disparities also contribute to constructing gender, class, and race hierarchies among Western residents. For instance, Jean-Baptiste, in his 30s, a finance executive working in a multinational company under secondment contract, got both a substantial salary raise, increased tenfold by tax advantages, the right to keep paying into the French retirement fund, and the inclusion of his years in Dubai when it came to calculating his seniority. During our interview, he explained that he would have to be leaving Dubai soon, not because he wasn't enjoying it, but to move forward in his career: "For my career, it's important to keep moving, to see other things." This statement was consistent with the classic discourse that valorizes professional mobility: the destination matters little; it is only one stage in the career of an executive.[64] Note that Jean-Baptiste, although married, presented this choice as an individual one, linked only to his own career; I met his wife, however, a woman with a graduate degree who interrupted her career to follow him. This made his statements all the more astonishing in my view, even though he was simply stating the obvious for males of his income bracket with regard to the division of labor within a couple.[65]

The majority of persons under local contract, however, did not correspond to the stereotypical expatriate: they benefitted from structural advantages (detailed in the next chapter) but their status was characterized by forms of uncertainty, however limited. Several felt they were underpaid. Among French residents, these situations especially affected nonwhites and women. The experience of recruitment and of arrival in Dubai strongly differentiated those who travelled to Dubai at their own expense—who spent a large part of their savings on rent and went into debt or attempted to find someone to put them up while they made the rounds of companies in search of a job—from those under expatriate or secondment contracts, who were offered comfortable residency conditions even before they arrived in country. For instance, Jean-Baptiste told me he benefitted from a "look and see" trip organized for him by his employer: a specialist in *relocation*—another word pertaining to upper-class migration—had him visit the city and the neighborhoods where he could live.

> "She showed me the places where expatriates live, and then I flew back to Paris. I chose the neighborhoods where I wanted her to find me an apartment. So, she made a choice, and in one morning, on the day I arrived, I visited the apartment and we signed a rental contract. She also handled connecting the utilities, water, electricity, and internet."

This highly privileged experience contrasts sharply with most world migrants' modalities for making the move to a new country. Other testimonials, however, did describe very different experiences. Several people indicated how hard it was to find work and reported cases of job-seekers who, after finding nothing, had to leave Dubai after having spent all their savings.

Because of this disparity among Western passport holders residing in Dubai, the term *expatriate* tends to be misleading. Different types of contracts give rise to different ways of relating to work, to career, and to the country. The expatriate contract represents a structural *superadvantage*, firstly because its beneficiaries avoid the precarious status of temporary worker, however circumscribed that precariousness might be in practice. Here, we can already glimpse not only hierarchies between persons holding a Western passport and those who don't, but also among Westerners themselves.

*   *   *

In the region and beyond, the historically constructed association between Westernness and expertise has shaped an advantageous status for Western residents, often considered de facto as skilled. The ambivalence between this advantageous status and the precariousness of the temporary worker visa still fuels fear among some—the fear of being treated like the "other" migrants, whom they view as radically distinct. The following chapters will focus on clarifying the structural advantages that the residents enjoy in the job market: despite a feeling of uncertainty expressed by some, their status is measurably privileged—disproportionately so—as compared to that of persons of other nationalities.

Temporary worker status also influences the construction of subjectivities, given the predominance of professional work in people's daily schedules and in the narratives of the individuals I interviewed. Their legally temporary status further reinforces their tendency to see themselves as outsiders in Dubai society, even though their Western passports situate them relatively high within its hierarchies. Some, as employers, take an obvious part in perpetuating and even reinforcing such hierarchies, as we shall now see.

CHAPTER 2

STRUCTURAL ADVANTAGES
IN THE JOB MARKET

"Westerners—they even get salary compensation for their pets!"

A WOMAN OF LIBYAN NATIONALITY from whom I was renting a room made this remark when I told her what my research was about. She is basically summarizing the bitterness aroused by the many advantages offered by organizations to their Western salaried employees. Naima, in her 50s, had had to accept a job well beneath her qualifications when she moved to Dubai with her husband a decade earlier—she has since divorced. In Libya, she was an engineer; she showed me photographs of trips with Yugoslav colleagues that she had made earlier in her career, a time she remembered fondly. After the fall of Qaddafi in 2011, she returned to Libya with the thought of settling back in, but the dangerous and chaotic situation compelled her to turn back. She remarried a man of Syrian nationality who, shortly after our interview, had to host a large part of his family in Dubai, at considerable expense. Times had been hard. To supplement his salary, Naima shared her little three-room apartment, to whatever extent feasible, with transient tenants like myself. Her situation regarding employment and salary stood in sharp contrast to that of most Westerners I met. In fact, though all Western passport holders do not occupy so-called skilled jobs, most achieve positions higher than what they would have reached in their home countries and also receive a more substantial salary for the equivalent function in the company.

This chapter bears on the structural advantages that Western passport holders enjoy in the job market but also, more broadly, on the way organizations contribute to shaping this privileged status by the differentiating ways they treat employees depending on their nationalities. It shows that companies located in Dubai, often multinationals, play a key role in the production of this city's social hierarchies. They are relatively unregulated, given how neoliberal ideology shapes local labor laws. Their differentiating treatment of nationalities combines with migration policies that favor Western passport holders. Both companies and migration policies also differentiate between men and women, in favor of the former, which shapes situated experiences of Western privilege, a point I delve into throughout this book.

These organizations create hierarchy and segmentation in a number of ways. Combining the postcolonial approach and the study of organizations has proven fruitful, notably by highlighting the material elements at the core of social hierarchies, beyond representations.[1] Intersectional approaches to organizations suggest analyzing various elements from salaries and careers to casual interactions at work in order to understand how organizations produce hierarchies.[2] In Dubai, salary inequality was often raised in the interviews as a major issue. But the organizations have various ways to differentiate their employees, such as salary amounts, contract and remuneration conditions, career possibilities, segmentation of jobs and spaces—the ways an essentializing discourse on the management of nationalities gets perpetuated. All these elements construct the hegemonic position of Westerners as a group, as well as hierarchies of gender, class, and race within this group. In general, Western passport holders are better paid, have more rapidly evolving careers, and often occupy supervisory positions. They play an important role in producing and perpetuating these structural advantages, notably due to their mostly senior positions in their organization's hierarchy. Most of those I interviewed validated and defended these advantages, developing their own reading of the work world in terms of nationalities. In the end, this configuration prompts us to question the social meaning attributed to nationality and the forms of its racialization in a globalized job market like Dubai's, including the ways in which persons of Western nationality are racialized *to their advantage*—that is, how they benefit from positive stereotypes associated with whiteness and Westernness. The issue of the differentiated management of labor is far from peculiar to Dubai,[3] and the idea here is to shed light on who stands to benefit from it.

The individuals whom I interviewed worked in human resources, sales, marketing, communications, finance, logistics, engineering, and urban planning and in a whole range of companies with different activities (luxury goods, banking, insurance, transportation, construction), different organizational structures, and different nationalities in their leadership. Several of these companies had a pyramidal structure: executive functions were held by men holding Western passports, while the middle and lower portions of the pyramid, where many of the jobs are considered unskilled, were occupied mostly by citizens of Asian countries. Other organizations were regional subsidiaries of multinationals in such sectors as finance or insurance and would hire only so-called skilled persons. Several interviewees started their own companies, and some, mostly married women, worked freelance as, for instance, tourist guides or as medical or psychological support staff.

NATIONALITIES AND SALARY DIFFERENTIALS

For residents employed in skilled positions but not holding a Western passport, the salary differential according to nationality is generally described as both an obvious fact and an injustice. This is notably the case with Sami, of Lebanese nationality and working for an American company. When I asked whether he thought the management of human resources was fair, he answered:

> "Once again, we're talking about Dubai here. And the thing is, not only in my company but in all the companies in Dubai . . . there is always a hierarchy of salaries they pay . . . and it has nothing to do with your experience, but rather, where you're from. I can tell you that first-hand. . . . There are managers who are American or British who are better paid than managers who are Jordanian or Egyptian. . . . I don't think that's fair. But those are, well, the tacit rules in Dubai, you see. Everybody knows them."

Statements like this and Naima's remark earlier in the chapter attest that the salary differential arouses bitterness but not resignation. Sami considered the situation unfair but he was willing to accept it, for it was a condition for furthering his career. Like other residents without Western passports, he considered Dubai as one step toward emigrating elsewhere, to Canada or Australia.

Western passport holders are the beneficiaries of this salary differential. They account for the highest salaries in the Emirates, even though most of those I interviewed were convinced that the Emiratis were better paid.[4] In this chapter, I explore how salary differentials are justified by the persons who benefit, and how salary differentiation is implemented at the time of hiring, how such practices get normalized, and how they contribute to defining groups. Western passport holders put forward three arguments to justify salary differentials: the first pointed to the purported superiority of Western credentials, the second involved the neoliberal ideology of the difference of opportunity, and the third dealt with the ideology of the temporary worker. I heard these arguments put forward especially among individuals working in human resources, whose statements are analyzed below. These arguments allowed them to legitimize salary differentials—so that people who hire and set pay rates can see the differentials as not unfair, and so they don't have to see themselves as perpetuating some kind of injustice.

The purported superiority of Western credentials

Ella, a graduate of a British university, worked at Startup Z, where she was in charge of public relations; Noor, in charge of human resources, was a graduate of a Pakistani university. During our discussion, they both justified the salary difference based on university degrees:

"We look at credentials and experience. We don't discriminate on the basis of nationality. It's not like that here. It's credentials and experience that count." [Noor]

"And of course, the degree the person has matters to us, as does the place he or she earned it. If it's a degree from one of the top twenty-five universities in the world, that necessarily raises the salary level; we know how hard it is to get into one of those highly selective universities." [Ella]

"In a way, you could say we discriminate positively for certain candidates, but we never discriminate negatively." [Noor]

On another day with them, I raised the issue of salary differences based on nationality. Ella asserted that "another type of company" practiced that kind of policy. According to her, within companies founded by "young internationals," there was no discrimination, because young internationals had "modern ideas"; the others were "stuck somewhere in the past." These statements matched up with the discourse surrounding the Dubai brand: promotion of modernity, cosmopolitanism, multiculturalism, and newness.

It accommodated the postcolonial hierarchy among countries and universities: salary differences pegged to the educational institution (and thus to the country as well) where the degree was obtained are not thought to constitute discrimination. The differentiation is based on the training, not the person. This hierarchy of training reflects the coloniality of knowledge: degrees earned in Western countries are considered better, and the individuals who hold them more competent. This is one way such hierarchies are renewed throughout the hiring process.

The purported "law" of supply and demand

A related argument claims that the difference in opportunity justifies salary differentials, based on belief in the law of supply and demand. Thus, it is not only because some credentials and skills are deemed superior but also because they are more sought after that companies offer higher salaries to degree holders from Western universities. Dieter, a German national who was once in charge of human resources for a French telecommunications firm and now was launching a new company, acknowledged the existence of salary differentials. Pointing to the argument of supply and demand, which he saw as an objective reality, he did not seem to consider them unfair:

> "For Westerners in general, there are more options. So, people come here because . . . they want to have a nice life, have a higher salary, and for example, if you come from East Asia, you have far fewer options, and the companies know it, and your college degree isn't worth much. . . . In the end, where you come from and where you got your degree determine your personal value in the market in terms of salary package and position in the hierarchy."

Salary differentials are legitimized here by two arguments presented as objective, logical, and linked to free competition. On the one hand, the claim is that training can vary greatly in quality and therefore is not always ascribed the same value; on the other, persons of different nationalities don't have access to the same opportunities. Based on this argument, it would be logical for a company to pay Filipinos less, because a low salary in the Emirates would always prove more attractive than a salary in the Philippines. This reasoning overlooks the Dubai job market: as long as the persons concerned are living in Dubai, they will compare the positions and salaries they are likely to earn there. Yet, most companies make salary offers based on nationality.

The ideology of the temporary worker

The third argument, presented by numerous interviewees, raised the difference of a Dubai salary's purchasing power in the salaried person's supposed
home country, as if people were in Dubai for the sole activity of working
and spent all they earned elsewhere. Consequently, the salary amount was
pegged to purchasing power in the country of the person's passport, as John,
a 42-year-old entrepreneur and consultant with US nationality, related:

> "They know where people come from and how much they can pay them. If
> someone comes from Egypt, they know they can pay them a certain amount.
> And they know that for the identical job, with the same requirements, if they
> want somebody from Great Britain or the United States, they will probably
> have to pay twice as much. But again, it's all relative, because if you receive the
> same amount—$5,000 in the US, it doesn't go very far, while with $5,000 in
> Egypt, that's someone who can live in Sharm Al Shaykh! . . . So, they pay them
> an equivalent amount."

This kind of rationale equates foreign residents with temporary workers
who would rather spend and work in their country of origin (or of passport)
than in Dubai. This is very reductive reasoning: most individuals working in
skilled professions settle in Dubai for several years or even decades and spend
a good share of their income in country.[5] Some, in fact, were born in Dubai
and have spent their entire life there.

In other words, salary differentials based on nationality cannot be
explained mechanically by globalization or by differences in education, opportunities, or purchasing power. Such arguments are more reflective of
beliefs that allow employers to rationalize their discriminatory practices.[6]
These beliefs are rooted in a vision of the economy as a set of objective principles applicable to any country, a vision historically conveyed by experts in
various colonial and postcolonial contexts.[7] They can be compared to the
"abstract liberalism" that Bonilla-Silva analyzed as a central frame of color-
blind racism in the United States.[8] Here, abstract economic principles, seen
as neutral, such as the "law" of supply and demand, purchasing power differentials, or the degrees' value, serve to justify structural discriminations
based on nationality. Nationality itself is presented as a neutral, administrative category in these moments, while at other times it is routinely associated

with racialized stereotypes. These extremely widespread beliefs, according to which salary differentiation is due to abstract economic principles, result in fixed norms via convergent practices in the Dubai labor market. This is how the tacit rule that salary depends on nationality takes root and contributes to perpetuating structural hierarchies among foreigners from different regions around the world.

Hiring as reproducing hierarchy

Several people who employed subordinates described for me the practices in use in Dubai to match salary to passport. For instance, Sarah, in her 30s, who worked as a sales manager in a company started and run by males of Indian nationality, gave this explanation:

> "In fact, every quote-unquote nationality, if I can put it that way, or each continent—I'm not sure if that makes sense—has a salary scale. For example, we as vendors offer 3,000 dirhams. . . . And at 3,000 dirhams, actually, we can recruit Filipinos, Pakistanis, and Indians. . . . If we want someone who can speak Arabic, we'll go after Lebanese, Syrians, Egyptians—it doesn't really matter. In that case, it will be a little more, somewhere between 4,500 and 5,000 dirhams minimum. Since our budget is at 3,000 dirhams, we generally don't have much of a choice. But then, I do actually like Filipinos a lot, because they are very, very good at customer service. They're always smiling, always personable."

Though hesitant at first, Sarah ended with an assertion that racialized Filipinos by attributing a behavioral trait across the board. This racialization of nationalities in the context of the Dubai job market is common, as evidenced in an interview with Deborah, 26, also a sales manager:

> "Firstly, we figure out the budget and how much I have available to pay someone, roughly. And I really did want to interview several people. Since everybody knows how much they can ask for according to their passport, there really aren't any big surprises. I met with a Swedish woman, a Jordanian man, and an Indian man. And for the same position, more or less identical credentials and experience in Dubai, . . . a Swedish woman asked for 15 [15,000 dirhams a month] while an Indian is okay with 6 [6,000]. . . . And the Jordanian, we didn't follow up because there are lots of Arabs who come and don't speak any English, it turns out."

These two interview extracts point to contradictory discourses. Sarah and Deborah had been living in Dubai for several years and had built their careers without having had much postsecondary education back in France. Although they seemed to cast a critical eye at times on the discrepant treatment of nationalities, at other moments, the hierarchical ranking of nationalities that structures the job market underpinned their narrative. For instance, in her last sentence, Deborah could very well have simply said that the Jordanian did not speak English, without making a sweeping statement about Arabs. Despite a certain critical distance, Sarah and Deborah integrated into their vision of the Dubai job market the structuring racialization of nationalities. They failed to question their own role in the perpetuation of this norm that benefitted them.

These interview extracts highlight two of the practices responsible for maintaining this norm in the Dubai job market: the individuals who do the recruiting select the nationalities of candidates depending on the budget at their disposal; and the candidates align their salary demands with the norms established for their nationality, a practice that has the effect of relieving the recruiters of feeling responsible for the salary differential. A third practice, probably the most common, consists of offering a salary on the basis of the candidate's nationality, as evidenced by the experience of Karim, an employee of French nationality in a French company:

> "When I left, the person who replaced me was Indian; he called me and asked how much I had been paid, and I asked him what he was being paid. It turned out he was paid half: 5,000 dirhams, and without a [company] car."

These differences result in major distortions between the professional hierarchy and the pay grade. Karim's company had made a company car available to him, unlike his immediate supervisor and his successor, and the latter earned half as much.

Claiming high salaries

In various situations, during interviews or informal conversations, I observed that salary levels were always routinely pegged to nationality. It was often my presence, as someone just passing through to conduct research and foreign to the Dubai context, that induced reluctance, disrupting the habitual spontaneity with which all decision-making about salaries is automatically linked to the nationality of the employee. Such was the case in this interview:

"The Filipina, it's a bit expensive for someone who, someone who is . . . for a Filipina. I pay her 5,000 dirhams a month, . . . but she's really great. A real treasure. I don't have to tell her anything, she's practically up to the standard of the assistants I had back in Paris. . . . But it was a choice for her, too, actually; she could have a higher salary, but she lives right next door. . . . I made her the offer to work five days a week instead of six. And my hours are pretty cool, too; we work from 8:30 to 5:30." [Céline, entrepreneur, French, 32 years old]

Her hesitation conveyed Céline's reluctance, as a white, college-educated woman, to state aloud to another French person, one who was not living in Dubai, this correlation between salary and nationality. She stepped into the role of boss who pays well and offers special work conditions to her employee. She also set Paris as the standard of professionalism, which feeds into the belief in French or, more broadly, Western superiority.

Most of the individuals constructed themselves, however ambivalently, by somehow rationalizing the salary differences that worked in their favor. Some even spoke of nationality as almost a professional interest group. A new arrival who browsed to a Facebook page for French-speakers living in Dubai asked about the price of apartment rentals, specifying his salary (12,500 dirhams for a trainee position). He received a number of comments, two of which were these:

"First of all, I hope you are not coming purposely from France for 12,500 DH, because that's the salary of a Filipino (with a few years of experience) living in Bur Dubai [a cheap area but far from everything] with a housemate."

"Don't come for that salary. A French degree is worth more than that. Go ahead at 20,000."

Using a similar rationale, several of my interviewees expressed the idea that certain French people, by accepting inadequate salaries, were "devaluing" that nationality. Such statements revealed that persons living in Dubai in privileged positions had gotten to the point where they no longer questioned the legitimacy of their inflated salaries and even defended the structural advantage they enjoyed. In their discourse, nationality was treated as a credential whose value the French should defend in the job market. Finally, many of those who arrived in Dubai assured that they would be working in highly advantageous conditions were disappointed: the employers often preferred candidates of other nationalities, mainly for budgetary reasons. Once again, this point reflects the disparateness of this group.

The individuals whom I have quoted here were all in Dubai on local contracts. The salaries and packages of those with an expatriate contract are overall far superior. They are negotiated prior to the move to Dubai and are rarely known to the employee's immediate colleagues. Thus, if Westerners are structurally advantaged in the job market, some can be said to be structurally *overadvantaged* by means of the expatriate contract, most of whose beneficiaries are white males.

Here is a typical French expatriate package, according to data gathered during my interviews:

Salary: $13,000 per month (net), plus bonus. Only this part is taxed in France.
Expenses covered by the company:
  Rent for a villa: 250,000 to 400,000 dirhams per year (approximately
    $75,000–$120,000)
  School fees: 40,000 dirhams per year per child
  Health insurance for the entire family
  Annual round-trip plane ticket to France for the entire family
  Utility bills (water and electricity)
  Company car

The base salary, around $156,000 per year not including the bonus, is more than doubled by the rest of the package, which is nontaxable.

Conversely, some Western passport holders benefit only to a lesser extent from such structural advantages. Some companies, rare though hardly the least important ones, practice policies of recruitment and remuneration that, for certain positions, differentiate very little among nationalities. This is the case for the flight crew of Emirates Airlines. During my study, I met with four individuals, two of whom were French, who worked for this Dubai-based airline and were flight crew members. They had been recruited during sessions organized in various large French cities, then integrated into highly diverse crews of several nationalities where, to their knowledge, contracts and salaries were identical for all, a relatively exceptional occurrence. This salary policy peculiar to flight crews does not preclude forms of differentiation at other higher levels of the professional hierarchy or in career development within the organization.

Career jumping

Although high salaries constituted the most obvious and most discussed topic in my interviews, it is not the only structural advantage that affects the distinct position of Westerners in Dubai, including those with local contracts. Among individuals who arrived in country without a contract, some experienced very rapid career trajectories through frequent changes of position, companies, and, in some cases, activity sectors. Several began at relatively low positions with commensurate salaries, and it was the rapid rise in their careers that defined the structural advantage of Westerners as compared to persons of non-Western nationalities. This was notably the case with several women I interviewed, all single without children. For instance, Charlotte, a woman of French nationality from a lower-middle-class background, nonwhite, experienced meteoric advancement. I reconstruct here her career based on her narrative.

After doing a master's in international trade in a mid-sized city, which she financed through a student loan, Charlotte came to Dubai for an unpaid internship in a hotel, though her housing, meals, and miscellaneous expenses were covered. This training stint had her working six days a week and sharing a room with a waitress of Chinese nationality. The company did not get her a visa, which meant that she was working illegally and had to leave the country every month. At the end of three months, she was offered a job, which she turned down, as she felt the pay was too low. She found another job through a colleague, which she also felt was underpaid (4,000 dirhams), but she made ends meet by continuing to live at the hotel without anyone in the company taking notice. At the end of two months, she found another job that paid 9,000 dirhams in a British company, which enabled her to afford shared rent. She got a raise within four months. At about the one-year point, a semipublic Emirati company offered her a job that was higher up in the professional hierarchy, with a sizable salary increase. She accepted. Within a year, she got a promotion with a salary hike. The pace was exhausting and stressful, and she came up against conflicts in the company, but the position was at a level that she could never have reached in France, she felt. She found a new job in 2014 with a company under Indian management, where she was paid 24,000 dirhams. Within a few months, the company started laying off a number of employees. Charlotte was not let go but she was asked to work six days a week and to work unpaid overtime. She proactively began looking for something else, for she reasoned that as an expat, she needed a bonus for being outside her own country in terms of social life. She found a job in a semipublic company that paid her 30,000 dirhams. In less than five years, then, she went from a salary of 4,000 to 30,000 dirhams (or from about $1,200 to $9,000) and switched companies five times, in addition to her initial internship. "Turnover is huge here. Two or three times a month you get contacted by recruiters," she said.

This career path discloses three peculiarities about the building of "local careers." First, Charlotte began at the low end of the salary scale, even accepting work that did not correspond to her credentials for her first job in the region. It is indeed much easier to find work once in the country than from a distance and to accept a job beneath one's expectations, hoping to get a foot in the door of the local job market.

Second, Charlotte proved resourceful and made a place for herself in Dubai. She notably housed herself in the premises made available free of charge by her previous job unbeknownst to her former employer, in order to avoid high rents. Other examples of resourcefulness include securing appointments with company heads, cold-calling for weeks on end, and going to every possible cocktail party to build up a local address book.

The third peculiarity of these local careers is perhaps the most important: the individuals who opt for this path work under a succession of local contracts to climb company hierarchies by "jumps," by regularly switching employers, as one of them told me (using the English word *jump* in an interview conducted in French). As soon as a job does not feel stimulating enough, when things "stagnate," they start "looking around," even if their present contract has only just started. This type of career is rooted in the *local* Dubai job market, punctuated by frequent switching of companies. A person's professional rank can often be transferable to other Gulf countries, though with great difficulty when it comes to France, Charlotte averred. These local trajectories differ considerably from those of salaried employees—mostly white males—under expatriate or secondment contracts whose employers offer transfers every two to four years within the same company, paying all the moving expenses. These employees may also request at any time to return to their home country. Conversely, the careers of local job-hoppers are unstable, precarious, and difficult to valorize outside Dubai; they build an ephemeral position of privilege (discussed in chapter 7).

These fast-paced local careers seem reserved for Westerners. I did not en-counter a similar case among residents not having a Western passport, even though some did experience a measurable rise, albeit slower, such as Angel-ica, of Filipino nationality, who within eleven years went from a receptionist job to director of human resources, multiplying her salary by nine.

Again, although the promotion rate of these careers amounts to a struc-tural advantage reinforcing the concentration of Westerners in senior positions, it does not characterize all the professional experiences within this group. Among the women I interviewed, those who had rapid career ad-vances were single, and not women with children to raise, against whom there appears to be a structural form of discrimination in Dubai. Although some women who had children after they had been working in Dubai for several years managed to negotiate unpaid extensions of their maternity leave (forty-five days) and felt that their situation did not pose any particular challenges, one interviewee, Lina, was fired after a trial period when she announced she was pregnant, undoubtedly an uncommon occurrence but not exceptional. The geographer Katie Walsh[9] has pointed to the "macho culture" sustained by white British males in elite professional positions in Dubai, which keeps women with children from getting jobs. This male chauvinism was also raised by several interviewees: one of them talked about the "BBC," the British Boys Club, pointing a finger at the solidarity among sexist white males in powerful positions. Others spoke out similarly against the sexism of French business-men in the French Business Council. More broadly, long working hours and the many business trips that high-level professionals have to make, especially those with expatriate contracts (regional directors, for instance) presuppose certain family arrangements, as we shall see in chapter 4.

It is also worth noting that women, even when their children live with them in Dubai, still receive less advantageous packages than men do. It is mainly men who receive the packages meant to cover a family's expenses in Dubai. Claire, a sales executive, moved to Dubai with her husband, who worked in sports and earned far less than she did. The couple was experienc-ing financial difficulties, primarily because the children's schooling was not covered by their contracts. In other words, despite her senior position, she failed to negotiate a family package—very rarely granted to women—which includes health insurance, an annual plane ticket for the family, and chil-dren's schooling covered by the company. With such packages practically inaccessible to women, it is nearly impossible for single mothers with children to afford to live in the city. Thus, these packages not only make the difference among nationalities, but also construct gender and sexuality relations within the group of Westerners. They shape specific forms of heterosexuality, characterized by a sharp labor division and women's financial dependence.

MANAGING NATIONALITIES

The differentiated management of labor is also reflected in forms of horizontal segmentation (in terms of departments and units) and vertical (hierarchical) segmentation among nationalities. Vertical segmentation translates into Western passport holders' overrepresentation in executive positions, in both local companies and multinational organizations.[10] These forms of segmentation differ greatly, however, from one company to another, and various nationalities can predominate in management positions. For instance, in French companies, French males are often overrepresented in positions at the highest level. The regional headquarters of an American company where Jean-Baptiste worked in finance was clearly segmented in terms of nationality and gender. The managers were almost always Western males, and the assistants were all Filipino and Sri Lankan females. Several persons I interviewed worked in so-called Indian companies, where the highest positions are held by Indians, or in semipublic companies under Emirati management. Most of the Westerners who work there, however, hold executive positions alongside other nationalities. Although the professional positions are indeed diversified,[11] Westerners do not occupy, or not for long, any job considered as unskilled.

As for horizontal segmentation, which varies according to sector of activity (a topic worthy of a whole study in itself), it places limits on whether different nationalities or groups of nationalities intermingle. Miguel, who worked for a French company in the luxury goods sector, explained that Indian employees are to be found in accounting, logistics, and finance but not in marketing, communication, or sales. These departments are divided across two different sites, separated by some thirty kilometers. This horizontal segmentation, materialized by physical distance, contributes to ensuring that salary and status differences do not become a source of tension: it impedes contact among persons assigned to different groups.

The hierarchy of nationalities constructed by organizations goes with widespread stereotypes, racializing nationalities (stereotypes about "Filipinos," etc.) or amalgamations of nationalities (stereotypes about "Arabs," etc.). For instance, Mike, a 60-year-old white American architect, based his point on the idea of a hierarchy in education and skills to develop a broader discourse assimilating several nationalities of the region into a single whole:

> "The [Egyptians] don't have the same quality of training. In the US, to become an architect, you have to pass exams, take courses. It's really very hard. Here, everybody's an architect overnight, just like that. And then, Egyptians hide things; they're not straightforward about things. They never want to take responsibility for decision-making. . . . I've actually worked with Jordanians and Lebanese too, but I've never really noticed any difference. Egyptians, Jordanians, Lebanese—it was always the same problems with all of them."

After ranking training and credentials according to country, to the point where he could assert that his colleagues' postsecondary degrees were worthless ("everybody's an architect overnight, just like that"), Mike linked individual behavior with their real or supposed national background. Assigning behavior to a specific nationality is quite common in the multinational work world, at both the top and the bottom of the professional ladder.[12] An essentialist, racializing reading of nationalities or groups of nationalities that ascribes specific qualities to each one combines with an assumption that members of these nationalities are automatically in solidarity with each other. Competition for control of an economic sector is often associated with fights between "mafias" of this or that nationality—the "Lebanese mafia" or the "Indian mafia," for example. One white Canadian female entrepreneur explained to me that she makes sure to gain access to these different mafias by seeking to win the trust of a friend or two within each group. Tensions inside companies are often described as clan contests among nationalities, a view expressed by Dieter, a white German human resource manager, with regard to a French company where he used to work:

> "Sometimes, Arab nationalities complain about other Arab nationalities, simply in a bid to self-promote, which I think is a very common thing in the region. So as soon as they have a critical mass of a certain nationality, they try to help each other out."

The interpretive framework of nationalities as involving set behaviors and solidarity groups is at the heart of the management strategies of numerous white Western males that I interviewed. It sometimes influenced the division of labor and the composition of work teams within companies, as revealed in an interview with Guillaume, a 40-year-old white French male who had spent his entire career in the region and was currently working in the logistics sector.

"I'm in charge of teams that are really made up of different nationalities. There are Filipinos; there are Indians, mainly in offices. Pakistanis. I also had some Egyptians. Now Jordanians and Egyptians. As for blue-collars, we had Indians, Pakistanis, Thais, Kenyans, a little of everything. Depending on the nationality, people work differently, so you have to know how to handle that—well, *handle* isn't perhaps the right word, but you have to know how to quote-unquote manage the nationalities."

"Do you have an example?"

". . . For instance, among the blue-collar workers, if there is a large group of workers of the same nationality, they're going to group together and form quote-unquote pressure groups. So what we do is to make sure their boss is of a different nationality. For Indians, we're not going to place a group who are all from the same state. Otherwise, it's the same thing, they get together and try to put pressure . . . Anyway, that's how we try to manage things. Or there are certain nationalities who are better than others. . . . Filipinos are great at anything having to do with repetitive, administrative work . . . not that they're—I mean, I'm not saying anything negative here. But when you give them a task, if it's one that involves repetition, they're great; they do a wonderful job. On the other hand, that means they're less creative, most probably. You need to know that when you hire somebody. That's the kind of thing you learn through experience on the job."

Many Western managers make use of national stereotypes in their management work. Nationality as a catchall explanation offers them a simple interpretive key to make sense out of complex configurations about which they know so little, without going any deeper or questioning their own position. These remarks about clans and mafias suggest that the speaker's position is neutral: I never heard anyone talk about a "Westerner mafia" or a "French mafia," even if the French did accuse the British of scooping up all the contracts. Western managers see themselves as outside these solidarities, which they describe as clannish. This sort of attitude can be compared to colonial stereotypes deployed with regard to this or that "ethnicity." The nationality rationale enables management to break up any solidarity among workers—even though trade unions are already forbidden—and to set the different nationalities in competition with one another inside each team. Guillaume's narrative, like so many others, offers a glimpse into the way racialized national origins are manipulated with the twin purpose of productivity and disciplining staff, in a manner comparable to how things operate in other contexts.[13]

Management of nationalities goes hand in hand with the construction of the "Western boss" figure, so key to the history of masculinity and whiteness, as demonstrated in other contexts.[14] In a hotel business under Emirati ownership where I conducted interviews, the managing directors of three hotels owned by the group are white males of European nationality. In one of these hotels, I observed how the one everybody calls *boss*, a man of German nationality named Karl, established his authority over his subordinates of diverse nationalities, mainly Indian and Pakistani. Karl embodied and performed a kind of domineering masculinity, positioned in the hierarchies of class, race, and nationality. For instance, during a meeting, he deployed a certain body language, like forcing a smile or gazing skyward or tapping on the table; he interrupted his subordinates and belittled them. He berated at length a manager of Indian nationality, with comments such as "Have you got a brain in your head or not? Well, take it out and use it," and he ended his rant with a degrading "All right, baba?" I found out later that he called all his Indian subordinates "baba." With this label, he relegated them all to an interchangeable national and racial group where they have no first names. This word, used in several countries of the region, connotes a kind of condescending familiarity. In Qatar, it was used by masters to address their male slaves.[15]

When he tried to justify himself after the meeting, behind closed doors, Karl said that his management style was probably not what I was used to. It is a fact that, depending on the sector of activity, high-placed males embody their executive function according to different codes. In Startup Z, their apparel, posture, and way of addressing employees, often tinged with humor and irony, conveyed a more relaxed managerial masculinity. But although such forms of exercising authority are more subtle, they are nonetheless effective. My observations at Hotel A, though not generalizable to all organizations, provide insight into what possibly goes on in highly hierarchical sectors, of which there are many in Dubai, where a handful of Westerners occupy positions of power and where virtually all salaried employees come from the working and middle classes of Southern countries and are kept at so-called unskilled jobs, apart from a few managers. Professional relations in the hospitality industry, a highly developed sector in Dubai and very explicitly hierarchized, contribute to establishing and perpetuating the association between Western masculinity and authority.

RACIALIZED OR INSTRUMENTAL NATIONALITIES?

This chapter has analyzed the various processes whereby organizations construct Westerners as an advantaged group: the salary differential, career jumping, forms of horizontal and vertical segmentation, and management styles. The people I interviewed had a stake in this differentiated management of labor. They contributed to both the valorization of Westerners and the racialization of different nationalities. This construction of the status of Westerner by work organizations results in two distinct but interdependent processes that link nationality and racialization: on the one hand, the development of an instrumental approach to the Western passport among elites in the region, and on the other, the projection of advantageous stereotypes onto persons socialized in Western countries as a function of their nationality.

Flexible citizenship and the Western passport

The way organizations manage labor is linked not only to the UAE's migration policies but also to those of other countries in the region and beyond. A shield against the precariousness of residency rights in the Emirates,[16] a Western passport also gives access to advantages in the job market and can even constitute a prerequisite for jobs that require travel across borders. This prompts the region's elites, especially people with Middle Eastern and North African passports, to try to obtain a second nationality, as explained to me by Amir, an Iranian-Canadian businessman with a Canadian master's degree:

> "Dubai was a happy in-between choice: I would be close enough to Iran—I mean, it is an hour-and-forty-minute flight to Teheran—and I would have all the flexibility and all the . . . I mean, at least the appearance of a Western lifestyle, or the comfort of a Western lifestyle, shall we say. . . . If I had an Iranian passport, I would not have the same flexibility to work here in Dubai. . . . I did not want to leave North America without a passport, basically. It is funny how countries in this region treat—afford a higher degree of respect—to Western

passports than to their own neighbors' passports, whereas it is exactly the opposite in, let's say, Europe. . . ."

"If you had an Iranian passport what would happen?"

". . . Given what has happened in the past two years with sanctions against Iran, I know a lot of Iranians got the residence visa canceled actually, so they had to go back home [to Iran]. You just show up to the police one day to renew your visa . . . , and when you arrive they tell you : 'We are sorry. The internal security department does not approve the renewal of your visa.' . . ."

"And in the job market, do you observe the same kind of thing? . . ."

"Of course. . . . A lot of my job involves travelling, so I cannot blame my employer because they would not hire me with an Iranian passport. . . . With an Iranian passport, I would have had to apply for a visa one month in advance every time I had a business trip."

Amir, son of a businessman, raised in Iran and Turkey, was referring to a strategic, or instrumental, use of nationality, with the effect of demystifying it as a source of belonging.[17] He wished to procure a Western passport, he said, for himself and then for his son, so as to escape the subaltern status to which his nationality consigned him in Dubai. He stated at one and the same time his aspiration to live a "Western style" of life and his Middle Eastern sense of belonging, expressing himself always as an Iranian, never as a Canadian. He also asserted his membership in the upper classes throughout the interview. His approach to the issue of passports in terms of unfairness distinguished him from most of the white people that I interviewed.

Of course, strategies in terms of migration and nationalities are not limited to elites. As underlined before, many inhabitants, including working-class ones, consider Dubai a "waiting room" before migrating elsewhere, especially to Europe or North America.[18] In this case, they develop a strategic use of Dubai rather than of the Western passport, which they don't have, at least as long as they stay in Dubai. The specificity of binational business elites like Amir is that they have a second passport not necessarily to settle in another country but rather to be able to move freely and have a good salary and status while living in Dubai by choice. These strategic uses of nationality partly blur the boundaries among the group of Westerners, since individuals like Amir do not clearly identify, or at least not consistently, with that group. In addition, such practices are not identified as such by others—for instance, a human resource manager of Sudanese nationality who described her boss as "a Moroccan with a British passport." For these members of the upper classes of non-hegemonic countries, naturalization typically tends to be "handled and experienced as a purely administrative procedural matter, irrespective of any other significations."[19] It allows for a certain "flexibility," the word Amir uses regarding Dubai. These elites' strategic use of nationality echoes the "flexible citizens" that Aihwa Ong describes as "mobile managers, techno-crats, and professionals seeking to both circumvent and benefit from different nation-state regimes by selecting different sites for investments, work, and family relocation."[20] This use of the Western passport contributes to destabi-lizing the connections between Westernness and whiteness.

Stereotypes regarding Westerners in the job market

Beyond the passport issue, the preference for Western nationals, or even specific Western nationalities, can assume a racialized dimension, especially when this preference bears on individuals socialized in those countries and not on elites of the Middle East region having double nationality like Amir. What motivates the hire is therefore not only the purported search for top credentials but also, as the interviews revealed, the quest for a cer-tain image. Individuals are chosen for the image they supposedly project by their appearance, their accent, and their behavior, considered typical of Westerners in general or of one specific nationality. In other words, physical and cultural characteristics get ascribed to them because of their supposed origin and their membership in a group (national or pan-national), which amounts to a process—unstable and fluctuating—of essentializing and at times racializing. For instance, French nationality can reflect a whole range of stereotypes projected onto French individuals, mixing purported skills, linked more broadly to a Western bloc thought to be at the cutting edge of professionalism, and so-called cultural, or even natural, features (whiteness, accent when speaking English, refinement, elegance in all circumstances, slenderness). These stereotypes are gendered. A white French woman told me she thought she was hired for a sales position precisely as a "young French woman":

> "When you have to work in sales, it's already a plus to be a girl, and French is even better; we have this image of luxury, fashion, good food, French cuisine . . . So, it's true that when you tell people you're French, they automatically view you favorably. And I noticed it over two years, it facilitates business, it facilitates

your relations with clients and suppliers. It can make a difference." [Jeanne, marketing employee, 26 years old]

Such statements were hardly exceptional. I heard similar reports from several other male and female interviewees, whose narratives attest that such stereotypes get projected onto people of French nationality whether they would be considered white or nonwhite in France. For instance, Inès and Fatima, both descendants of Moroccan migrants in France, emphasized the advantage of being "French" in the Dubai professional world, when it came to image.

"Having a French girl in the company, that can improve the company's image, you know." [Inès, manager, 30 years old]

"We're well-educated, after all, we're so much more rigorous at work than some other nationalities . . . which means that you always have that little extra something when you're French. We always have a better reputation. When they hear our accent, when we speak on the phone, right away they trust us more. They always get all interested in where you live in France. . . . If I were Indian, if I were Filipina—you see, I wouldn't have had that kind of thing happen." [Fatima, entrepreneur, 34 years old]

Khaled, a 30-year-old who had had a local "jump" career in Dubai for seven years, told me how being French mattered in one of the companies where he worked. He had earned a two-year associate degree in international trade and had been working the same job in France for three years (a job that it had taken a year to find) when he left for Dubai. In less than four months after his arrival, he left the business for which he came to Dubai and was hired by a Lebanese company that emphasized the fact that he is French.

"They sold it like it was added value for the company. Every time they met someone, they would say, especially the boss, who was Lebanese: 'He's a French employee, one of my employees is French.' It was a plus, value added. . . . A company where there are Europeans, where they have lots of European employees, is a company that's, let's say—how should I put it? An organized company. With a more cutting-edge organization. That's the image they give, anyway."

Khaled was immediately paid more than his co-workers for the same job even though they had more experience, and he was moved up to manager within a few months. He attributed the promotion to his status as a French-man "beyond his actual professional capacities."

> "Here's the thing, I brought a lot to the company, but I think that I would have moved up much more slowly if I had been Indian or something else."

Uneasy with the management methods that put him in an awkward position vis-à-vis his co-workers, he left the company for another job elsewhere. He then switched companies again, climbing the corporate ladder with each move. In the meantime, he acquired a "professionally useful" level of Middle Eastern Arabic. In seven years in Dubai, his salary multiplied by seven. Although he was staying there for professional reasons, he criticized the "arrogance" of the Dubai inhabitants and was thinking about leaving in the medium term, perhaps for Asia.

In the range of stereotypes conveyed by these interviews, the tourist's image of France—luxury, taste, refinement, and so on—combines with that of professional expertise. These individuals emphasized the fact that they had been hired and advantaged compared with their co-workers not only for their professional skills or college degrees but also for the prestige they supposedly would bring to the company. Their nationality entered into the organization's branding, the construction of its image. In Dubai, these stereotypes can in certain cases decouple European nationalities from whiteness. This stands in contrast with what is happening in most European countries today, where Europeanness is tacitly associated with whiteness, constituting an implicit norm, while nonwhite European citizens are structurally depreciated and discriminated against.[21] The way Europeanness, Westernness, and Frenchness are conceived in Dubai differs, therefore, from how they are thought about in Europe, particularly in France. In the Dubai job market, the structural advantages that construct the status of Westerner seem to depict a group with vague, ill-defined borders. On the one hand, persons born and socialized in the region, like Amir, make an instrumental use of the Western passport, obtaining it later in life, to overcome certain well-defined obstacles in their professional career. On the other hand, advantageous stereotypes that go beyond the professional sphere are projected onto persons socialized in European countries, who, whether white or nonwhite, by their mere presence are assumed to add value to the organizations where they work. Still, nonwhites with Western passports can be ascribed various stereotypes, even some contradictory ones, depending on whether they get assigned to their passport nationality or to another nationality or membership, as we shall see in the following chapters.

*   *   *

This chapter exposed the various processes whereby Westerners are differentiated in the job market to their advantage in terms of salary, career development, job segmentation, and nationality-based management, all of which contribute to constructing them as a structurally privileged group. The companies where they are often decision-makers play an important role in shaping and preserving the overlapping hierarchies of gender, class, race, and nationality through the apportionment of contracts, salaries and packages, positions and roles. The racial reconfigurations at work in the job market prompt us to question the image of Westernness as embodied by the individuals concerned.

CHAPTER 3

PERFORMING STEREOTYPICAL WESTERNNESS

"Their paths are perfectly straight and smooth, you feel like these are people who are completely carefree. Dubai is a city of winners." [Emilie, 34]

EARLY IN MY SECOND STAY IN DUBAI, I took part in a considerable number of networking events, gatherings intended to broaden everyone's circle of business contacts. In this regard, my experience in Dubai was comparable to that of many recent arrivals seeking employment or hoping to fill their address book with potential business acquaintances. Networking events are numerous in Dubai and there is no need to know someone in order to attend: all information is web-based and openly available. This does not mean, as we shall see, that everybody has access, nor are the chances for success necessarily equal. Networking events are there for people to appear in public and "sell themselves." The first cocktail party I attended brought together the French-speaking community, and people looking for jobs were advised to go.

The entrance fee to the cocktail party was 50 dirhams, about $15. I'm standing at the bar when the first person comes up to talk. He's a 27-year-old man, tall, dark hair, olive-skinned, wearing a suit and tie. He shakes my hand and says, "This is the first time I've come to this kind of event," which puts me at ease. We talk a little. He explains that he's from southern France, where he was a tennis coach, and works today in the hotel business. It turns out that he left France in 2006, spent two years in Qatar again as a tennis coach, and then he came to the Emirates. That's when he started doing something different. Tennis coach, he explained, that doesn't pay very well: "Here, it's mostly Indians and Filipinos, so the pay is low." I ask him what he means by "low." How much exactly? He answers that it's often less than €1,000. For the hotel, it was a way to get his foot in the door, and he was able to climb the ladder very quickly. Within three years, he had a management position. Later, he tells me his father is Lebanese and his mother French, that French nationality is a real asset, because here in Dubai, "the French are well-regarded." He then offers to reserve me a hotel apartment in his establishment for 19,000 dirhams (around $5,700) a month. I tell him that's really too much for my budget. He asks me if I enjoy this sort of cocktail party, and I tell him I'm here for my study. He replies that he is "really here for work, but in Dubai, everything is business. It's all fake." And with that, he takes his leave, saying, "Madame, it was a pleasure, I'm going to keep making the rounds," and he shakes my hand.

There I am, alone amid a highly primed crowd, a glass of Perrier in my hand. Two persons are making their way to the bar, and I am standing between them and the barman. I am first struck by how tall the young woman is; then, when I look down at her feet, I see she is wearing spike heels—I'd say over four inches. Her nails are done in bright red; her long, straight hair is chestnut with blond highlights; tan skin; lipstick. She's in trousers and a jacket, but at the same time, she doesn't look dressed to the nines like everybody else; she looks more relaxed. We make our introductions, and Maud puts me immediately at ease. She's quite informal and immediately suggests that we switch out of the formal French *vous* and use *tu* with each other. She offers to take me along with her friend for the tour of introductions and business card exchanges. She has been in Dubai for only two months and says that she has already found everything she needs: friends, housing, a car, activities; she feels like she has always lived here. She works as a headhunter. She worked in Paris for several years, then took a year off to travel, came through Dubai, where she met her current partner, and decided to move here. She contacted her former employer and was hired by the same company but in the Dubai office. "I haven't seen any downsides yet to living here. I see only advantages; everything is easy," she tells me. "It's all about networking here." Networking is all she does: even when she goes out to nightclubs, she brings her business cards. She thinks it's fantastic to be able to meet very senior businesspeople and to talk simply, something she feels would be impossible in France. A bit later, I get to talking with the person she came with to the cocktail party, a man who works in a relocation company, while she turns around to talk with two men in their 50s, the oldest at this gathering, where nearly everyone looks to be between 20 and 35. About an hour later, I catch up with Maud again: she has nearly run out of business cards, even though she brought a supply of fifty or so. I tell her she's very good at this game. She politely takes the cards of people looking for work, but actually, the people she's most eager to meet are the executives to whom she can "sell" candidates. She moves in the direction of the older men.

This cocktail party initiated me to an important skill: what is known in Dubai and elsewhere as "selling yourself." It is a key skill for many of those who move to Dubai or who are in the sales professions there, but not only sales. I met people in the health professions, for instance, who were trying to spread the word about their "business" at these networking events. Whether or not it is thought of in such terms, these performances of self-promotion involve real bodily and emotional labor. The notion of performance here refers to self-presentation, partly conscious—in this sense, we can talk of staging oneself—but largely unconscious, shaped by different socializations that are hard to monitor. To participate in this kind of event, people must be able to put themselves forward, to self-present in a way that is adapted to the venue, and to speak English (or here, French). Not everybody has such skills.

Attendees mustn't be intimidated by the luxurious hotel décor. Although very few people outside the upper crust are accustomed to these five-star venues, it is a setting that Westerners adjust to very quickly, since a large part of Dubai social life takes place in hotel bars—one of the few places where the sale of alcohol was authorized before 2020 (when the ban was lifted). Nor should they feel uncomfortable in a crowd of stylishly dressed people who conform to hegemonic binary gender norms: for the men, closely cropped hair, suit and tie; for the women, heavy makeup, long hair, high heels. Guests are constantly looking around to see who might prove useful, trusting certain signs to assess how much power this or that person might wield: age, gender, self-assurance, skin color, style of dress. Finally, once a target has been identified, it takes a certain composure to approach someone, to perhaps interrupt a conversation, to know just the appropriate or clever thing to say, to attract attention, to be comfortable and relaxed, and all of this at virtually the same instant: no one will waste time with a person they judge uninteresting.

Undoubtedly, because my presence seemed somewhat offbeat, or because I'd done a poor job at hiding my lack of self-assurance, several persons dropped the mask of expected behavior for a moment and confessed that they felt ill at ease, before setting off again to sell themselves. This was not Maud's case. For her, such a performance seemed utterly spontaneous: not a single detail gave away how hard and how consciously she might have been working emotionally to appear so relaxed and sociable.

Westernness is constructed like a sales pitch in service of the Dubai brand. It is tacitly expected that people will perform an essentialized Westernness, one that has been shaped in a singular manner. To conform to norms of behavior and self-presentation that reflect Westernness in Dubai requires a particular bodily and emotional kind of labor. This labor makes it possible to sell not only the Dubai brand but other company brands as well—and to *sell yourself*, an often-used expression. Selling yourself in this corporate city consists of promoting yourself in the job market and compiling a network of useful contacts. The routine use of this expression reveals an individualistic approach that tends to conceal the inequality of opportunity due to factors independent of the people concerned—in particular, their position in inter-locking hierarchies of gender, class, race, and nationality. A person's capacity to sell themself is facilitated, though not determined, by socialization in a par-ticular milieu: individuals who succeed in playing this game have contrasting trajectories; to adapt to these norms, they have to work on themselves, con-sciously or unconsciously, and are transformed as a result. For some, this work fits into an ongoing learning process that began at business school,[1] where the curriculum addresses "self-marketing." Others, who have not had this kind of training, gradually learn to incorporate and perform a stereotypi-cal professional Westernness.

Emotional labor, a concept from sociological analysis developed notably in the wake of Arlie Hochschild,[2] highlights the ways that people adapt and respond to what she calls *feeling rules* by striving to experience the emo-tions that correspond to those expected of them or to a given situation (e.g., to feel sad at a funeral or happy at a wedding). While Hochschild was in-terested in cognitive, bodily and expressive aspects of emotional labor in professional situations, feminist geographer Linda McDowell[3] analyzed bodily labor more specifically by studying gender performance and its link to heteronormativity in the field of finance in London. In her estimation, many jobs require "the marketing of personal attributes, including sexual-ity."[4] Analyzing sexualized performances in London merchant banks, she shows that the emotional labor of interaction with clients is also bodily labor, engaging body disciplines, dress codes, and implicit performance rules of a certain sexual identity at the workplace. Although many of her conclusions resonate with my observations, one limit of her theory lies in her focus on masculinity and femininity by isolating them from other dimensions of social hierarchies that contribute to their construction, especially class and race. Sociologist Beverley Skeggs,[5] by linking emotions and bodies, has scrutinized the way bodily practices and expression of emotion are read, coded, and interpreted in terms of class, race, and gender: certain behavior types are expected of certain persons, and this does not come down to a binary classification in terms of gender. As I will show, the Dubai job market valorizes an emphatically (hetero) sexualized Western femininity, situated in terms of race, class, and gender.

In this chapter, I am interested most specifically in the gendered and racialized incorporation of Westernness, in the way a person can be perceived as Western and in the effort exerted toward that objective. I shall be analyzing both the coding of self-performance observed in Dubai and the bodily and emotional labor required to conform to the corporeal and behavioral norms that allow an individual to be identified with the group of Westerners and valorized as a member of that group. We shall see ultimately that this bodily labor involves other persons, considered non-Western. Incorporation is to be considered broadly here, including the effects of transformative technologies (clothing, makeup, exercise, plastic surgery), self-presentation, posture and movement, voice intonation, and even accent and speech mannerisms.

BODY IMAGES

The foreign residents of Dubai are selected according to health standards. Medical testing is required to obtain residency status, and the presence of viruses like HIV is grounds for refusal. More broadly, given the connection in Dubai between work contracts and residency rights on the one hand and the high cost of insurance and health care on the other, persons who are sick, handicapped, or aged are exceedingly rare, and mostly national citizens. Representations of the city's inhabitants, deployed to signify its modernity and cosmopolitanism, reveal certain expectations in this regard.

Dubai, as a global city and a "city-corporation," is engaged in a strategy of branding. The urban landscape is shaped by "starchitecture,"[6] investment in buildings and facilities meant to enhance the country's greatness through architectural innovation. Many recent structures are designed to be photo-graphed and viewed throughout the world rather than by the people who physically inhabit the space. Gigantic billboards, like those on Sheykh Zayed Road, a twelve-lane highway above which runs an elevated railway that spans the city from north to south, boast of a new luxury residential complex or convey an enthusiastic message from the emir about Expo 2020 Dubai. As a corporate city, Dubai not only advertises itself but is also flooded by the ad campaigns of a huge range of companies.

The image of whiteness is used by leaders to sell the city.[7] Although Indian nationals make up the numerical majority, the advertising images repre-senting Dubai's inhabitants, such as those intended to promote real estate projects or entertainment venues, rarely show people that spontaneously call to mind persons of that nationality. Some show Emiratis, as suggested by a manner of dress recognized today as national. Dubai's foreign residents are most often represented as fair or olive-complexioned blond women or fair-complexioned men, sometimes accompanied by children. This is notably the case for advertisements for a supermarket in the Marina quarter, a pricey neighborhood inhabited by people of various nationalities, as well as for the handbook of Hotel A, the overwhelming majority of whose employees are not white. In other words, whether or not the target population for the ads is white, the bodies represented in them are fair-skinned.

The city also displays images of visibly wealthy persons with sophis-ticated self-presentations, whose skin can be more olive though never dark-complexioned. A billboard advertising a real estate development, the "Beverly Hills of Dubai," depicts a scene with an olive-skinned woman, curly blond hair, looking both dressed up and partly undressed, in a come-hither pose. An ad for a public fountain under construction in the Marina quarter shows an olive-skinned child playing in the future facility. These representations contribute to constructing the Dubai brand as a modern, global city that attracts whites but also as a multicultural city, open and tolerant—a city where wealthy and sophisticated people from a variety of cultures cross paths, all in a soothing climate of security. These images are also consistent with a neoliberal discourse at work in other contexts, advocating consumerist multiculturalism and diversity via notions such as cosmopolitanism or hybridity, while obscuring structural power relations, especially structural racism.[8]

Lastly, the visual representations in the city are imbued with stereotypical gender identities, often associated with consumer products. During one of my stays in the city, ads in the subway indicated the expansion of space reserved for "women and children" in railcars by featuring a tube of lipstick and a baby bottle: the inhabitants of Dubai, women in particular, are prompted to turn themselves into sophisticated consumerist subjects in line with binary gender identities.

NEGOTIATING THE "RIGHT LOOK"

The professional world is obsessed by brand imaging. People I met who headed work teams or were involved in human resources placed only a relative value on college degrees, favoring instead more nebulous criteria that might make all the difference during the recruitment process: the "right look" or the "personality." I asked them what they meant by these vague terms. Melanie, a salaried employee (French) in a recruitment office, attempted to clarify them during our interview:

> "Image is very important here. This means that no matter what your position is, you're an ambassador for the brand. So somebody with the right image and great presentation will often get favorable treatment, more so than for their college degree. They're looking more for a personality than a profile. . . . In France, your degree is the access code to get past the first stage. Your CV. Here, they're looking to see whether the person is friendly, nice, if they present well—that's it. They'll base recruitment more on your soft skills, which means your life skills. . . . For administrative positions, they do often ask for someone who presents well; a photo is always required with the CV, for example. . . ."
>
> "So, what is meant by right image?"
>
> "A good presentation. . . . For a job as executive assistant, it means you have to have a businesswoman look, I guess. Take extra care to be dressed just right, I think that's what it means. I've actually never asked them the question."

What is peculiar about the skills mentioned is that none is clearly defined; they sound more like characteristics or qualities than skills. During the interviews, "good presentation" and "right attitude" returned again and again as key recruitment criteria. Ella, a salaried employee at Startup Z (Norwegian nationality), explained to me that she needed to recruit someone for her team, and she was looking for "personality" above all else. When I asked her what she meant by that, she replied:

"I'm looking for someone with a good attitude. Someone who works well in a team, who has a positive attitude. Who's friendly and relaxed. Open-minded. Who has the same mindset as we do, transparent, positive, relaxed, open."

The "good presentation" and soft skills are not particular to Dubai. In other contexts, what are also called relational skills are valued by employers.[9] Still, in such a multinational job market as Dubai's, college degrees are ascribed only a relative value. Although they are weighed on the basis of the country where they are earned, and even if a degree issued by a Western university is seen as a valuable asset, soft skills can partly compensate for the absence of a strong degree, at least for Western passport holders. Good presentation and the right people skills, both highly valued, cover quite a range of specific criteria, as I understood them throughout my interviews, even though they were most often implicit: displaying outward signs of wealth, concealing any signs of religious affiliation, dressing in a way that reflects a certain construction of professional Westernness, speaking English with a European or American accent, and cultivating the art of ordinary interactions, including a sense of culturally situated humor.

DISPLAYING OUTWARD SIGNS OF WEALTH

A French entrepreneur, Fatima, in her 30s, stressed the importance of displaying visibly expensive objects in order to be taken seriously. For her, this was a prime criterion of "good presentation":

"In Dubai, when you have a meeting for a major company, if you're a guy, they're going to look at your watch, and if you're a girl, they'll look to see how smartly you're dressed, if you're wearing a diamond. . . . In France, if you have a Chanel handbag at a [professional appointment], it's considered tacky, if you know what I mean. . . . [Here] you had better be decked out with things of value. . . . So it was hard for me at first, because I had to get used to all that. When I first got here, I felt really uncomfortable."

For Fatima, displaying outward signs of wealth was a judgment criterion for an entrepreneur, and more broadly for any person working in sales. She herself had to learn how to best present herself according to the codes, quite different from those she had learned in France, in her village, or at the small-town business school where she got her three-year degree. Her professors there recommended that students should not display conspicuous signs of wealth, explaining that they would arouse distrust.

> "I come from a village of 5,000 inhabitants . . . even though I've traveled a lot . . . So I started with London, which was already—all the girls had Chanel bags . . . After that, I came here, where it's all about excessive luxury . . . [. . .] I was a little shocked by all the excess, the luxury. After a while, I realized that you kind of had to play along to be able to—here, if you're not well dressed, you're not successful."

When we got together, she conformed to this model. For the interview, she set our appointment in the lobby of a luxury hotel in an expensive part of town, arrived dressed in what for me are sophisticated, expensive clothes, though her look was casual; she ordered several drinks and paid the bill. Consumerism, the performance of spending money and showing off brands considered prestigious, is central to interpreting people's membership in a given class. There are obviously other kinds of capital within Dubai society, like family capital that distinguishes certain "important families" or the importance of degrees obtained from universities in the US or the UK. Nevertheless, in a professional world where many are just passing through and where everyone has to be able to quickly situate a new acquaintance, looking wealthy constitutes a criterion that links with that of nationality. Still, it is possible to fake it in these international social environments.[10] Before starting her business, Fatima had lived in Dubai for a year with the status granted by a tourist visa, which obliged her to leave the country every forty days. She was working illegally and was thus in a precarious situation, all the while displaying outward signs of wealth.

DISSIMULATING THE PRACTICE OF ISLAM

In order to conform to a certain construction of professional Westernness, a second implicit criterion is the absence of signs indicating the practice of Islam.[11] Several individuals report cases of discrimination in hiring candidates whose practice of the religion was deemed too overt by the recruiters (such as a veil or beard); dismissals of salaried Muslims who wanted to pray during working hours were also cited in Emirati, French, and American companies. Several factors explain why such discrimination is common, in apparent contradiction with the Emirates' Islamic image constructed through other measures (proclamation of Islam as state religion, limitation of alcohol sales). Firstly, companies enjoy considerable autonomy in Dubai's neoliberal economy. The absence of anti-discrimination laws allows them to adopt the same practices they would in other contexts with regard to persons whose practice of Islam is deemed too conspicuous, as I was told by Melanie, an employee of a recruitment firm, cited above:

"The recruiters tell me overtly, for instance, 'I don't want any veiled women.' No one here has a problem with saying that.... There's no taboo in that regard."

Secondly, although the stereotyped construction of Westernness benefits the group concerned, it also shapes normative expectations. People hired in this setting are expected to perform a stereotypical professional Western identity, where women wear tailored suits, and men wear suits and ties, so as to embody the Dubai image as a global city. Esteban told me that as a job candidate wearing a short beard and having declared that he was Muslim (religious affiliation is often asked on the job application), he met with opposition during a final interview:

"He says to me: 'So, the beard, what do you think about it?' I said: 'I don't understand.' He went on: 'Do you wear it all the time?' I answered: 'Well, yes!' ... It's a question I had never thought to ask myself, so I asked him why. He says: 'Well, here's the thing, in the luxury goods industry, it's not something that's done, really.' ... He asked me if I was religious. I didn't quite know how to reply. So I said: 'It's a little bit of both. It's a fashion.' Because it's a nice beard, close cut most of the time; it's clean. So he says: 'Oh, I was afraid that during Ramadan, you would let it grow really long.' I say: 'No, no, but if you'd like, I can go to the barber's every day.' We ended up talking about it for five minutes, and I closed by saying: 'We can discuss it again later.' ... They never followed up."

During the same conversation, the potential employer explained that not having wine with a business lunch projected the wrong image of the company. This reference to wine on the part of an American interlocutor in a professional context where alcohol was unavailable except in hotel restaurants and very expensive is not trivial. Certain positions are said to require employees to adopt behavior typical of European business classes. This directive is specifically addressed to persons whom employers expect to correspond to a certain image of Frenchness and/or Westernness.

Such practices result from a combination of discriminatory practices against Muslims brought in from different countries, linked to forms of racialization of individuals assumed to be Muslim,[12] and the construction in the job market of a stereotypical Westernness that excludes outward signs deemed too overtly Islamic. Within administrations and companies, only Emiratis, with their traditional dress (*dishdasha* for men, '*abaya* for women), are encouraged to display signs likely to be associated with Islam and thereby perform a kind of national authenticity.

SPECIFIC PRESSURE ON PEOPLE OF COLOR

As such discrimination shows, specific normative pressure weighs on the behavior of persons expected to embody Westernness, and this is all the more applicable to nonwhites. Others in their environment continuously try to figure out where to place them racially, whether they should be considered French, Western, or Arab, or some combination, for instance. They come under a kind of scrutiny that they find oppressive. A young Frenchman from the Caribbean recalled a casual conversation where the other person "was looking me up and down." This ceaseless scrutiny and questioning signify and reproduce power relations.[13] Such recurring hesitation outlines normative Westernness, which remains associated with whiteness, though without being reduced to whiteness alone. Liminal and unstable, the Westernness of nonwhites can be jeopardized at any moment.

Irrespective of presumed religious signifiers, in the professional sphere, nonwhites can be summoned to reassert their "Western" national status when faced with competing categorizations. "I was advised to 'wear my passport on my sleeve' and unfortunately it's very true here! As others have said, where you come from is vitally important to people here," explained a participant in a discussion forum entitled "UK Indians in the UAE."[14] During a first encounter, there always seems to be the need to clear up some doubt, as affirmed by Tony, a resident of French nationality:

> "I am of Bangladeshi origin, and in most cases, I'm thought to be Bangladeshi at first. But very quickly, because of my style of dress, and as soon as I start to speak, they understand that I'm not . . . that I'm from somewhere else. So, at that point, I get treated a little differently. But at the outset, people are definitely wondering."

This extract from an interview suggests how central self-presentation is in the performance, whether unconscious or strategic, of a status that is different from other, less-valorized statuses. He cited "style of dress" as one of the criteria that enabled him to be classified in a certain category. We can assume that displaying outward signs of wealth, the criterion put forward by Fatima, takes on all the more importance when a person is not white, since it contributes to removing any uncertainty. This self-presentation also involves language and bodily practices. For instance, Neha Vora analyzes her own experience in a comparable context. In Qatar, where she was teaching at a university, she recalls, "I consciously performed as a Western anthropologist in front of my classroom, emphasizing my American accent and asserting my positionality as someone who was not Indian 'from India' in order to maintain authority."[15]

The structural advantages to being Western thus come laden with normative expectations that specifically constrain the behaviors of nonwhites. "Do I look French enough?" This comment a young woman posted on her Facebook page next to her selfie, showing her in a navy blue striped skirt and a little scarf around her neck, is making fun of the directive to perform one's nationality. Made explicit on an official "multicultural day" at her company, this message is tacit but ever-present on other days as well.

Nonwhites with Western passports can at times be subject to contradictory expectations. For instance, Bilal, of French nationality, working in the "intercultural" area, reported that his direct superior reassured a female collaborator of Brazilian nationality, fearful that he was to become her manager, by reminding her that he is "French" and not "Arab." This rationale reestablished her professional credibility in a way, he explained to me. On the other hand, Bilal told me that he felt valued in the job market because of his Arabic language skills. He found this paradoxical, since Arabic was almost never used in the professional setting: no negotiation, no presentation was ever done in Arabic in his company. In his view, "Arab" (his family is in fact Kabyle, he would clarify later) was valorized for the trust it might inspire. He added that, according to him, there was an actual difference in terms of know-how and mentality, as he preferred to meet with people in person, a better strategy, in his opinion, while Europeans communicate by email or phone. During our conversation, Bilal described his "double" affiliation as a source of specific cultural skills, endorsing essentialist stereotypes according to a mechanism brought to light by Nacira Guénif Souilamas.[16] Bilal's narrative reveals the contradictory expectations that weigh upon many nonwhites socialized in Western countries: even though some situations allow these individuals to foreground double belongings in a valorizing manner, at other times they are called upon to justify their Westernness.

I met with several persons to whom their co-workers attributed only one affiliation: they were not prompted to justify their Westernness but were assigned to whiteness, which also came at a cost. For instance, an Iraqi-American architect confessed how uneasy she felt at a meeting when one of her British collaborators circulated a caricature that represented Iraqis as sectarian, backward, and incapable of agreeing about how to build their country's future. "I don't think they realized that I'm Arab," she says. This sort of ordinary workday interaction reveals the assumption of whiteness that prevails in certain sectors and at the highest echelons of the professional world. Complicity feeds on this presumed identification.

Although the normative pressure that coerces individuals to match Western stereotypes mainly concerns residents who are Western passport holders, it also weighs on persons originating from non-Western countries who occupy, or seek to occupy, skilled positions. Gayatri, an architect of Indian nationality, reported that the sari, considered an "ethnic garment," was forbidden by most companies in Dubai, with the exception of Indian-owned companies: "You have to dress Western."

> "The unspoken rule here is to include a photo with your CV. One of my friends looked very Indian on her CV. A consultant friend of hers told her: 'Don't dress like that, you'll never find a job.'"

These different situations show how the job market produces norms of self-presentation and forms of exclusion in terms of gender, class, race, and nationality. The norm consists of considering one type of so-called Western dress—broken into various versions that reaffirm binary gender—as neutral and professional, while any other style of dress, perceived as "ethnic" or as religiously inspired (in the case of the hijab), discredits the person wearing it and limits job opportunities and advancement. Once this hurdle is passed, some people are still seen as more desirable than others in the job market. Certain attitudes are valorized, especially whether you are seen as nice or fun, which requires particular bodily and emotional labor.

ACQUIRING SOFT SKILLS

At times, the bodily and emotional labor of acquiring soft skills is made visible. Various techniques are taught at meetings devoted to that purpose. This is the case of the Business Mixer, where a group gets initiated into the art of networking through practice.

The gathering takes place at a café in the Dubai International Financial Center, a free zone devoted to finance. The organizer, Mike, greets me. Tall, wearing a suit and tie, in his 50s, brown hair, fair skin, and a little goatee, he explains that he comes from Miami and started a networking firm that organizes this type of event (free of charge). He calls himself a Yankee. I then talk with the other organizer, Sean, a financial analyst in his 30s. He doesn't work for Mike's business and explains that he is just helping, that it's his hobby. This is also true of Paola, a woman in her 50s to whom Mike suggests I should give my contact information.

Before long, the workshop starts. Mike and Sean describe their endeavor to launch weekly meetings devoted to networking. This week, they decided to work on the elevator pitch. The meaning of this term needed no explanation, for it seemed obvious to everyone. Luckily, I had learned what it meant at some other meeting: "Imagine that you find yourself in an elevator with the CEO that you've been dying to meet, and you have two minutes to get his attention." This evening, then, we're going to learn a few tricks to improve our elevator pitch. We go once around the table to start. There are ten of us. Everything is in English. "Each person will state his name, profession, and . . . you have to add something fun," says Mike. Paola suggests, "Your ideal professional title." Mike adds, "What do you want to be when you grow up?" Paola comes up with "What are you doing for Christmas?" (it's early November), and that's what is chosen.

Mike is standing. He has a voice that projects and he occupies the space with his size and gestures in an almost theatrical way, sounding articulate and professional. Later on, he talks about his interest in body language, asserting that "words make up only 7 percent of a sentence's meaning." Once we've gone around the table, Mike begins his PowerPoint presentation about how to give an effective elevator pitch. The first thing you have to do, he says, is to say your name, and then a funny quip that will make people remember you. And "in the Dubai context, you generally also say your nationality."

The elevator pitch makes sense in the social spaces of the middle- to upper-class hypermobile society of global cities like Dubai. Nationality is one of the first pieces of information exchanged during these brief conversations. Likewise, at cocktail parties organized under the banner of Internations (described online as an "expat network"), which bring together foreign residents from all over the world, each participant is given a name tag with his or her nationality and the country's flag. This confirms how central nationality is to routine categorizing, and it suggests at the same time that people don't necessarily prejudge.

While being Anglophone from birth is definitely an asset, not all English accents are equally valorized. YouTuber Reenie, who presents as black and British and works as a flight attendant based in Dubai, tells the story in her video *Black Living in Dubai* of how certain passengers would snap their fingers to call her—a contemptuous and even dehumanizing treatment—but then radically change their behavior once they heard her British accent.[17] Accent is included in the signs that code affiliation to a certain social group: even though many of Dubai's Indian inhabitants learned English from a very early age, their fluency in the language is not valorized in the same way as that of Americans or British. I heard several American, New Zealander, and French nationals characterize the Indian accent as incomprehensible—never questioning their own accents. Moreover, speaking fluent English does not necessarily guarantee that a person can master various valorized registers of expression and humor. The way Mike leads the meeting is shaped by bodily and relational norms that he designates in a later interview under the term "informal American attitudes." In his view, this type of behavior puts those attending the networking meetings at ease. One of the dispositions most cultivated by the participants is humor, even though humor always refers to a very specific cultural universe. The meeting organizers nevertheless exhibit their way of presenting, expressing emotions, or even standing and moving as the right way, as somehow universal.

Neha Vora refers to a "Western habitus" valorized in the Gulf.[18] As this chapter shows, this habitus is also situated in terms of nationality, class, and gender. Being fluent in English, with a valued accent, and able to interact and use humor in the "right" way are assets, especially for British and North American nationals. However, other European nationalities, while not native English speaking, are also associated with the "right" way to interact, through other dimensions. At another point in my field research, a woman of French nationality explained that she had led coaching sessions in "business etiquette" for persons of "non-Western background," intended for Indian and Pakistani businessmen. In this light, Dubai appears as a hub in the circulation of bodily and behavioral norms originating in the business circles and upper classes of hegemonic countries.

NETWORKING AS TEST

The key importance of networking in Dubai stems from certain features specific to the professional world. A number of professions exercised by Westerners, whether in sales, marketing, or human resources, rely heavily on an available network. Dubai is often described in the interviews as the Middle East's business hub. Many companies set up their regional headquarters there—the definition of *region* varies according to the company and often includes nearby South Asia (India, Pakistan) and stretches sometimes all the way to Morocco or Senegal. For a broad spectrum of activities, it is the city where suppliers, clients, and so-called skilled labor are to be found. Once on the job, persons must be able to quickly mobilize a network of collaborators, to be regularly refreshed, since turnover rates are very high. Finally, fast careers, characterized by job jumping for salary hikes as presented in chapter 2, are also based upon the mobilization of a network to meet recruiters, but having a good network can also work in one's favor during the hiring process, as Sarah said:

> "At no time did he [her current employer] ever ask me about my college degree. He recruited me because I have experience and I know a lot of people."

Sarah's extensive experience in the Gulf—she had been living there for ten years, five of them in Dubai—and the fact that she had proven herself and had accumulated a substantial number of contacts had earned her a managerial position even without a college degree. Daughter of a working-class couple—a father of Tunisian origin and a white mother—she left France at the age of 20 because she could not find an internship required to validate her two-year degree, which she failed to obtain in the end.

These ad hoc training events aside, networking invades every space of a Western resident's social existence. Unlike what happens in certain fractions of the upper class in other contexts, where sociability is presented as disinterested,[19] any and every situation here represents an explicit opportunity to make professional contacts. Maud, the headhunter in my introduction, never went out dancing without her business cards; another interviewee had a card handed to him by someone on his team, a lawyer as it happened, at a pop-up volleyball match on a beach frequented mostly by Westerners. Networking is ubiquitous and often considered the hallmark of Dubai and the key to professional success. The effort exerted to control the impression one makes on any person seen as potentially useful to one's career, no matter the circumstance, gives one the sense, expressed by Emilie, that Western residents follow paths that "are perfectly straight and smooth; you feel like these are people who are completely carefree. Dubai is a city of winners."

These various gatherings result in a relative breaking down of barriers between persons of differing classes who, in European countries, would probably not have had any occasion to meet each other. One might posit that the bodily and emotional labor required to pass this kind of test is less difficult for those accustomed to doing so since they were very young, having been raised in well-to-do families. Still, a large number of persons encountered at these networking events did not come from upper-class families and were seeking precisely that, to acquire the codes through intensive bodily and emotional labor. Several confided that they felt uneasy, finding it hard to conform to the rules of these gatherings. Conversely, during interviews with persons belonging to the upper classes, the topic of networking was rarely raised, which suggests that this type of interaction is not an issue for them, but also that there is much less at stake for them where networking is concerned. Many had already secured their job before coming to Dubai and had no need to attend this kind of event to search for a job. Nor do they necessarily attend subsequently, because their immediate circle of friends and neighbors are often already people in high places or because their longer-term careers play out in locations other than Dubai. More precisely, it is *men* that have no need to attend these networking sessions. The women who have followed their husbands as spouses do have to submit to this kind of ordeal, one that requires free time—which they do not necessarily have as they are the children's primary caregivers—if they wish to find employment. These events are attended by individuals unaccustomed to five-star hotels or to approaching strangers at cocktail parties; they are discovering these norms and codes for the first time in their adult lives. In this regard, Western passport holders often see the professional world as more open than they had previously experienced.

During my study, I was unable to conduct interviews with persons who had failed to secure a relatively stable job. I did cross paths with people who were having trouble, whom I would later learn had decided to leave for that reason, but they declined my requests for follow-up interviews, most likely because it would have been painful to relive what they experienced as a failure. Several residents knew people who had stayed for three months, six months, a year, before going back home without ever finding a job and having spent considerable funds. Karim, 27, whom I interviewed after his return to France, had found work right away in Dubai but was unhappy with the salary. After spending two years without getting a raise, a promotion, or any other kind of offer, he decided to go home, even though his return would involve going back to his former place of employment and a job he had had while in school, far beneath his qualifications, until something better came up. At any rate, the professional situation in Dubai had not met his expectations, given the lack of opportunities to advance and the intensive work pace (six days a week).

If other residents began their Dubai stay in relatively underpaid jobs, their "jump" careers took off thanks to the networks they were able to build. This was not Karim's case, however. He despised Dubai social life, which he defined on three separate occasions as "prefabricated." He failed to meet the behavioral standards expected of Westerners in Dubai, or he simply did not feel like playing the game.

> "Social life isn't so easy [in Dubai]. . . . There were weeks at a stretch where I did nothing but work and sleep. . . . There are Facebook groups and that kind of thing, sure . . . but every time I tried to join in, it felt a bit too prefabricated. That's not my way of getting to know people. So . . . I made a few friends here, but it was more about—I mean, they were already French, and then I had a few co-workers I could go out with in the evening. I didn't really expand my circle of friends. . . . I have to say, I went from New York, where, when it came to social life, I really felt great, to Dubai, where my life was much more solitary."

As the child of parents who had come from Tunisia to France as a laborer and stay-at-home mother, Karim did international studies at college, followed by a master's degree in New York, a city he very much enjoyed. Over the five years since, he has spent all his money travelling, mainly in Europe and Asia, to "make up for the lost time" caused by his parents, who only ever took him back to Tunisia. It was not therefore because of an inability to build relationships in an international, multicultural setting that he failed to enjoy himself in Dubai, but because he refused to conform to expected behaviors. The people he met, particularly among the French, "lacked humility," he told me.

The only benefit to his life there was to be able to "walk around wearing a djellaba" on Fridays ("It was something of a luxury for me"), but he felt that, to quote the terms he used, socializing among "Muslims" was just as "prefabricated" as among "Europeans." Karim did not undertake the necessary emotional labor to feel right in Dubai—in terms of acquiring soft skills, certain useful behaviors in ordinary social encounters. He remained outside the game of social codes specific to Westerners' social spaces; he refused to take part. In hindsight, he also said he felt uneasy about the privileged treatment his company offered him compared to his co-workers, especially Filipinos and Egyptians, who were paid far less and lived "under pressure." Not only did he refuse the networking game, but he also failed to achieve the "promise of happiness" ascribed to Dubai that allows so many Western residents to feel fulfilled, thanks to their "quality of life" and their "sense of success."[20]

EMPHATIC, SEXUALIZED FEMININITIES AT WORK

If Westernness relies on a particular bodily and emotional labor, a specific relationship to the body governs this social construction. The persons I interviewed generally attempted to shape their bodies into one seen as slim, healthy, beautiful, and feminine or masculine. This gendered construction was further articulated during interviews conducted with women: several interviewees mentioned the advantage of being "a woman" in the Dubai job market, or even "a pretty woman." The case of Cindy exemplifies this valorization of a certain kind of emphatic Western femininity. I borrow the term "emphatic femininity" from Raewyn Connell's theory; it refers to the most socially valorized model of femininity, constructed in relation with, and as subaltern to, hegemonic masculinity.[21] This image of femininity is used to sell various brands in the city. I analyze here its underpinnings.

Cindy, a 35-year-old American, changed jobs five times in five years without ever having to search. Her status as a white American woman meant that people spontaneously came up to talk with her, as she observed on her very first visit to the Emirates, a work trip, which made her want to move there to work. At one point in our interview, she displayed a partial and contradictory moment of self-reflection regarding the structural advantages she enjoyed socially as a Western, American, white, and pretty woman—terms that she herself used:

> "I think it's the most racist society I've ever lived in. . . . I think there is power to being white, number one. . . . I think Western people, with their education and specifically Americans, we happen to be very systematic and organized, generally speaking, and, um, . . . advanced in many skill sets. So even if I was coming fresh out of college, I would still be desirable, but coincidentally I have a lot more experience than that to bring to the table. It's just being able to run a business better than many people in this town, and even . . . it's grammar, you know, as simple as grammar. Being able to write English and read English, you know, that's a strength. . . . And if you are in sales, and being a pretty woman, . . . you have a huge advantage in the marketplace."

Her self-reflection is partial here, for although she acknowledged the advantages she enjoyed as a white American woman in a society she called racist, Cindy implied that they were justified by her skills and education, as well as her fluency in English which, in the Dubai context, is considered a skill in itself.[22] Cindy also pointed out how a body coded as feminine and attractive (and white and Western, as she takes for granted) amounted to an advantage in the job market. In the open space of her workplace, Startup Z, I observed how the division of roles got established between her and the company manager according to a very particular script during appointments with potential purchasers. Here are a few lines that I wrote about this prior to the interview, when I was sitting with my computer in my lap, on one of the two large couches set around a coffee table at the center of the open space:

> A woman is talking with a potential purchaser, of Indian nationality. The purchaser is wearing a suit. The woman is in a short pencil skirt and beige jacket over a tight top, her nails are polished red, shoes are white flats, chestnut hair is worn shoulder-length, blue eyes, designer sunglasses worn like a headband. They are sitting side by side on the same couch in the middle of the open space, which allows them to keep their voices low and establish a certain physical proximity. The man, in a beige suit over a checked shirt, is explaining the business he already has, the woman explains to him all the procedures and modalities. A little later, Nabil, one of the company heads, dressed more casually, no

jacket or tie, but trousers and a shirt that look to me like very expensive brands, arrives on the scene, sits down on the other couch across from them (next to me), which means he has to speak louder. He seems to be "testing" the potential purchaser, and asks him why he wants to get involved in this new area. He warns him that it is hard work, speaking to him rather condescendingly.

The sales head, Cindy, adopts a personable attitude of invitation, openness, proposal, support, proximity, and accessibility, while the company head, Nabil, embodies the position of authority, sits facing the client, between scrutiny of his skills and paternalism. This sharing of professional roles, according to a script most likely set beforehand, relies in part on bodily performances coded in terms of gender, sexuality, class, race, and nationality. The image of femininity that Cindy performs contributes to her professional success, though it stops short of freeing her from masculine domination—she remains under the authority of the bosses, who are men. Even if Cindy does not present it thus, she is predisposed to this sort of performance by virtue of her socialization (being American, white, middle class, and having worked in Washington, DC), but she has also invested work, time, and financial means to maintain her network and perfect her self-presentation. On the one hand, she goes regularly to the spa, does cardio workouts at the gym after work and estimates that she spends 5 percent of her monthly earnings on clothes (about 20,000 dirhams, or $6,000), which comes to $300 per month, the approximate salary of a construction worker in Dubai. On the other, outside her work, which is very time-consuming, she attends many networking gatherings and other cultural events to develop her personal network:

> "It's very easy to meet new people. I went to Sundance [music festival for which standard tickets cost about $90 an evening] two weeks ago. I just started chatting with a girl and she was really nice, and we swapped numbers, and we started walking around the marina, exercising together. I wanted to meet some more girls, like professional and successful and classy, and . . . I met this girl! I was just partying, just listening to music. So you just never know!"

Here, Cindy enumerates the qualities that she believes qualify a person as a useful, desirable contact, professionally and personally, for the two seem inextricable: "professional and successful and classy." The latter adjective reflects self-presentation and conformity to the gendered bodily norms of the upper classes, which are at the heart of the relationship that gets established: Cindy connected with this new acquaintance by working out at the gym with her.

The type of femininity that Cindy displays in a professional world dominated by men combines professionalism as a token of respectability with elements coded as feminine and (hetero) sexualized—that is, ones that ensure that a woman will be considered sexy within the norms of heterosexuality. Her narrative recalls the analyses of Linda McDowell[23] of the performance of heterosexual identities in the workplace involving an emotional labor that is also, for many women, a form of sexual labor, to the extent that they are required to make themselves sexually attractive in the eyes of their co-workers and business clients. In the multinational companies in Dubai, high heels, low-cut tops, and lipstick are the rule, which might explain a certain permeability between spaces of sociability at work and the nightspots, bars, and clubs, spaces patronized mostly by Western residents. But they might also translate as a willingness to demonstrate the freewheeling lifestyle that is supposed to distinguish the Westerners from other segments of the middle and upper classes (chapters 4 and 6). In other words, women not only must be available for long working and social hours, but they are also encouraged to perform a sexualized self-presentation. This puts a specific pressure on women in the job market, as it takes time, money, and emotional work to conform to this model. It is also excluding. When women are beyond a certain age or do not have time to work on their appearance or fail to correspond to the norm of femininity constructed as desirable or are construed as sexually unavailable, they are liable to face discrimination in this context, alongside other factors, notably being married with children to raise. They do not meet the image criteria expected of women—Western women in particular—in this job market.

Cindy embodies a type of femininity coded as sexy, heterosexual, Western, modern, professional, and respectable, further facilitated by the fact that she is white. In other words, it is because she is identified as white and Western that her appearance is coded as feminine, professional, and sexy, and not as a sign that she is selling sexual services. She is thus rarely exposed to the kind of unsolicited propositioning by men looking for prostitutes that several nonwhite women complained about; however, she has been the target of inappropriate flirting in the professional context, including one case of sexual harassment by a superior.

The performance of a (hetero) sexualized, Western femininity in the professional world is specific to certain women, those without children and most of whom are single. Especially noticeable in the sales area, it is also central to networking events and job interviews, even for less exposed professions. This emphatic Western femininity is subordinated to certain forms of masculinity but valorized in relation to subaltern femininities. Alongside the masculine image of the "boss,"[24] it constitutes one of the stereotypical figures of Westernness.

TECHNOLOGIES OF BODY TRANSFORMATION

A Western resident's performance of the "right presentation" is based on an infrastructure of care for certain people by other people. Technologies of body transformation, such as fitness room bodybuilding, beauty treatments, or even plastic surgery, occupy a prominent place in Dubai. Many apartment buildings intended for foreign residents come equipped with fitness centers (for weight lifting, cardio training) designed exclusively for the building's tenants, who nevertheless also sign up at better-equipped gyms nearby. More broadly, beauty salons, spas, and fitness centers flourish in neighborhoods designed for the middle and upper classes: nearly every building has them at ground level, and in the villa neighborhood of Jumeirah, they take up an entire avenue.

Western residents are by no means the only ones to frequent gyms and spas, but many do go on a regular basis, more so than they would back in their home context. In Dubai, all the facilities are nearby, requiring almost no transit time, and most of their domestic chores are outsourced, as is their children's education, for some, which leaves them lots of time to indulge in workouts and various sorts of grooming and body care. As a result, Westerners' bodies often correspond to the dominant social norms: healthy, athletic, muscular, sophisticated, and shaped by their apparel, all signs of an always-gendered affiliation with the middle and upper classes. As is the case nearly everywhere, a particular pressure weighs upon feminine bodies, often subject to disciplines such as fitness regimens or diets and further transformed by makeup, jewelry, and tight, belted fashions.

Several women admitted they had considered plastic surgery or fitness and dietary coaching, something they would never have thought of doing before. "Here, you see lots of really fabulous-looking girls. . . . Sometimes I tell myself I could make a little effort to look great like that, and other times, I say I just don't care," confessed Emily, 34, an employee at a startup. She explained that she hired a personal trainer at a gym, which cost "only 600 dirhams" (about $180) for ten personal sessions, and that she also went to spas, which she loved and which were not that expensive: "It's not always very well done, but it costs next to nothing." Spas are places of intimate body contact between the wellness staff (in salons, spas, or fitness centers) and the clients, usually highly paid professionals. These contacts, although frequent, are mainly limited to work situations during which one group is servicing the other. Most Western residents I met never went to the more working-class neighborhoods of the city, nor did they make friends or forge affective relationships with anyone from there.

Exercise, weight, and diets often came up in conversation. Many feel that the "expatriate" lifestyle in Dubai is unhealthy. Fearing weight gain from eating out so often at restaurants and getting around only by car, many try to work out and diet. The efforts exerted by Western residents to stay fit, to keep moving in a city designed for the automobile, contrast starkly with the bodily life of less wealthy inhabitants, who need to walk quite a bit when taking the subway (stations are often very far from destinations) or whose professional activities involve considerable physical exertion, such as those of cleaning staff, construction workers, or cashiers, who carry things all day long. In public spaces in Dubai, as in other global cities, Western people's bodies kept fit to appear healthy and seductive, often unclothed and glistening with suntan oil (especially during their leisure time at the beach or poolside), contrast with the bodies of laborers who work at the countless construction sites, completely covered to shelter their bodies from the sun.

*   *   *

This chapter has described the expectation differential with regard to bodily and emotional labor not only in terms of gender and class[25] but also of nationality and race, between persons whose bodies are predominantly considered as a workforce and those whose bodies are seen as an asset to sell the company, to attract contacts and build up the Dubai brand. Of course, many poorly paid service jobs, the analysis of which lies beyond the scope of this study, also require "selling oneself," and here again, many skilled jobs are occupied by persons without Western passports.[26] Other groups of workers cannot be studied in detail here, and binary oppositions are always too simplistic. This schematic opposition nevertheless helps explain the specificities of expectations for Westerners in a job market where they are employed partly for what they represent.

The construction of Westernness as a privileged position in the professional world implies particular performances in terms of self-presentation, behavior, social interaction, and the use of humor. Research reveals the importance ascribed to displays of wealth and to the absence of any sign evoking the practice of Islam. These signs contribute to constructing a stereotyped image of Westernness, associated with wealth and secularism. It also highlights specific expectations with regard to women in terms of sexualized self-presentation. All these norms sharply differentiate women and men, with separate expectations for each; they are also central to the differentiation between hierarchized social groups, certain of which are in the service of the others. Although, among Westerners, a particular pressure weighs on people of color to conform to these norms, these very norms are often experienced as more inclusive than those they experienced before their departure, back home in European and North American societies, as chapter 7 explores.

CHAPTER 4

THE HETERONORMATIVITY
OF "GUEST FAMILIES"

Old life

Pull up to pump. Get out, fill up the tank. Get everyone out of the car after filling the tank, troop into the fuel station, try to block shelves filled with sweets with your knees as you queue. Pay (faint at price—perhaps we could re-mortgage?), then herd everyone back in the car. Second scenario: fill up, lock car with kids in it, join queue of drivers waiting to pay at the till, whilst staring out the window with panic as both kids hurl themselves around the car as if it were a soft play centre.

New life

Pull up to petrol pump in your roomy, air-conditioned SUV. "Fill it up special please!" Smiling man fills your car up. Asks you if there is anything else—you request a coffee and a SALIK top up card—both brought promptly to your car window. Pay, give him a tip (you still have change from that Dhs100 note after all), and then drive off. Kids barely notice—they are too busy watching *Frozen* on the in-built car DVD system.[1]

This somewhat tongue-in-cheek description opens an online article, published on a website popular among Western residents, comparing family life in Dubai and "elsewhere," intended for parents wondering whether to move to the city. If this is never made explicit elsewhere, the examples and accompanying photos, showing white, blond parents and children, clearly indicate what kind of families are being targeted here. Affluence—a roomy, air-conditioned car—and constant, almost complimentary assistance by service personnel who handle all the more unpleasant tasks are reflected in the comments of parents I met, many of whom emphasize how "easy" it is to raise children in Dubai. The concerns raised by other residents—the high cost and limited availability of spots in private schools, for example—get no mention. "If we hadn't been here, we never would have had a third child," I was told by Philippe (a heterosexual male, married, white, French nationality), speaking about the UAE. "It was very tempting for a mom with a second child to come here, where we can find domestic help," said Marie (a heterosexual female, married, white, French nationality), to explain why she chose to move to Dubai with her husband and children. These statements suggest that moving to Dubai allows for a harmonious family life conducive to raising several children in favorable conditions. As in other global cities, the state and companies intervene in the private lives of foreign residents in a number of ways that reinforce social differentiating and hierarchizing. Certain residents are induced to adopt a comfortable family life in villas, delegating most domestic and parental work to live-in employees, or to attend lavish parties in luxurious venues, while others are considered as having no private life at all—which is obviously not the case.[2]

The point here and in the two subsequent chapters is to show how the formation of distinctly Western intimate subjectivities contributes to constructing differentiated and hierarchized social groups.[3] This chapter analyzes the organization of intimacy within Western heterosexual couples and their children, called "guest families," who identify with a distinctive hetero-conjugality by means of specific masculinities and femininities.

WHITE MIGRANTS' INTIMACIES

Apart from their professional and social position, white migrants from the upper classes are set apart by their familial and affective practices. For instance, many women with graduate degrees do not work professionally:[4] numerous studies have shown that transnational mobility accentuates professional inequality within heterosexual couples. If not the sole breadwinner, the husbands become at least the "career leader";[5] wives often abandon their professional activity, investing instead in supporting their partner and raising the children and deploy strategies to "re-create the family home abroad."[6] Companies play an important role in this process. Regarding British residents in Dubai, Katie Walsh points out that employers often require their staff to work long hours and to travel, which, in addition to the prevalence of a "macho culture" among expatriate males, makes it hard for the "wives" to sustain a professional career.[7] Wives occupy an ambivalent position, however. According to Daniella Arieli, who worked on similar situations in Beijing,[8] they take part in a "patriarchal bargain": "They cooperate with a structure that excludes them, but at the same time they enjoy numerous economic and social privileges."

While these studies have explored the ways that intimate, sexual, affective, conjugal, and familial life has been transformed during the "expatriation" process and have also pointed to an underlying gender inequality within the couple, they do present two shortcomings. First, heterosexuality in these social settings is often taken for granted and, for this reason, tends to be naturalized. Based on queer approaches to migration,[9] several studies that consider heterosexuality as "specific and contingent" have shown how "various performances of migrant heterosexuality" are located outside the heteronormative frame that so often defines the research.[10] Other more recent work sheds light on more specific forms of heteronormativity performed by expatriate women.[11] The aim here is to pursue this discussion about migrant heterosexuality and heteronormativity.

The second shortcoming of these studies is their failure to link conjugal dynamics with race and class, a limitation that more recent work has remedied.[12] Ann Laura Stoler's work on colonial situations,[13] which has informed my own research, describes how the regulating of intimate relations has aimed to draw and redraw racial boundaries: my starting point involved testing this idea within the contemporary context of a global city like Dubai. Intimacy will be taken here in its broadest sense, including domestic life as well as a variety of affective relations. In Dubai, there is no corpus of texts, legal or otherwise, that regulates intimate relations between persons of different nationalities. And yet, an array of state and organizational provisions combined with social norms do orient and differentiate the intimate lives of foreign residents and tend to maximize the possibility of profiting from these lives. The governing of intimacies is intrinsically linked to the development of Dubai as a neoliberal corporate city. For maximum profit, foreigners here are induced to adopt particular lifestyles that imply specific constructions in terms of gender and sexuality and contribute to differentiating them from other social groups. In other words, intimate relations translate and reinforce hierarchies not only of gender and sexuality but also of class, race, and nationality.

If state institutions and companies steer intimate lives in a certain direction, the hierarchies are co-produced and perpetuated by the kinds of relationships that the foreign residents sustain, the kinds of attachment or detachment they cultivate. Their intimate subjectivities contribute to differentiating and hierarchizing individuals and groups. It is mainly these subjectivities that I am studying here, with a focus on the links between heteronormativity and the construction of social hierarchies. And indeed, the boundaries of a distinctive Westernness get reasserted or renegotiated via these different intimate relations.

DUBAI'S BIOPOLITICS

The differentiated treatment of intimacies by Emirati institutions conveys specific ways of thinking about nation, migrants, and the economy. In a country where the majority of the population does not have nationality, the state constructs a discourse of national purity, encouraging marriage and reproduction among Emirati citizens,[14] although Emirati males can legally marry women of any nationality, and many do marry foreigners, which has become a matter of public discussion.[15] Nevertheless, Emirati women have been designated as the most legitimate spouses for Emirati men, and the best possible mothers for Emirati children, responsible for transmitting an imagined form of cultural authenticity.[16] Among foreign residents, heterosexual marriage is regulated through national consulates, except for couples who wish to be married before an Emirati Islamic court, which is possible only if the husband is Muslim. Thus, there is no local law regulating heterosexual marriage between foreigners. Still, there are provisions and limitations concerning their mobility, their activities, and their practices that shape an oversight of intimacy, producing de facto hierarchies in terms of gender, sexuality, class, and race.

As in many settings where migration policies define foreign residents as temporary workers and where migration somehow constitutes a profit-seeking industry,[17] salary is often the factor that determines whether dependents can accompany the foreign worker. Wage earners at the bottom of the job hierarchy are considered to be single and cannot "sponsor" their families—that is, obtain residency rights for them on the basis of marriage or kinship—because they earn less than the minimum wage allowing that to happen. The state, more broadly, has imposed "highly constrained forms of sexual citizenship on migrant builders,"[18] constructing them as potential rapists of women and children.[19] On the basis of this imagined threat, their mobility is closely monitored, notably by means of curfews. Even though much research has assigned victimhood status to the masculine figure of construction worker, the quintessential casualty of neoliberal biopolitics, certain women—domestic workers in particular—as well as specific categories of feminized men[20] are also constrained, monitored, and exposed to various orders of violence. Many employers limit how often they can go out and with whom. Women of certain nationalities are suspected of being prostitutes and are thus subjected to close police surveillance.[21] These individuals do still develop intimate relationships and personal plans that no amount of surveillance can undo.[22] In Kuwait, Attiya Ahmad analyzes the "suspended belongings" of domestic employees: "dual agents of reproduction," they develop forms of intimacy with the employer's family, becoming "a part of yet apart from," and feel they are "in between the lives of others, in their home countries as in Kuwait."[23]

The economic diversification strategy promoted over the past few decades has impacted the lifestyles and family models endorsed for the more advantaged residents. Beyond migration policy, this strategy is implemented through a variety of initiatives undertaken by both the government of Dubai and the semipublic companies, the urban megaprojects and private multinationals. In all these organizations, Western residents work and make decisions and are thus both actors and targets of these policies. As we shall see, Western residents are encouraged to adopt a particular form of family life or to experience Dubai nightlife by embracing a hedonistic lifestyle as a single person.[24] These two lifestyles come with consumer practices that shape Dubai as a corporate city. Both involve imaginaries of Westernness as well as particular affective economies.

THE GUEST FAMILY AS NEOLIBERAL PARADIGM

Brenda Yeoh, Shirlena Huang, and Katie Willis,[25] writing about Singapore, state that global cities are based on specific family ideologies. This observation applies equally to Dubai. The corporate city promotes a specific model of the nuclear family for foreign residents. I call this model the "guest family" with reference to the term *guest worker* used in certain languages to describe "temporary workers," migrants whose residence permit is linked to a fixed-term professional activity. Although migration policies do consider all foreign residents as temporary workers with no possible access to citizenship, they differentiate in practice, especially through government of intimacy, between those who earn high salaries and those whose wages are low. Once above a certain earnings level, the figure of temporary worker is paralleled by the guest family paradigm. Their status mixes the different meanings of the word *guest*, because they are invited (or encouraged to come) and pampered, but they are also considered to be foreigners whose stay is temporary and, most importantly, to be clients. These guest families are envisioned as married heterosexual couples and their children. As a direct resource for the local economy through their consumer habits, they also participate in constructing the image of the Emirates and of Dubai as an ideal relocation site for highly qualified professionals.

A range of infrastructures aim to attract well-to-do families to Dubai: luxurious housing developments featuring spacious villas with swimming pools, a wide assortment of entertainment and leisure activities, distinguished international schools, intensive police surveillance that many interpret as a guarantee of security, and a range of inexpensive services, particularly full-time live-in domestic employees. The urban plan and architecture of the neighborhoods intended for wealthy residents take into account the specific needs of children by means of enclosures, speed limits, secure playgrounds, and shopping areas that include play areas for them. Many interviewees insist that raising children in Dubai is easier than in other European or North American contexts (and notably less tiring than in Paris) and that their children love living there. The city thus appears as the perfect place to live with children for married heterosexual couples of substantial means. Companies, in fact, often choose to relocate to Dubai the families of their regional directors even when the job does not require such a move. This choice has to do with the infrastructures and security that the city has to offer, considered exceptional for the region, as well as with its situation as airline hub.

Guest families are envisioned as consumers via their full array of activities. The state finances public infrastructure such as education and health mainly for its own citizens. For the same services, foreign residents depend entirely on the market. The daily life of wealthy foreign families in Dubai therefore represents a significant source of revenue for the local economy.

One Emirati expert on institutions in charge of nationalizing jobs sums up his rather stereotypical vision of things thus: "Expatriates come with their families, their children attend school, the wives shop at the malls." The salaries of executives in particular are structured in such a way that a portion will be spent in country. Among the "compensations" added to the base salary is the "housing compensation," one of the largest, intended to pay the rent, enormously expensive in Dubai. This sum cannot be transferred to any other country. Other compensations include education costs for children in private schools—according to one interviewee, certain companies are believed to even reserve places in prestigious schools for the children of their high-ranking managers—and health insurance for all the dependents, as stipulated by the family package. Companies do not pay for childcare of infants, an indicator of how little concern they have for the professional career of the wife. In this way, they are co-producing the regulation of family practices and the division of labor among couples. Furthermore, married women are almost never offered family packages. Generally speaking, working conditions, notably the legally binding forty-five-hour week as well as business travel, which is very frequent for those in management or regional coordinator positions, make double careers for couples with children a very rare phenomenon. In this context, most married women with children tend to be reduced to their migration status of spouse (and mother). Men and women living in Dubai as guest families inhabit, reproduce, and reinforce or (scarcely) transform these norms of conjugality, masculinity, and femininity in various ways.

SELECTION AND TRANSFORMATION OF FAMILIES

The family model advocated in Dubai results in the selection of particular kinds of families that fit the heteronormative model that this migration reinforces. Foreigners who relocate to the corporate city with their children do so as married heterosexual couples, or they marry in order to relocate: only legally married couples are recognized. Very few are single or divorced. Raising children in Dubai is costly; between housing, schooling, and insurance, only those earning the highest salaries can afford it. And earning such a salary involves spending most of one's time at work and travelling on a regular basis, thereby making it difficult to care for children. This construction of lucrative jobs has two consequences: on the one hand, many non-Western parents, since they earn lower salaries, forego raising their children in Dubai;

on the other, raising children would appear practically impossible for a single or divorced person, regardless of their passport. The only one that I met, who had divorced while living in Dubai, left the country as a result. Since the salary figure required in order to bring dependents is higher for women than for men, the couples who relocate to Dubai are overwhelmingly heterosexual couples where the career of the husband takes precedence over the wife's—most of the rare couples who deviate from this norm end up conforming once they arrive.

The French people I interviewed who were raising children shared certain characteristics: aged between 30 and 50, they were more often white and well-to-do than the single interviewees, and one member of the couple was generally under an expatriate contract (or had been)—the male in thirteen out of fourteen cases. Perhaps people with children are more reluctant to relocate to Dubai than those without children, given the unpredictability of temporary worker status under local contract and the cost of raising children in Dubai. This could explain the overrepresentation of persons under expatriate contract among couples with children. Migration policies combined with company strategies have the effect of selecting for couples where the division of labor between husband (entirely consumed by his professional career) and wife (devoted to domestic, conjugal, and parental tasks) is particularly well delineated. Marc, the only husband I interviewed whose wife was the one with the expatriate contract, confirmed my hunch as to how rare it is for couples not to conform to the standard model, and he complained that the emails from his children's school are always addressed to the moms. His case, exceptional far beyond Dubai, so rare is it for women to relocate their families for their career,[26] does still adhere to the classic scheme. Marc's distance work as an entrepreneur provided him a substantial income, albeit lower than his spouse's but far greater than that of wives interviewed for this study, despite the women's higher graduate degrees. If he followed his spouse, it was because he had grown bored with his salaried job in Paris and wanted to quit; none of my female interviewees reported anything similar. This exception does not challenge the gendered dynamics in heterosexual couples from middle- and upper-class backgrounds: Marc's narrative showed no signs of sacrifice on his part, unlike what was clearly perceptible in many of my interviews with wives.

This division of labor can nevertheless be framed as a choice that favors conjugal and familial cohesion. Among couples for whom this was their first

experience of living abroad, getting closer to one's spouse to live a more fulfilling "family life" often motivated the move to Dubai. "We decided to go
abroad to be together," I was told by Patricia, 45, whose husband used to work
a great deal more in the Paris region than in the Emirates. This family togetherness was made possible by the couple's very high pay, which enables them
to reduce the time spent not only at work but also at domestic chores, by
virtue of the hierarchy of intimacies that puts certain persons in the service of
other people's family life. Claire, 38, a full-time salaried employee and mother
of two children, also confided:

> "My women friends who have two children, who work, who have to go get
> them at daycare, who get home every night and give the kids a bath before do-
> ing the dishes, . . . I think that the reason people divorce—if they had a maid,
> I mean, they wouldn't divorce. . . . Being able to have a maid is one of Dubai's
> real assets."

Still, Claire found herself in a relatively more precarious situation than the
other couples I interviewed: she worked full time for a company under local
contract, her salary was vital for the family, but she and her husband experienced financial troubles because neither of them benefitted from a family
package (and even less from an expatriation contract), clearly an anxiety-
inducing situation. For her, the ability to afford a full-time live-in nanny was
one of the great assets of life in Dubai; despite difficulties, she was getting
what she bargained for in terms of conjugal and familial harmony.

As in other contexts, hiring a third party puts an end to the "housework
war" among middle- to upper-class white heterosexual couples.[27] Thanks to
this hire, the resistance of women to forever being assigned the housework
becomes compatible with their husbands' reluctance to get involved in it.
The nanny allows couples a more harmonious life with more leisure time,
less tension. The family togetherness that Dubai affords contrasts with the
separation and long-distance relationships experienced by many residents
in low-paid jobs coming from poorer countries. Among middle-class non-
Western passport holders, Sami (previously quoted), born in Dubai, spoke
of his relocation to Lebanon after his father's business failed. His parents
no longer had the means to raise children in Dubai, and this forced departure remained a painful memory for Sami, who was very young at the time.
Angelica, human resources manager at a hotel, had lived away from her son

since he was born. Her financial situation had recently improved, which meant she could now "sponsor" him, but he was in his teens and preferred to continue living with his grandmother in the environment where he grew up, in Dacca. If she mentioned this without showing any particular emotion during the interview, her situation echoed the "suspended belongings" described by Attiya Ahmad, a reality very different from the one experienced by Western guest families.

For many, the life of a guest family takes place against the backdrop of a spacious villa in the residential neighborhoods of Jumeirah and Umm Suqeim—where rents can amount to $65,000 a year, an expense generally covered by the husband's employer—surrounded by similar houses inhabited by upper-class Emirati and Western families. These neighborhoods are located along the relatively well-preserved, noncommercial beachfront, between "old Dubai" and "new Dubai." Old Dubai is inhabited by mainly middle-class residents, notably Indians. New Dubai, which includes the high-rise neighborhoods meant for middle and upper classes, went into development during the 2000s: the Marina, Jumeirah Beach Residence, Jumeirah Lake Towers, and the artificial island, The Palm. These so-called old and new parts of Dubai, separated by several dozen kilometers, are connected by a highway and an elevated train. Between the two on the beachfront side stretch residential neighborhoods of opulent villas, and on the desert side, the recently built business quarter, Downtown (arranged around the gigantic Dubai Mall) and a variety of residential towers.

The villa neighborhood where the guest families live is distinct from the ones featuring towers and apartments. As a rule, villas should house only families and are forbidden to single men, unless they are household employees or are living with members of their family (parents, adult brothers and sisters), a measure intended to prevent close contact between poor men and rich families. This rule also has the effect of strengthening a certain isolation of families, particularly with regard to unmarried residents, whether or not they have Western passports. Families mingle mainly with other guest families that they meet in the neighborhood or at their children's school.

These guest families can differ in several respects. Some reside in a succession of different countries, others see Dubai as a beneficial hiatus to the husband's career in France, and still others end up staying for the long term. Some place their children in French schools, others in English-speaking schools, which has implications for their sociability. Women who arrive with the status of spouse, administratively speaking, can follow various professional tracks: some have already experienced life as an "expatriate wife" in other countries; others give up their careers to follow their husband in the hope of turning the Dubai experience into something interesting for themselves. Yet, despite these differences, guest families tend to converge via their common lifestyle.

GOOD FAMILY MEN?

Some of the women I interviewed lived in Dubai with their children while their husband was away on business, coming home only on weekends. These couples were based on a gendered division of labor and space: as in other contexts, the men selected "different sites for investment, work and family life."[28] The opposition between the husband's hypermobility and the wife's sedentariness characterizes these masculinities and the forms of hetero-conjugality upon which they are built. Certain quarters of the city seem to have been designed in accordance with this ideology of gender, sexuality, and family so that hypermobile family men would find them attractive. David, in his 40s, British, white, a regional manager for a large company, recruited in Great Britain by a headhunter, addressed thus his family life during the interview he granted me in his professional setting. He considered the Dubai environment "secure and respectful for [his] wife and two children"; he said he devoted his weekends to family life—his weekdays were spent on business travel; and he asserted that "Dubai is a fantastic place to build a family and raise children." He performed both as a busy, important man at the professional level—it was one of my shortest interviews—and as a good family man, concerned about his family's comfort. In these couples, the man is constructed as busy, consumed by his professional life and "serious things," and the woman as sociable and available. Unsurprisingly then, the people living with a spouse and children in Dubai who agreed to be interviewed were mostly wives, some of whom then agreed to set up an interview with their husband for me.

Raewyn Connell and Julian Wood have noticed a certain transformation of transnational business masculinities:[29] the Australian men interviewed for their study distanced themselves, expressing some uncertainty about gender order and the traditional bourgeois model. This stands in contrast to the results of my study: based on the persons I interviewed, life in Dubai tended to reinforce certain components of this model, notably the gendered assignment of roles.[30] Nevertheless, virtually none of the wives I met perceived the status of dependent as normal or natural, which undoubtedly differentiates them from previous generations. Nearly all of them were in the workforce before leaving their country, and nearly all have abandoned their career since then, either by ceasing all professional activity or by maintaining it as a secondary activity. Being a "dependent" therefore entails, for them, a change of status—a change often presented by the men as their spouse's choice, made possible by their additional remuneration, or even as a goal set by the couple together. For instance, David explained to me that migration to Dubai was motivated by a desire for a more fulfilling family life. His wife stopped working, which would have been difficult in London, he said, but possible in Dubai given the highly advantageous conditions of his contract as regional manager of a company department.

Men with expatriate contracts also depict themselves as good husbands and fathers by casting other men into a cultural otherness. In several anecdotes, they presented theirs as the right kind of masculinity, which they claimed as modern and focused on the couple and the family, unlike other masculinities more shaped by masculine homo-sociability. Take Jean-Paul, who mixed with Emiratis in the semipublic company where he was employed. When I asked, "Do you have any relations with Emiratis outside work?" he gave this answer:

> "There aren't many that I'd care to make friends with . . . ! We just don't operate in the same way. We French have stuff we like to do as couples, man-woman. . . . In a restaurant, you can see Emirati couples, or groups of Emirati friends, but never groups of Emirati couples out together as friends. . . . At first, I had just got here and a colleague had gone to Tunisia on vacation. When he came back, I asked: 'So, did you have fun with the wife and kids?' And he looked at me and said: 'I don't go on vacation with my wife and kids.'"

Jean-Paul situates Emiratis in a radical otherness with respect to an "us" that encompasses Westerners. In his statement, the gender order emerges as one of the principle criteria of distinction between "Emiratis" and "us." For Jean-Paul, Emiratis are not believed to have the same sociability standards for dining out as do Western guest families. In his view, they do not perform their married life in public, which he deems less modern, less egalitarian. During our interview, Jean-Paul kept wavering between casting Emiratis into an absolute otherness and a less dichotomist vision: he put the difference into perspective, making it a question of degree, and acknowledged that not all Emiratis behave in the same way. Still, this less dichotomist vision only comes into play within the professional sphere, outside of which the difference is not nuanced but affirmed.

The performance of couple and family is described as an insurmountable difference in a number of interviews. The homo-sociability attributed to Emiratis is associated with a greater inequality in male-female relations. We enter here into a vast debate concerning gender order, forms of sociability and conjugal norms, one that has been stirring the region's intellectual elites, whether Arabic speaking, Persian speaking, Turkish speaking, modernist, feminist, nationalist, Islamic reformist, or Salafist since the early twentieth century.[31] By projecting onto Emirati society a homogenous and timeless cultural practice, these persons are disregarding this undercurrent of debates and disparities. They also avoid any self-questioning, notably about the real cost to women of publicly performing hetero-conjugality.

If Emirati men are seen as different because of their non-egalitarian values, another foil to Western masculinity emerges from my interviews: the frustrated masculinity attributed to subaltern males. The common narrative regarding frustrated celibate males concerns "Indians," a racializing term used to designate persons from the Indian subcontinent. Benoît, 32, under expatriate contract, put it thus:

> "The way Indians and Pakistanis look at the children is a little disturbing sometimes. You wonder a bit what they're thinking—is there something unhealthy about it? . . . When you ask around, you find that most people feel the same: . . . that the men who come to work here without going back home for months at a time, who live all together, all men, I think there are some strange behaviors, a bit dubious, on the beaches for example, and sometimes you have to wonder. . . . We've seen guys taking photos of my daughter, for example. . . . We've stopped going to that beach. There are too many groups of Indians and Pakistanis, and we wonder what they're thinking. . . . I mean, there's nothing wrong with looking at women in bathing suits, I guess, but when it's children, there you have to wonder. . . . There was one time when I saw he'd taken a photo, I went over to him and asked him to delete it, and asked him why he took the photo. And he deleted it right away. So, you see, . . . there's something wrong about that. The guy was fully clothed, right at water's edge, with a thing on his head to protect from sun."

This narrative suggests various scenarios of self-segregation on the part of Western residents and their distancing strategies from certain men dismissed as belonging to a deviant masculinity. While Dubai is relatively segregated when it comes to housing, the wealthiest neighborhoods are also the workplaces of subaltern service personnel. Working day and night at worksites all over the city, construction workers are ubiquitous. Some Westerners like Benoît try to avoid them, deeming them dangerous and threatening to their wives and children: they seem to believe that the women and children, Western and white as they are, would necessarily spark the desire of these men represented in a stereotypically heteronormative way as having no sexual practice, since they are far from their countries and are housed exclusively among other men. For Benoît, the manner of dress alone—"fully clothed," a description that takes on its complete meaning only by contrast with the bathing suits worn by the family—makes these men suspicious. He looks upon such men with a mixture of pity and disgust, considers them abnormal, weird, unwholesome. Through such representations, Western residents contribute to the fantasized image of the dangerous "bachelor" from whom women and children must be separated and protected.[32] They also resonate with the construction of brown men as "always already dangerous," whatever their acts, in various past and contemporary white-majority social contexts. In Dubai, this collective fantasy legitimates policies of tightened security and segregation.

The distinctively Western masculinities of married men and fathers are constructed in opposition to two counter-images of racialized masculinity. On the one hand, these men assert their desire to take advantage of Dubai "as a family" and defend a hetero-conjugal practice they consider horizontal and shared (despite actual practices), as compared to Emirati masculinity, described as non-egalitarian and segregated. And on the other hand, they pose as protectors of children, and sometimes of women, faced with men whose masculinities they consider deviant. Married women hierarchize masculinities in a similar way; for example, Stéphanie implied that the clients of sex workers in Dubai were mostly Emiratis, Saudis, or even Russians, even though their clients are in fact of all nationalities.[33] Assigning a stigmatized practice to only certain nationalities amounts to placing Western men above all others, since they don't have to pay to have sexual relations.

The model guest family as embodied by certain Western residents comes with a particular kind of discourse on masculinities. It sets up Western males as good family men, responsible, devoted to their wives and children even while subject to the demands of the professional world, in contrast to men considered as more sexist or sexually frustrated, suspected of adopting deviant practices. Such a model also implies specific femininities, as we shall now see.

BECOMING DEPENDENT WOMEN

The married women I met in Dubai, most of whom are white college graduates, inhabited their status as dependent in a variety of ways. Among this group, I will pinpoint two types of experiences: those for whom this was their first migration and who had to either switch professional activities or abandon them altogether; and those who had lived for several years, or even decades, in countries other than the country of their passport, and who saw in Dubai, on the contrary, the possibility of investing more in extra-familial activities. Their trajectories tended to converge once in place, with most exercising a professional or volunteer activity that they considered secondary as compared to their husband's.

A status that combines privilege and social scorn

The status of dependent, let alone "expat wife" (for those whose husband is under expatriate contract), comes with a degree of ambivalence. These women's living conditions—starting with where they reside—are determined by their husband's employer, who can compel them to supply forms of labor even though the women have no formal connection to the company.[34] They enjoy privileged material conditions but often experience forms of social scorn.[35] The status of dependent, in a context where professional work and career are core values, gives rise to a particular kind of social scorn, as revealed by statements made by a French woman entrepreneur, in her 30s, single, with no children:

> "I never go to any of that stuff for the French—the dinners and French events—because there are too many housewives. It's just not interesting for me. . . . There are lots of women who followed their husbands and who don't work . . . so it just doesn't fit my networking needs to meet them. . . . I think they're very nice—I've been invited before—but they stay home with the kids all day, the ones who aren't grown up and . . . I don't know what else to tell you: I'm someone who works like crazy."

In a society organized around professional work where many seek useful sociability, these women are not seen as strategic contacts. A bit further on, this French entrepreneur explained that she avoided hiring women married to highly paid men or women whose husbands she assumes were highly paid:

"Personally, I see things from the entrepreneur's perspective. It's not that I don't take her seriously, but I have to ask myself: 'She doesn't actually need the job. Is she really going to go all in for this job? Is she going to go the extra mile?' Because there's fixed pay plus commissions. . . . They're not going to complicate things, since they have their base salary plus what the husband earns. So they're unlikely to take risks, if you get what I mean—there won't be any challenge. . . . From my perspective as an entrepreneur, that's how it would go."

This neoliberal discourse speaks to the expectations weighing on the professional world in Dubai: you have to "go all in," an expectation that wives of men under expatriate contracts—and, more broadly, raising children in Dubai—would seem unable to meet. The narrative circulating with regard to "expat wives" presents them as women of leisure, a bit depressive, who wander around the house or spend their life at beauty salons.

The ambivalent status of expat wife is experienced by these women in a variety of ways. While some manage to defy the stereotypes that accompany the label—notably, those who have chosen to interrupt a very time-intensive professional career (in Paris, London, Brussels) to take advantage of life with their children in Dubai—others, particularly when the absence of a professional activity is not of their choosing, have trouble getting excited about their new lifestyle. Generally speaking, being a wife in Dubai requires a particular emotional labor in order to enjoy oneself in a city where everything is new, including one's own status; where the tasks of household organization are deemed trivial; and where poorly paid professional activity is not taken seriously.

Those who give up their career

Most of the married women I interviewed had never envisioned living in Dubai before the opportunity arose for their husband. Among the couples where both spouses had comparable university degrees and highly lucrative careers, it was nearly always the husband's job that determined the move to Dubai. This relocation sometimes coincided for the wives with plans to have

a child, as some of them confided. Thus, without taking the initiative to relocate to Dubai, they accepted the idea because they were going to have a baby,
or had just had one, or figured that such a move would facilitate such a plan.

In Dubai, the wife generally has the migrant status of spouse—even if she
has a job—which means that her right to reside in Dubai depends upon her
husband: if he is dismissed and has to leave, she has to go, too. Life in Dubai
creates or reinforces these women's dependency, in other words. It accentuates
the gendered division of labor within the couple, as Clotilde's story suggests.
In her 30s, she negotiated a part-time distance job with her former employer
based in Europe. She suffered from not being able to interact physically with
her colleagues, but after an unsuccessful job search in Dubai, she finally gave
up. "Wives of expats are not exactly welcome. Employers often think that
they're just looking for some way to pass the time, so they make very low offers," she explained. She figured it wasn't worth it, especially because there is
less vacation time and "maternity leave is only forty-five days." For that reason,
she preferred to slow things down to be able to adapt to her husband's schedule and spend as much time with him as possible. Even if "it's weird to have a
housewife visa that doesn't allow me to work," she said she's pleased with the
situation. The latter assertion reveals an aspect of emotional labor peculiar to
Western women migrating as wives, as analyzed by Daniella Arieli:[36] despite
having to suspend or give up their careers, they *labor* to see the positive side of
their situation. Clotilde summed up her choice, saying she has

"a flexible job, I can adapt it to my husband's needs. We have an expat life that
we have chosen to live, when it comes down to it. Many women do that. At
any rate, school here ends at 1 p.m. and there isn't any daycare.... People have
nannies at home since it costs next to nothing here, but still, even if they're
very nice, I don't know anybody who trusts the nannies here. That's why many
women choose to just take it easy here. To live a fulfilling family life. Well, I'm
talking mainly about French women here whose husbands are executives at
companies, career women who used to work in big firms in Paris in plush conditions. The issue for me here is salary and vacation time."

Other married women reported that their bids for a job are not taken seriously: assuming that they wish to work just to "pass the time," employers fail
to make them acceptable offers, in their estimation. Perhaps the feeling that
they are excluded from the structural advantages that most Western passport

holders enjoy and their determination not to lower themselves to a subaltern status[37] could be factors in their decision to drop the search for full-time employment, deemed not "cost effective" enough and too restrictive. Many have carved out a part-time independent professional activity—with a modular schedule that they make compatible with the responsibilities of running a household according to bourgeois standards (even when the women do not come from that particular milieu)—as substitute teacher, translator, freelance journalist, coach, decorator, or artist. Several generally referred to this as a leisure activity, gauging it as poorly paid in comparison to their husband's income. Most presented the transformation of their role and status as a situation they had come to terms with, one that offered advantages, at least for a few years. A minority among them do pursue a full-time career, either with a company or as an entrepreneur.

It is worth noting that the rare males arriving on the Dubai job market as their wife's "dependent" are greeted very differently. One man who followed his fiancée, a local contract recruit, explained to me that his situation was interpreted as proof that he was serious about staying in Dubai. Here again, the cases seem asymmetrical.

Those who develop a new activity

Other women follow a path that is quite the reverse: they live abroad many years or decades with their husband under an expatriate contract, after long ago leaving a professional career behind or, in rare cases, never having had one. They have gotten used to devoting themselves to their husband and children, adapting to the situation and trying to see the positive sides to this life choice. "We go with the interesting job," says one woman, referring to her husband's career, to explain all the relocations that have marked her adult life. "I just like to live wherever I am," another tells me. At any rate, family life is "pretty much the same everywhere" and so is that of a wife, says a third: do the shopping, make the meals, and take care of the house and kids. Still, in Dubai, the lifestyles of married women tend to merge, whether they claimed a professional identity upon arrival or have always considered themselves as an "expatriate wife." Marianne, in her 40s, a mother of two, tells me that she feels fulfilled, even though she has "followed," with ups and downs, the professional career of her husband, an engineer of German nationality, for the past fifteen years:

"He just follows his career path. As for me, I have to find a new one each time ...
which means that there have been places where I've had to try harder than in
others, but here, I think we've found a good balance."

Among the women I interviewed, Marianne is one of the few to never have
had a professional career, due to the constant relocations of her husband, who
earns a very comfortable salary. It had been hard for her at first to forego investing in a meaningful profession for herself. That seems to be the case for most
women of that generation, who came of age in a period when professional
work for women was promoted as a source of equality and fulfillment, notably
in the middle and upper classes. Despite Marianne's lifestyle as a wife following her husband in his professional assignments around the world, what she
calls "expat wives" and their forms of sociability are repugnant to her: "women
who don't work, who spend their time buying gold to have jewelry made for
themselves, going to the beach, having luncheons and all that." She declares
that "women who get together for coffee and to chat," that's not a life. She
dislikes "social obligations" and has a very small circle of friends. One of her
major concerns throughout her successive "expatriations" has been "to keep
busy." She lists the various volunteer projects she has been involved in:

"When you're an expatriate, ... it's not always easy to organize your day-to-day
life. You buy your milk here, your meat there ... It's a hassle to find good-quality
produce.... In the end, you can keep pretty busy with a little volunteer job, about
the equivalent of a part-time. It fills the day, I guess. I was fine with that; in fact,
it was pretty satisfying. And then I got here. So it's very different here.... I think
that [about three months after we arrived], everything was taken care of: the
house, the schools, the activities.... And I had someone at home who did all the
housework and such ... So, ... pretty soon I didn't have anything to do.... And
all my women friends here were mostly on their first expat experience.... I didn't
really fit in, since they were all coming directly from Paris or London, this was a
first-time gig for them. They didn't have the same life experience as me, not at
all. And especially, they had all had real jobs before. I hadn't ever really worked."

Several women arriving in Dubai after many years abroad saw in the city
a place where they could launch a professional activity, the reverse of what
Clotilde said about "career women" who cannot find a job that meets their
standards. Marianne said she felt intimidated by these women "with their

positions of responsibility, their super salaries." This feeling may be what prompted her to look for a paid professional activity. When we met, she was working as a part-time freelancer and was not financially independent, but she "does participate in family life," she explained. As for her friends, who looked down their noses at the salaries they were offered when they first arrived from Paris, they started to see salaried work the same way she did and to take part-time, flexible, and low-paying independent jobs.

"At first, my friends would say: 'We've always worked, but we're not going to go work for €2,000 [about $2,600]. In Paris we always earned [a lot] more than that.' Today, all of them have taken a step back from that attitude. What I mean here is you need to work to keep busy because you can't . . . go to the beach every day. There are limits . . . reading, that kind of thing. . . . Some people can do it, but I hardly know anyone around here who can live like that. . . . Today, my friends have accepted to earn less but at least to be doing something they enjoy, something personal, that brings everything else into balance, I guess."

It should be noted here that €2,000 is not a low salary in France, where the median wage in 2015 (at the time of the interview) was €1,797. Before they came to Dubai, these women had high-paying jobs relative to the French job market. In Dubai, these women would rather invent other, distinctive ways to work part-time than to work full-time for salaries comparable to those given to non-Western employees.[38]

The ways these women relate to professional work, despite their dissimilar paths, do seem to converge. What they report reveals more broadly a complex relation to their dependency status. Quite often, they have no desire to join "expatriate wives" clubs, disparaging these women's activities and distancing themselves from any association with the "expat wife" image. Any activity, whether professional or volunteer, is often a way to move beyond dependency status, even if migration policies, like those inside companies, as well as the division of labor prevalent within couples, still prevent them in practice from being financially independent.

Participating in the family's upward mobility

Women's contribution to the professional career of their husband and to the family's upward mobility tends to go unrecognized,[39] including by the women themselves. If that were not the case, perhaps they would speak differently about their own status. However, the patriarchal negotiation that binds their dependence to a privileged lifestyle plays a central role in the couple's upward mobility. A good number of the women I interviewed were assigned to be "custodians of family welfare and respectability and dedicated and willing subordinates to and supporters of men," not unlike the wives of colonists in colonial contexts.[40] Their role is to ensure the family's comfort, continuity, and cohesion in a situation of mobility, but also to perpetuate and, if possible, improve the family's class position and move it toward a distinctive model of the cosmopolitan Western family. These concerns require considerable labor, even though the family discharges some of their domestic chores to a salaried employee. The wives handle the furnishing and decorating of the home, often a spacious villa, in accordance with upper-class codes; monitor their children's educational setting and oversee their day-to-day schooling, often multilingual, in prestigious international schools; keep in touch with friends and relatives abroad; and finally, organize the family's and the couple's social commitments in Dubai. They organize dinners, excursions, vacations, and, generally speaking, all of their husband's leisure time, so that he might better deal with his extensive work schedule, while consolidating the couple's social network, whether or not of the same nationality. Living in Dubai, then, reinforces both division of labor and role differentiation between the two members of the couple, while bringing about a lifestyle transformation, increasingly integrating the coded practices typical of the upper classes: dining or brunching in prestigious hotel restaurants,[41] enrolling one's children in expensive private schools, driving a shiny new SUV or sports car, having a pool in the backyard, playing golf or jet-skiing on weekends, and finally, having a live-in domestic employee. I devote the next chapter to this practice.

These women occupy a preeminent role in the family's upward social mobility but also in maintaining a certain upper-class cliquishness and affirming their distinctive Western positioning. Guest families, especially when the husband is under expatriate contract, represent only a fraction of Dubai's upper classes, which include people of many nationalities. Among these, it is especially with regard to the Emiratis that the men and women I interviewed seek to position themselves, notably by asserting their own values when it comes to gender equality, despite the relatively unequal practices described within their own marriages. The villa neighborhoods of Jumeirah and Umm Suqeim, where the majority of these couples live, present the peculiarity of being divided into several zones. The line of homes nearest to the beaches is reserved for Emirati inhabitants, while the homes directly behind them are lived in by well-to-do families of various nationalities, notably Emirati and European. Thus, guest families can have Emirati neighbors. Neighborly relations with the latter, however, often remain distant. Westerners easily slip into concluding that Emirati women are confined, as Stéphanie asserts: "They are hidden behind their *abaya*; they're bullied by their husbands, poor things." Despite their own dependence, these Western women think of themselves as emancipated and see their Emirati neighbors as submissive and oppressed, which they believe is the cause of their inaccessibility—they cannot imagine that some Emirati women might actually choose not to interact with them. Statements of this type feed the neo-orientalist and Islamophobic mentality toward women assigned to an "oriental" and/or "Muslim" culture, in continuity with colonial stereotypes.

And lastly, women in Western guest families play a role in consolidating the class clique. To illustrate, although Marianne says she is happy to live in a "fairly tolerant, fairly open" Muslim country, which gives her "a window onto this religion," she realizes, after my asking the question, that she has no Muslim friends, male or female, in Dubai. She attributes this to her having very few friends in general but also to the fact that those she calls "of French origin" do not live in the same neighborhoods and are often younger and childless. She explains that, in any case, she seeks above all to construct an "expatriate community" that is nearby. In this regard, she feels it is easier to be "an expatriate abroad" than in a European capital: "When you're an expatriate abroad, you always come together into an expatriate circle, or in compounds like they have here, in special subdivisions," which makes it easier to meet people in comparable situations and social positions. An assertion of this sort reveals her geographic imaginary: "abroad" stands in contrast to "Europe," on the one hand; on the other, living in a cluster with other "expatriates" of similar social status is experienced as a good thing, since these are the relationships she is seeking, to the exclusion of others.

LIVING IN AN ENCLAVE

The enclave of guest families is not merely the result of an urban plan separating family residences from housing for singles. It is also built upon practices that distance nonwhites, including Western passport holders, in more mixed spaces. Tony, a French male of Bangladeshi descent, quoted earlier, told me of his experience at a French-language Catholic Mass, a space where white French families are notably present:

"It's my own personal France; in fact. . . . I felt like I was in France. . . . It was the France that I missed . . ."

"And you made friends thanks to this particular venue?"

"Oddly, because of the way I look, because obviously there are so many Indians and Filipinos who are very fervent Catholics, . . . in the church there weren't necessarily only French people, there were also Indians, etc., sitting a little further back. I think that at first, they [the French] didn't see me as necessarily—but . . . Yes, I'll say I've seen more welcoming churches in my day."

Tony describes the way the French who attend Mass, since they automatically categorize him as non-French, fail to *see* him at all.

Even though the white French people I interviewed were hardly regular church attendees, this example nevertheless reveals one of the exclusion mechanisms that define the "French community" or, rather, its wealthier segment. Several nonwhite French interviewees explicitly denounced these mechanisms: "Here, there are the 'French' French and the 'hyphenated' French," one of them told me during a conversation with a group of his friends, also of color, who were in complete agreement. The word *hyphenated* signifies that their category was seen as not quite French, especially by white French people. Another explained that a white French male had asked him what he was doing there, implying that by wearing a suit and tie in a Dubai high-rise, he was out of place. During an interview, Fatima, an entrepreneur, complained about the lack of mutual assistance among the French. She feels "taken seriously," "encouraged," and "respected" by citizens from other regions, especially the Gulf Cooperation Council, unlike her interactions with French males in business circles, which she described as "curt"—forms of exclusion revealing inextricable power relations of gender, class, and race.

As a consequence of these forms of exclusion, French men and women in Dubai do not form a "community" in the commonly accepted sense of the term but, rather, different groups that have little to do with one another: on the one hand, white men under expatriate contracts with their spouses and children, living mostly in spacious villas and employing domestic workers, and on the other, younger persons, white or of color, recent graduates who have come looking for their first job in Dubai and living in a rent-sharing situation or even sharing a room or studio—and all the possible variations between these two situations. The first category cultivates cosmopolitan sociabilities that often exclude nonwhite French persons, giving precedence to class homogeneity and the search for exoticism. Social networks often form through the children's (private) schools or via the housing compounds, with their shared facilities such as swimming pools, an arrangement somewhere between the subdivision and the gated community. These are relatively homogenous ensembles as far as class is concerned and are reserved for families. This would partially explain why these couples generally have only white French friends despite the large number of people of color among French residents in Dubai. What the narratives of French nonwhite persons and some whites reveal is the extent to which this exclusion is maintained, consciously or not, by forms of ignorance, contempt, or condescension. Sociability among singles, surely not exempt from this type of practice, seems nevertheless to promote more mixing between white and nonwhite French.

*   *   *

Guest families take part in the biopolitics of Dubai by adhering by and large to the consumerist and heteronormative lifestyles promoted for them within the corporate city. The regulation of intimacy means that, among foreign residents, only those whose income exceeds a certain threshold have the option of living as a family in Dubai; such people then become a resource for the local economy by way of their consumer practices.

Some married couples with children that I interviewed, attracted to Dubai by the prospect of a more harmonious family life, do participate in hierarchizing and segregation among social groups constructed as different via their social practices and representations, thereby reinforcing a certain enclave mentality among Western guest families. Despite a particularly salient division of labor within their marriage and the construction of highly differentiated masculinities and femininities, these couples identify with a gender equality whose outward sign is the public performance of their hetero-conjugality, which distinguishes them from other segments of the upper class seen as sexist—notably Emirati and Middle Eastern. Within Western guest families, the division of labor is often presented as concerted and the couple as in agreement and harmonious, sharing successes and having fun, supporting each other in difficult moments. What they have to say about domestic personnel confirms, as we shall see, this emphatic division of labor between members of the couple, enabling me to go deeper in my analysis of their claim to distinctive egalitarianism.

CHAPTER 5

RELATIONS WITH DOMESTIC EMPLOYEES

"There are people who are too disgusted by what they see on a daily basis, the
segregation, the labor camps, the nannies. We're wary about a lot of things, but we
still think there are more positives about being here than being in a Paris suburb."

THIS STATEMENT BY A FEMALE RESIDENT of French nationality presents
the choice of living in Dubai as a compromise: accessing a certain "quality of
life," to quote the term so often heard during this study, is thought to compensate for the daily unpleasantness of seeing an array of injustices, among which
is the situation of nannies. Seeing? The use of this verb implies that the persons
she is talking about—herself, her husband, her acquaintances—were bystand-
ers to segregation, labor camps, and nannies. And yet, this woman and her
husband, like other couples in their circle of friends, employ a full-time nanny
to care for their children. What are the issues involved for the employers of a
domestic worker living in their home, as they present the employment of domestics as a practice at once morally reprehensible and that somehow does not
involve them? It is this paradox that the present chapter will seek to elucidate.

Numerous studies within various disciplines have been devoted to domestic employees and the historically gendered and racialized construction of
their jobs, such as the now-classic text by Evelyn Nakano Glenn (1992) about
the United States. While much research focuses on female domestic workers
in the Arabian Peninsula,[1] little has centered on the employers of these workers. My inquiry here draws on the studies of other societies.[2] In her pioneering
work, Judith Rollins, a sociologist who got herself hired as a live-in maid for
her study in the US, showed how female employers used their maids to assert
their own middle-class identity, both to themselves and to others.[3] But unlike

the female employers in the US described by Rollins, most of the employers of both sexes that I interviewed in Dubai did not seek to valorize themselves through the employment of a live-in domestic worker, but instead tended to distance themselves from it—and not only from the person, as was recommended to white female employers in colonial situations,[4] but beyond that, from the employment of domestics as a practice. This willingness to disassociate from the employment of domestics is key to the construction of their positioning as Westerners—to set themselves apart from both the domestic employees and other employers of domestics.

Out of the ninety-eight persons I interviewed in Dubai, fifteen told me that they employed a live-in, and a large majority of the others only occasionally sought the services of a housekeeper. Several elements differentiate the persons employing a full-time live-in from those who call in a domestic on an as-needed basis: only married couples, unlike "singles" (based on their migration status), can "sponsor" a domestic employee, which entails requesting a visa for her as the employer. French residents who employ a live-in nanny (a dozen among my interviewees), the focus of this chapter, share specific features: all are white, belong to the middle and upper classes, live in a married heterosexual couple, and are raising children.

By analyzing the paradox of engaging in a practice and making moralizing statements that denounce it, I shed light on the ambivalent stances of these privileged persons in the social order that these same persons perceive as exceptionally unfair. Although some did previously employ live-out nannies, they experience this practice as a break with their earlier way of life, and it causes some soul-searching, presented as unprecedented and specific to their Dubai life. This questioning reflects contextual variations of migrant whiteness: the flip side of these people's denunciation of Dubai is their idealization of their own society of origin, structured by a relation between majority (white) and minority (racialized) favoring forms of "white ignorance" with regard to structural racism.[5] The discourse on domestic employees reveals patterns of how Westernness gets defined and how whiteness is reconfigured in a global city where only a fraction of the middle and upper classes is white Western passport holders.

WIVES AS EMPLOYERS

During the interviews, it was predominantly women who brought up the issue of employer–domestic employee relations; thus, in this context, when I speak of "employers," I mainly mean the women, unless otherwise specified. In effect, even when delegated, domestic labor continues to be the woman's responsibility, in Dubai as in other contexts,[6] and this is true even though, administratively speaking, the employer is the husband. The construction of jobs by organizations plays an important role in this division of domestic labor, of care work, and of education.

Employers whose stories are analyzed here are aged between 30 and 45 and are raising at least one child. Some work as full-time professionals. Others devote themselves first and foremost to their family while also having activities on the side, either paid or volunteer, regularly scheduled or ad hoc, outside their domestic chores and caring for the family members. Although the social milieus where they grew up are diverse, from working-class backgrounds to the upper bourgeoisie, they all moved in middle- and upper-class circles before leaving for Dubai, and mostly in France. Most enjoy comfortable lifestyles thanks to their husband's work contract and are residents with dependency status under the husband.

Although, from the perspective of migrant status and financial resources, both the wives and domestic employees are dependent on the husband, the wives still do assume in practice a role of employer and boss in relation to the employee. The domestic employee, most often of Filipino nationality, was designated during our interview as either the maid or the nanny—French interviewees used these English words or talked about *la nounou*, an infantilizing term that comes from *nourrice*, or "nurse."[7] Regardless of the term used, the employees are in charge of various tasks, from housecleaning to childcare, though proportions may vary. Several employers had already recruited salaried employees to take care of their children and/or do the housework prior to their arrival in Dubai, but it is not the idea of delegating domestic or parental work that has raised issues. They have already experienced what it is like to be "the boss" and have acquired the skill of "knowing how to dominate."[8] However, employing a live-in—that is, actually living with a domestic employee under one's roof—is unfamiliar for them: in France, this practice is reserved for the very wealthiest elite[9] and is broadly decried outside those circles.[10]

The discrepancy between Emirati and French public policy when it comes to early childcare calls for a contextualization of these statements regarding the hiring of domestic workers. Unlike the French state, the Emirati state subsidizes neither infant daycare nor the education sector for most foreign children. What Emirati society does engage in, however, as do European societies, is the globalization of care work more broadly, analyzed by numerous studies:[11] the workers are for the most part migrant women from poorer countries who assume the duties of childcare in these societies. Infant care policies in these contexts are intrinsically bound up with migration policy.[12] The Emirati state encourages the influx of large numbers of women working as low-paid domestic employees; their residence visas, about $1,300 annually, paid by the employers, guarantee the state an important revenue source. Representing a range of ages, most of the employees arrive in Dubai with an unmarried migrant status—which does not necessarily correspond to their actual status but signifies that they are not authorized to come with their partner or children or any other member of their affective entourage. During the compulsory annual medical checkup (also paid for by the employer), a pregnancy test is required and must prove negative—just like tests for HIV, syphilis, hepatitis B, and leprosy. Although there is no minimum wage law in the Emirates, minimum wages for domestic employees are set through agreements with the embassies of their country of passport and thus depend on their nationality: 750 dirhams (about $225) per month for a Bangladeshi national and almost twice that (1,469 dirhams) for a Filipino national, in addition to housing, round-trip airfare every two years to their home country, medical insurance, and visa fees.[13] Private daycare centers, which are very rare, are costly, and schools tend to let out early in the day. There is clear incentive for middle- and upper-class couples with children to hire a domestic employee, especially since the salary is trivial compared to that of the husband: for instance, the husband of one of the women I interviewed earned a monthly salary of 80,000 dirhams ($24,000), or forty times the salary of the nanny, who was paid 2,000 dirhams ($600).

"Maids and live-in help are synonymous with family life in Dubai," asserts a feature article on the topic in a guidebook intended for Westerners relocating to Dubai.[14] Live-in nannies and maids are a standard feature of middle- and upper-class families in Dubai, so much so that housing almost always includes a maid's room. Most of the employers I interviewed lived in a villa that included a maid's room with a separate entrance. Some, like Claire, lived in apartments, a slightly less costly option, where the maid's room amounts to a tiny, windowless space near the kitchen with a small adjacent bathroom reserved for the employee's use.

EGALITARIAN CONVICTIONS

The wives' moral labor

In Paris, sociologist Caroline Ibos observed that many employers of full-time, live-out nannies knew very little about their employee's life, the country she came from, her legal status (documented or undocumented), and the like.[15] They seemed to reserve their "pity for victims much further afield than her."[16] Such disregard proves more difficult in Dubai: it is the employers, both husbands and wives, who handle all the necessary paperwork for obtaining a residence visa for the domestic employee and who pay the relevant fees. Beyond this administrative dimension, several employers did seem to take interest in their employee's life: they talked with them about their background, their family life back home, and if pertinent, their children, and so on. I attribute this heightened concern to the way Dubai is represented as a place of exploitation, a notion widespread among the employers and their social circles in France. Some employers told me they had suffered criticism of their lifestyle from friends and family in France, criticism linked to negative visions of Dubai that those people had nurtured. Unsurprisingly then, the employers confront these issues and develop justifications.

This attitude is gendered. It is especially women interviewees that questioned, from a moral standpoint, the act of delegating a part of the household's domestic labor to an employee from a poor country, where she has perhaps left her own children behind. This kind of soul-searching would suggest that they are undertaking a form of moral labor to arrive at a justification, unlike their husbands.[17] The men in the couples, whether or not they hired a live-in maid, were far less likely to perform any work of moral self-reflection on this issue. For instance, one of them when asked whether he "has hired a domestic employee," answered point-blank: "No, my wife stays at home," with no further elaboration. Delegating domestic work appears to come naturally to this man. Though a few reported reluctance to hire a domestic employee, it was more a matter of personal comfort. They fear experiencing a live-in person as an intrusion: "I like to walk around in my underwear when I get up in the morning and . . . I don't want to run into a maid when I'm in my underwear," one of them told me.

Within several employer couples, their differentiated professional roles reinforced the construction of femininity as altruistic. The husbands perform managerial functions in the private sector, while several of the wives work or have worked, professionally or as volunteers, in areas with a marked emphasis on the social, where hierarchies are less visible. Heterosexuality does take on diverse and contingent forms,[18] and this division of roles is a specific feature of the mobile heterosexual conjugality adopted by a fraction of the upper classes. The moral labor appears therefore as an additional component of the unpaid work performed by expatriate spouses, alongside the emotional, parental, conjugal, and community labor highlighted by Daniella Arieli.[19]

This allocation of moral labor is specific to these couples. Among the unmarried French men and women who require occasional housekeeping services, several expressed certain moral qualms in this regard, independent of gender. For instance, Javed, whose father worked his whole life as a janitor in France, replied to my question about engaging housekeeping services by saying, "I try not to overuse them." Bilel explained at length that he pays the maid the equivalent of the French minimum wage for her to clean his two-room apartment, because he considers the going rate for cleaning services in the Emirates too low:

> "You shouldn't exploit the person either. . . . I had a salary that allowed me to pay her. I considered that the job deserved the wage I set. . . . All work deserves decent pay, and this work deserved to be paid fairly."

Among the persons experiencing upward social mobility, class socialization influenced how they talked about domestic employment in a number of ways. For instance, the interviewees of French nationality and working-class backgrounds (four of whom had fathers who worked as janitors, like Javed) expressed a range of opinions when it came to employing domestic workers, considering it normal, reprehensible, or acceptable in certain conditions. Conversely, white female employers from middle- and upper-class backgrounds and belonging to the Dubai upper class were more likely to have developed a moral stance on the matter, marked by the recurrence of certain rationales that demonstrate their concern to appear fair-minded.

Only one woman among my female interviewees made the choice of assuming all domestic work, family care, and child education, thereby avoiding the need for a nanny or maid, which acted as a factor in her decision. The other women raising young children all availed themselves of these services, including women with no professional activity. By delegating part of their household and parental chores that the drive toward upward mobility makes more burdensome, they can spend more time on personal athletic, artistic, and associative activities, while still maintaining conjugal and family cohesion by organizing various entertainments and outings and developing a local social network. Most felt the need to justify this choice by three types of arguments, often deployed in tandem.

A non-choice?

A first type of justification consists of presenting the job of live-in maid as a non-choice. All but two interviewees—Claire referred to maids as "one of Dubai's real assets," and Marie as a motivation for her relocation—shared an initial reluctance to hire a domestic. Some regretted what they consider as a lack of alternatives in Dubai, especially when both spouses work professionally. This is precisely the case of Aurélie, a full-time salaried professional, who specified in her interview that she had never employed a nanny before coming to Dubai.

> "So, to my great consternation, I find out that school lets out at 3 p.m., which doesn't work at all with my having a job, so I'm feeling helpless, how am I going to make this happen. . . . 'Well, of course, Madame, everybody has a nanny.' . . . At any rate, I had to go to work somehow, so I got a nanny."

This absence of choice, linked to Emirati state policies, does need to be put into perspective, however. The people concerned did *choose* to come live in Dubai for a few years with their children, often in order to earn a higher income than they would have in France and to build their savings and/or to enjoy a more pleasant, less stressful lifestyle than that available in large European cities. The gender hierarchy that materializes within most couples, however, does construct women as relatively subordinate in this decision;[20] moreover, they are expected, for their husband's benefit, to arrange things such that domestic chores get done and the children cared for, whether by themselves or with a female helper—in Dubai or any other place they live. This has to do with the particularly sharp division of roles within these couples. Among the few working professional couples who were parents of young children, the choice to live in Dubai and hold down two salaried jobs prevailed over their initial reluctance. In other words, hiring a live-in disturbed them at first, but this concern seemed incidental compared to the advantages of living in Dubai with two salaries. Other reasons, like the desire to have the children cared for at all times by the same person or to save money (compared to the cost of private daycare centers, for example), also came into play.

Most of the women who at least temporarily had to give up their professional activity, like Sophie, a salaried professional, before moving to Dubai, also expressed their initial reluctance to hire domestic workers, considered a reprehensible practice. Still, they could not present their eventual recourse to this solution as a non-choice, as did the women working full-time jobs.

> "For two years, we refused to have a live-in. It's an easy thing to do here, to have live-in help, but we felt that it was a kind of modern slavery. Then later on, with all the activities there are here, we had to admit that it was a little silly not to take advantage of what was on offer."

This interview extract is hard to interpret, given the striking contradiction between the reference to modern slavery and the breezy tone that follows. Perhaps this woman was somehow conveying how much her position changed within a few years, from the time she arrived, when she was passing a clear moral judgment on the employment of domestics, and her gradual socialization to the lifestyle of well-to-do families in the Emirates. A short while later in the interview, she explained that hiring a live-in domestic employee costs less than four hours a week of housekeeping and babysitting, which weakens her original argument all the more.

Hiring a live-in nanny is not trivial, as we have seen. Most employers represent this working relationship as unjust, and yet, they still do assume the role of employer. They later grow accustomed to the benefits that a live-in employee provides, such as allowing the couple to go out at night, leaving the children in her care, without any prior scheduling.

Denial of coevalness and interconnection

Another type of justification refers to these temporary residents' supposed non-impact on the situation of domestic employees in Dubai: many feel that they have no role in the Dubai social order. This argument is best summed up by Philippe, under expatriate contract: "Whether we're here or not changes nothing." The self-perception of being outside the social order in which one participates is all the easier to achieve when that order is cast as an absolute temporal and spatial alterity. For several persons, the employment of a live-in domestic worker belongs to a non-egalitarian past. The situation of domestic employees in Dubai, although very much a contemporary phenomenon, gets cast back into a distant time and place over which French residents believe they have no control. Philippe, who admitted that he and his wife (on parental leave) would never have envisioned having a third child if they had not been living in Dubai and benefitting from the presence of a nanny, explained:

> "It's always important to keep in perspective the way we see people as compared to life in their own country. For instance, we used to say sometimes that the nanny was earning almost nothing, but that gave her access to a lot of things back home. She was a mother herself; she had children back in the Philippines. That might sound strange to us now, but in France, one hundred years ago, that's how it was, too. The system of governesses . . . so what that means is that the grandparents are raising their grandchildren."

Philippe's story is typical of a world vision marked by the "denial of coevalness,"[21] which consists of situating persons or groups of persons in a past anterior to a present conceived as Western. Thus, the nanny is a throwback of another era—a century behind. According to this teleological vision of history, the Philippines, to which he compares the nanny's living conditions, is less advanced than France in terms of development and social justice. This vision presupposes an absence of interaction between the situations under consideration. In other words, the denial of coevalness also has to do with a denial of interconnection between different contexts and situations, a mindset prevalent in the West's way of imagining the "global South,"[22] as if societies had parallel evolutions that never intersected or had any influence on one another. It is a denial of colonial history and contemporary power relations.

The denial of coevalness amounts to a way for employers to distance themselves from the employment of domestics. According to this imaginary vision of radically different and disconnected worlds, Westerners take no part in this practice, since it belongs to the past, and they decidedly belong to the present. This vision of a line of historical progress along which Western countries are ahead of those in the Gulf also underpins two ideas that I heard among the interviewees, beyond the employers of maids: firstly, at Dubai's current stage of economic development, exploitation is believed inevitable, and secondly, Emiratis are not yet ready for democracy.

Virtuous employers?

As the third type of justification, most employers self-represent as virtuous, so that their relation to the maid is cloaked in a charitable exterior. This type of justification was particularly salient during the interview with Stéphanie, who has no profession, an upper-class background, and is very engaged in volunteer work.

> "I actually didn't want to have her live with us. Still, we had no choice, because when you want to sponsor someone, you have to house them. But I didn't want to, since we don't have a small child at home to take care of, and I really didn't want her around. As it turns out, if we don't house them, they live with twenty other girls in some rat hole; it's really horrible. So I went ahead, and I don't regret it now, because ever since, she's doing great, she's very happy."

This narrative, which turns an employment relationship into a charitable one, emerged in several interviews. Though the same discourse can be heard elsewhere,[23] it does relate to forms of distinction that are specific to this context. Seeking to soften the image often projected back in France—the exploitation of housemaids in Dubai—the employers include themselves in the "we" which refers to "expats" or "Westerners," represented as virtuous and charitable employers, unlike the "local" or "Arab" employers. According to their report, their maid is better paid, better treated, and works less.

> "An expat pays a nanny twice what a local does, while having her work half as much." [Philippe]

> "In addition to her salary, I buy her food separately, because that way, I can be certain she isn't skimping, that she's getting enough to eat. . . . They talk a lot among themselves, the Filipinas, . . . and their main goal is to especially avoid working for Arab families, of whatever nationality, because . . . she has some friends who practically live in slave conditions." [Stéphanie]

On the one hand, the narrative that turns the housemaid's job into a charitable act reinforces the hierarchy between employers and employed, already considerably strong in a situation where the maid's residency papers depend on her job. On the other hand, this distancing applies to both the maid and to those who mistreat their maids. While nonetheless employing a housemaid, these employers seek to set themselves apart from the whole issue of domestic employment, which they say harkens back to another era and other societies. In this way, they construct themselves as Western by differentiating themselves not only from the maids, of course, but also from the "locals," branded as slave-driving employers.

Beyond these narratives, the purported generosity of the employers is framed by precise behavioral norms: although most of those I encountered paid their employee above the minimum wage set by the relevant embassy, some admitted that this factored into a strategy intended to curb turnover, and that they also made sure not to pay her "too much." Stéphanie said she pays her maid above the going rate to induce her to stay, but not too much either, so as not to "create unfair competition."

An unusual case encountered during the study confirms the strict norms that govern relations between employers and employed and limit the forms they can take. Aurélie had a more horizontal relationship than most employers with the employee who took care of her children, so much so that she became a reference for the other domestic employees in the neighborhood. She even attempted to intervene in conflicts between the housemaids and their employers, in favor of the former. These initiatives got her into trouble in her neighborhood. She received threats from some of her (Western) employer neighbors for having deviated from the agreed-upon conduct: maintain a polite relationship, including charitable actions, with "your" maid, proclaim your indignation among your compatriots about how the "Arab" employers are reportedly mistreating their domestic personnel, but do not get involved in what's going on with your own neighbors. These types of behaviors contribute to specific positionalities and forms of distinction of employers as Westerners in the Dubai social order.

WHITE EMPLOYERS' SPECIFIC DEMANDS

The paradoxical positioning of employers gives rise to specific demands with regard to domestic employees. On the one hand, they attempt to circumscribe the maid's presence with the family, and on the other, they ask her to avoid certain deferential behaviors that make the family uncomfortable.

A particular insistence on invisibility

The social convention of invisibility that would have live-in domestic employees treated as nonpersons, as if they were not there, makes this work, according to Judith Rollins, a particularly trying experience.[24] I observed the way maids are rendered invisible throughout my study. For instance, the women who invited me into their homes, with a maid present, did not introduce me to her, even though they did introduce their family members. However, the employers' very reluctance to live with their employee gives rise to another way to produce invisibility. Unlike employers for whom a maid's presence is routine, the employers I met can never feel quite alone as long as the maid is in the house. They sense her presence as obtrusive and uncomfortable, as revealed by entrepreneur Céline's story. Céline had a prestigious career as a consultant before relocating to Dubai. At that time, she did have a full-time employee come to take care of her child, but she was not a live-in. During the interview, Céline spoke extensively about her relationship with her current domestic employee, addressing the issue in far more detail than the other interviewees; she seemed visibly concerned by the situation. If she is quoted in such depth for the details she divulges, her story is far from exceptional and resonates with those of several others. When I asked if there was a room in the house for her domestic employee, Céline gave this answer:

> "It's set apart, a separate studio, with its own entrance; she can come and go as she pleases; she has her own bathroom, toilet, bedroom, her own kitchen, etc. Otherwise it would have been no, no way! I can't stand having someone in the house. . . . Even when she's here in the house, I don't like that she's here when we are. . . . Even though she would love to be with us when we're here, we just want to be left alone, have the place to ourselves. It really intrudes on our personal lives, it's invasive. . . . I would always ask her to finish everything before the kids are back from school, so that when they get home, she'll have nothing to do but look after them, and I never asked her to stay in the evening with us, . . . and if she did, I would tell her to leave and come back in the morning to finish whatever it was."

Céline imposes invisibility on her nanny because she experiences her presence as an intrusion into her home, even calling it invasive. All the work has to be done in the family's absence: she refuses to *see* the nanny. Even while benefitting from the domestic's services, she wishes to preserve the kind of privacy of the home that one would logically enjoy if the housework were done by employees not living under the same roof. If most employers I interviewed set a rough work schedule for their domestic employees, they also made clear their limit for the domestic's presence, beyond which the employee must retreat to her own quarters or go out, so as to be invisible to the family.

This insistence upon invisibility is also present among women who pay for housekeeping services on an as-needed basis, like Sabrina, who is 26.

> "I have two house cleaners who come in once a week. There are two of them because the apartment is pretty big, so it's faster with two, right? Because I don't want to have someone spending the whole day in my house. When I come home from work, I'm tired and don't feel like having to deal with a maid, to tell the truth. So there are two of them, one morning, once a week."

These women prefer that the household chores get done without their having to *see* the person doing the work, perhaps because of their early reluctance to consider themselves as employers—that is, as privileged and having a certain relative power over the women they employ.

Deference as a source of unease

If certain employers claim to seek out encounters with persons from other countries and cultures, relations with the maid do not enter into their cosmopolitan imaginary. The domestic employee is thought to be a stranger[25] whose influence over the children is a source of concern. This fear of the nanny's malign influence is not specific to Dubai,[26] but it is accompanied here by the peculiarities linked to the imaginary that Western residents project onto non-hegemonic countries: the racialization of qualifications and skills and the belief in Western superiority also mark this work relationship.

> "The problem with nannies here is that they come from developing countries, they aren't educated, and they especially don't want any responsibilities. Maybe it's just a question of culture, but . . . They aren't really nannies, in fact. . . . The term *maid* is more like it. They really are nothing but enhanced housemaids that can do a little babysitting. And as far as I'm concerned, these are clearly not the women I want raising my children." [Céline]

Céline's story focuses on the maid's lack of skills, which she explains by her culture and by the fact that she's from "a developing country," which is also a way of holding her at a distance, to cast her as an absolute Other. Céline is one of the interviewees who came out as strongly critical of the bad influence nannies have on children: she fears, she said, that they will end up "ill-mannered" from their contact with nannies. Among my interviewees, few so roundly criticized their nanny's supposed incompetence. Several, on the contrary, praised their nanny's qualities, rather vaguely in most cases, evaluating their domestic employee as "very good" or describing her as "a pearl." Still, other interview extracts, as well as certain Facebook posts on pages intended for francophone residents, demonstrate that this suspicion of incompetence that weighs upon nannies, though not ubiquitous, is widespread and not specific to Céline.

> "Europe's leading daycare group made up of early childhood specialists has moved to Dubai! . . . All their educators have degrees in early childhood education (no nannies . . .) and their standards are apparently very high."[27]

The parenthetical remark "no nannies . . ." refers here to a presumed complicity among the francophone women residents of Dubai, who seemingly fault nannies for their lack of training or skills. Their use of language was a reproach that returned time and again in the interviews. Even if the language of communication between the nanny and the children is English, a language that the parents believe their children need to master for a proper education, the nanny's accent is considered problematic by the parents, who fear that the children will pick it up. This pervasive fear of the nanny's influence through a kind of contagion recalls a certain colonial mentality that counseled distrust with regard to "native" nannies.[28] An additional factor, however, seems to feed this fear in the configuration under study. The women I interviewed did indeed fear that the nanny would transmit debased cultural content to their children, but what they really held against the nanny was her tendency to serve the children instead of educating them.

> "All the women I talk to here, the ones who leave too many things . . . up to the nanny, they have problems when the kids grow up. They're ill-mannered. Even with us, their behavior is sometimes borderline. They'll be sitting with us on the couch and say, . . . 'Take my shoes off.' Or 'Go get me some water.' Without saying please or anything, even if we repeat it fifteen times. It's because the nanny will just say OK; she won't ever reprimand them for it, even if we tell her to. We ask her to tell him to say please, something a nanny would do automatically in France. Because it's just so basic, isn't it?"
> (*Later in the same interview*)
> "So, it sounds like you're planning to stay quite a while in Dubai . . ."

"Sure, we really do like it here, I guess. So, at first we said we'd stay for three years, but I think we're going to add another three. Between three and five years, I think. After, we'll just—I don't think we'll stay once our kids are teens."

"Because..."

"The values being conveyed... I feel that when it's the early years, it's kind of complicated to explain. You know. The social differences, the..."

"So, when you say social differences and all that, and values, it's..."

"The fact that we have people serving us all the time in the house, even though we're pretty much used to it now, that's what I mean." [Céline]

In this interview extract, the nanny's deference to the children is a source of unease. In other words, despite the sharply delineated hierarchy between employer and nanny, the employer would prefer that the relationship she develops with the child invert that hierarchy to become that of an adult to a child, not in the interest of the nanny per se but in the interest of the child. The structural inequality of conditions between the nanny and the child must not, in this case, impact the child's education: the nanny must act in such a way as to render this inequality invisible. Céline blames the nanny for failing to make this effort. The nanny does not live up to her expectations: in her view, she should build a connection of attention and affection with the child that is not based in a relationship of service.

In the media and in articles in English, mothers explain how they assign a few household chores to their children, neither out of need nor a desire to unburden the service personnel, but so that the children will be able to adapt to other contexts in the future:

"I think some children get used to having day to day chores done for them and that they are exposed to the kind of 5 star lifestyle that doesn't necessarily exist in their home countries. I worry that when the time comes for university or to start work that the children will not have learnt the necessary coping mechanisms. I worry about the kids learning to be self-reliant, I remind them of how lucky they are and that some of the benefits they take for granted are not usual in other countries. It is difficult for them: but with so many things done for us, who can blame people for thinking life is served on a silver platter?" [a teacher at a British school in Dubai][29]

The concern that emerges in statements such as this has less to do with the exploitation of domestic employees than with the education of children. It is this educational imperative that justifies leaving Dubai, in the eyes of some.

SHELTERING WESTERN CHILDREN FROM DUBAI

A number of parents, like Céline, explain that even though they enjoy living in Dubai, they have set an age threshold for the children—often
adolescence—beyond which it will be appropriate to leave, fearing that the
children might have "no grasp of reality" and develop bad habits, notably that
of always being served. Several women, including some who did not have
children but intended to in the near future, put forward similar assessments.

> "I can't see myself having teenage children here. What most of my friends tell
> me is that they want their children to see another reality. Otherwise, these are
> children who will go back to France and wait for the door to open all by itself.
> It's good that children learn that everything isn't this easy." [Clotilde]

This kind of statement pertains to an exceptionalist vision of Dubai, according to which this city is incomparably non-egalitarian and unfair, as opposed
to an idealized, egalitarian France.

The plan to leave Dubai for reasons of education reveals a particular positioning in the city's social order. According to this logic, the adults claim they
benefit, with no ethical qualms, from a hegemonic position in a highly unequal society, while also claiming that their children are harmed by it, in the
mid to long term. In other words, what disturbs the parents the most about
persons they employ as domestic workers is the impact on their children,
who they imagine get exposed to them as if to some toxic substance.

Sophie's story is interesting in this respect. The woman she had been employing as a maid for several years was jailed, prosecuted, and expelled for a
money matter not related to her employers. Sophie and her husband tried to
help and defend her, though only within certain limits, since they were warned
that they could have problems themselves if they got too involved. Sophie concluded her narrative with these words: "This was not exactly a great experience
for my youngest." Of course, that statement reveals unsurprisingly that Sophie's affective investments in her daughter, on the one hand, and in the nanny,
on the other, are of two very different orders. But what also emerges from
this testimony, as from other interviews, is that in the final analysis, what is
considered most problematic about the exploitation of nannies is the impression it leaves on the children. It is for them, and not for what they nevertheless
identify as a situation of unfairness, that most of the Western residents I interviewed do not plan to stay in the city for the long term.

*   *   *

Egalitarianism is not performative:[30] making statements critical of forms of inequality does not preclude adopting strongly non-egalitarian practices. If these statements can nevertheless have an impact, it is by shaping these non-egalitarian practices, by giving them specific forms. This chapter has shown what is at issue for white female employers when morally distancing the employment of domestics while at the same time engaging in the practice. Materially, the possibility for Westerners to cheaply hire a live-in employee, who devotes most of her daily life to caring for their family, encourages them to have children. This advantage available to the middle and upper classes contributes to building the Dubai trademark as a welcoming city for families, where it is easy to raise children and where domestic work seems to get done as if by magic. This advantage relies on a form of exploitation that features close surveillance of domestic employees, whose mobility is limited and whose reproductive rights are nonexistent—surveillance exercised by the combined actions of state authorities and employers, both male and female.

Within this hierarchy of intimacies, Emirati citizens occupy positions comparable to those of French residents. For the latter, in this context, distancing oneself from the employment of domestics is a key element of distinction (racial, civilizational) with regard to the "locals" and of identity-building as a Westerner, self-defined as more egalitarian than the rest of the world. When the logic of some of these statements is pushed to the limit, Emiratis who employ domestic workers are slave-owners, but when Westerners do likewise, it is an act of charity. Consequently, Western employers require nannies to behave as if the relationship were not non-egalitarian; they see this as a way of instilling so-called Western values in their children, including a form of discursive egalitarianism.

These remarks shed light on certain contextual transformations of whiteness in migration. Between female employers in France[31] and in Dubai, a few invariables emerge. It is always the women and not their husbands who deal with childcare, even when this duty is delegated to a third party. In this respect, relocating to Dubai does not mitigate the prevailing gender hierarchy within different couples. The moral labor deployed by the wives (and a few rare husbands) to justify the employment of live-in domestic employees, however, conveys a reconfiguration of whiteness and class belonging: if, when in France, an employer did not question her social position as employer, she now feels it necessary to assert the egalitarian values that help define her affiliation to a specific social group, that of Westerner, among the upper classes of Dubai. Through this Westernness, a positive and explicit content is thereby added to whiteness, not overtly formulated for the most part and therefore cast as neutral and normative among whites in societies where whiteness accounts for the majority status. In Dubai, for Westerners, it is about foregrounding distinctive values and, in the end, a hegemony thought of as better, more just, and therefore more legitimate than that of "others." The self-reflectiveness of the people I interviewed, while it reveals complex positionings, does contribute to constructing forms of distinction by asserting difference with other segments of the middle and upper classes.

CHAPTER 6

HEDONISTIC LIFESTYLES

"The region is in a state of utter turmoil, but the country is super-stable, and I for one believe that it will always be stable here. You don't see any of it from here. And it's true that if you look around, you see people decked out like jetsetters, sipping cocktails around a pool, listening to hip-hop." [A resident of French nationality, during a night out at a bar]

IN CONNECTION WITH ECONOMIC DIVERSIFICATION, a number of bars and nightclubs opened in many luxury hotels, outside of which the sale of alcohol used to be tightly controlled (until 2020). Dubai nightlife has become part of the city's branding effort as a more liberal lifestyle space compared to neighboring emirates and countries. When Western passport holders refer to their Dubai experience, many of them, singles in particular, speak of a hedonistic lifestyle.

This category of "single" requires clarification. The married/single distinction is insufficient when it comes to understanding the hierarchies among the affective, intimate lives of foreign residents, male and female. These categories cover a range of different situations. For instance, not all married persons have equal opportunity to raise children. Neha Vora points out,[1] for instance, with reference to women of Indian nationality, that the internal rules of certain companies allow them to dismiss a pregnant employee, even if she is married. Beyond these rules, bringing one's partner to Dubai or raising children there, if one does not have Emirati nationality, is in practice impossible for anyone not earning a very high salary. The administrative category of single thus covers a variety of situations: some persons are not married anywhere in the world, but others, married elsewhere, are categorized as single from the viewpoint of the authorities because their salary does not allow them to come with a spouse unless that spouse has a separate work visa. While the mobility and sociability of single residents working at so-called unskilled jobs and coming from relatively poor countries are narrowly limited, nightlife represents one of the corporate city's strategies to leverage the presence of the better-off, especially those holding Western passports.

This chapter explores how single Western residents, male and female, relate to this consumerist nightlife. The persons I interviewed advocated a temporary hedonism: they had decided to take advantage of it, while at the same time regarding this lifestyle as just a phase. During the interviews, my subjects often spoke of consumerism and materialism, seen as features of Dubai life, as negative aspects that made it difficult to develop "serious" affective relationships. The selective identity of potentially "serious" partners reveals a distinctive heteronormativity. Nightlife and intimate relationships prove to be sites of reinforcement of hierarchies between Westerners and others, but also within the group of Westerners itself.

PRIVILEGE AS A FEELING OF ACCESSIBILITY

In the opinion of many unmarried Westerners, the parties held in lavishly decorated hotel bars and clubs are part of the Dubai experience, at least early on, and taking full advantage of this nightlife is a key component of their lifestyles. This was the case for Juliette, a young engineer with a passion for clubbing. With an upper-class upbringing in a provincial city, a graduate of a prestigious French *grande école*, she came to Dubai in search of her first job because "that's where it's all happening." She was working for a British company, where she found the culture "closer to French culture" than in companies where they celebrate Ramadan—that was the example she gave. She expressed her hope to "have an international career" and complained about the ambient "pessimism" in France. At 22, she went from student status in France to a Western salaried employee in Dubai earning 15,000 dirhams (about $4,500) a month. She built a social network starting with a friend of a friend and moved into the Marina neighborhood to be closer to the bars and nightclubs, a world she greatly enjoyed, even though she considered the policy regulating alcohol "a bit hypocritical," as do many white people.[2] Juliette loved to go out dancing. She felt that Dubai's night world was more accessible and less elitist than in Paris. She planned to stay for "three to five years" but did not see herself "raising kids, having a family" in Dubai, where it would be difficult to "instill true values" in children. She could easily see herself moving to the United States for the long term. Four years later, she was preparing to leave for Australia after her company made her an offer, matched with a promotion and a significant salary hike.

Juliette's story introduces several aspects of the lifestyles adopted by well-to-do single residents: the choice of living in the part of the city where the most sought-after nightspots are located; the perspective that this nightlife is accessible; and the representation of hedonism as a temporary phase. Many single Westerners live in Dubai Marina, as did Juliette, a very expensive mixed commercial and residential neighborhood for the upper classes, composed of high-rises surrounding a vast marina—an artificial yacht harbor. This sea inlet with its scalloped outline, yachts and tourist boats sailing in and out, is edged by a pedestrian promenade lined with cafés and restaurants, a shopping mall, and several luxury hotels that include bars and clubs. Several persons explained that they wanted to live there because they could go everywhere on foot, unlike many other districts of the city where a car is a must. Some find this neighborhood beautiful, corresponding to the image they had of Dubai: yachts, shiny new high-rises, luxurious bars, cafés where you can smoke a hookah out on a terrace by the water. Many say that it is practical to live in the Marina, since all the nightspots are right there. It is accessible by metro, located at the other end of the city from "old" Dubai, which includes the neighborhoods inhabited mostly by the less well-to-do groups. Getting from one to the other takes at least an hour, with long stretches on foot to reach the station, and more walking once inside the metro, whose stations are very distant from one another. Kate, 26, a human resources manager of Australian nationality, sharing rent with a friend, adds another reason to all the above:

> "I live with a man. Normally, that's forbidden. Here in this neighborhood [Marina], there are only Westerners. I prefer living far from the locals, in this situation where I'm living with a man."

Kate referred here to the ban on unmarried men and women living together, which was ended in 2020. Her relatively unusual statement conveys both a search for a "Western" enclave and the desire to keep a certain distance from the "locals" represented here as more conservative, or even potentially menacing toward the hedonistic lifestyles of the single Westerners.

At Dubai Marina, it is not uncommon to pay 80,000 dirhams ($24,000) a year for a two-room apartment, which is a considerable outlay even for those earning around $55,000, like Juliette. While some are willing to spend such an amount, many live in shared rentals, which is slightly less expensive (and theoretically illegal). Apart from commuting to work, Juliette rarely leaves her neighborhood and surrounding area, where all her friends live. Near the Marina is another even more expensive neighborhood, JBR—Jumeirah Beach Residence—composed of high-rises right on the waterfront, whose beach has recently been the focus of a vast architectural project involving stores, bars, cafés, and restaurants, as well as an IMAX theater and sports facilities. Opposite the Marina, on the other side of Sheykh Zayed Road, a high-rise neighborhood built around artificial lakes, JLT (Jumeirah Lakes Towers), slightly less costly, represents a compromise for all those who enjoy going to the bars and clubs of the adjacent neighborhood without having to pay the corresponding rents. These are the three neighborhoods where most of my unmarried interviewees were living. Their inhabitants belong to the upper classes and are not necessarily white.

Most describe Dubai's nightspots as accessible. Still, going out in these neighborhoods is costly: one cocktail in a hotel bar often costs the equivalent of $25, and a hookah in one of the surrounding outdoor cafés costs $13. Profiling is another limit to accessibility in these establishments, notably for South Asians.[3] Some are barred long before they get to the entrance of these bars and clubs, due to the rules that govern their mobility. Consequently, the interviewees' emphasis on the accessibility of nightlife and luxury leisure activities was all the more striking. It would appear that this extolling of accessibility refers rather to the pleasure of being a member of an advantaged group, as a Western passport holder, Mehdi, 30, tells me:

> "Right now . . . , I'll have to get back to work and start saving a little money, but I won't lie to you, I've been eating at restaurants in five-star hotels. . . . I eat in places where I would never eat in France. It's a good life here: I've gone out on quads, I've jet-skied, I've rented yachts with friends. . . . I've done things that I never could have afforded to do in France."

Mehdi's emphasis is all the more surprising in that his situation is one of the most precarious and least well-paid of all the people I interviewed. Even when money is tight, it is conceivable, even normal, to frequent luxurious spaces, including for those who are not members of the upper classes in their home countries, let alone for some interviewees of color who had the experience of being refused entry to clubs in France. In Dubai, they do not feel they are being screened when they go to luxury venues. This impression can be explained by their affiliation with an advantaged group: they do not risk being refused entry, unlike others. Enjoying automatic access to luxury spaces constitutes a component of "the wages of Westernness" in Dubai.[4] Even for persons like Mehdi, who enjoy few benefits from the structural advantages that most Westerners enjoy in the job market, living in Dubai allows them to feel they belong to an advantaged group and to experience that group's lifestyle, even when it means going into debt.

The pleasure of assimilating into a social universe seen as jet-set—the word evokes parties in fashionable, luxurious hotels, where everyone dresses expensively—justifies the sizable expenditures. Further, this sort of prodigal spending is done ostentatiously, considered a de rigueur part of the Dubai "experience." During a night out with a group of Western residents at a bar, I observe some of them, as they talk about their nighttime adventures, perform a kind of narrative display, as this extract from my notes for that evening demonstrates:

> Max explains that he goes to some really crazy parties out on the beach where cocktails cost 250 dirhams apiece [about $75]. He talks about an electronic music festival he went to in Abu Dhabi. He and his friends were at a hotel and were drinking champagne, and got drunk in their rooms before going out to parties. It cost him something like 3,000 dirhams [about $900] but it was really worth it, he said.

Lavish spending is valorized. At another party, at the home of a man of French nationality, the conversation turned toward how much a night out costs. The guests estimated that "if you can get away with spending only 500 dirhams [$150] on an evening out, you're ahead of the game. It's because you've been careful." This social practice is made possible by the high salaries of Western passport holders in Dubai, as well as the easy credit terms available. Dubai allows Westerners both to live beyond their accustomed financial means, via credit and/or a higher salary, and to consume products and services considered as more luxurious. The lavishness of the restaurants, bars, and clubs relies on the cheap labor of construction workers, cleaning staff, and other service personnel. The persons I interviewed did not make the connection between the accessibility to all this luxury and the harsh conditions of those employed as so-called unskilled labor, whom they denounce in other contexts.

"Everything is easy, you can have dinner delivered to your home or go out to restaurants. It's all much more accessible than in France. It's super gorgeous for a standard price." [Valérie, 42]

"Parties are lots of fun. You meet all kinds of people. And it's always really well-planned. Recently, I was at a party at a girl's place. . . . She had hired staff to handle the bar and clean up while we were dancing." [Juan, 27]

Valérie's use of the word *standard* assumes that everybody has access to this kind of luxury. It renders invisible the structural advantages and the cheap service work that the Western residents enjoy.

SURVEILLED HETERONORMATIVITY

One aspect particularly appreciated by certain women I interviewed—Western passport holders, white and nonwhite, as well as one middle-class Indian woman—is the security surveillance of public spaces and nightspots. For instance, Juliette explained that there are a lot of security guards in clubs and they will intervene directly "if a guy makes unwanted advances on a girl, and keeps insisting when it's clear she isn't interested." Nawel, 21, who returned to France after one year in Dubai, also pointed out this particular asset of the city.

"And what I also loved about Dubai was the security. As a woman, I mean, when you talk [about Dubai in France], they say, 'Yeah, you'll see when you get there, how women are treated.' . . . But as it turns out, women are treated really well there. Personally, I never had a problem. I could walk home at four in the morning. . . . I could do whatever I wanted. I could go out wearing short shorts. Later, I moved to the Marina, which by definition made things even easier. . . . There [in Dubai], it's against the law to be drunk, in fact. You can't get drunk. . . . It's not like here [in France]. And frankly, that changes how your evening goes. You've got people who've had a little to drink, but they're cool. They're just there to have fun; they're not there to grope you."

Surveillance of the dance floor and the feeling of security when it's time to go home makes nightlife all the more accessible to single middle- and upper-class women. Public drunkenness is outlawed and prosecuted, as Nawel recalled, even though others report that drunken behavior is hardly rare. In addition to the ban on drunkenness, it is the surveillance of dance floors and nightclubs in general that explains how rare harassment and sexual aggression are in these spaces, and a number of women pointed this out. Bars and clubs try to attract a female clientele in order to attract the male clientele in a city where men make up the clear majority.[5] The city's nightspots compete with ladies' nights, special once-a-week events where women can drink free of charge.

Nightlife in Dubai features a surveilled heteronormativity, to be understood in two ways here. On the one hand, body-to-body relations are closely monitored by police or security guards. Certain sexually connoted gestures, like kissing on the mouth, are banned in public, irrespective of gender. On the other hand, inhabitants can report any outlawed behaviors, such as forbidden gestures, cohabitation of unmarried men and women (until 2020), or sexual relations between persons of the same sex. In this respect, surveillance can reinforce the gendered binary of self-presentation. Geographer Katie Walsh analyzes how this binary, notably in the nightlife world, affected her during her study in Dubai:

My own everyday performances and experiences of sexuality and gender changed in the field. I began to embody a much more exaggerated white, feminine, heterosexual identity (both consciously and unconsciously) than I ever have in other spaces, which began to materialise in the manipulation and also in my corporeal gesture. The sense of belonging I experienced as a result . . . was seductive.[6]

Although many gay men take part in Dubai nightlife, an interviewee defining himself as gay felt that they often complied with a self-presentation that conforms to dominant norms: "Here in Dubai, the gays are mostly straight-looking. In dress-up." To a certain extent, this observation is also related to the forms of surveillance described earlier. It is felt that looking straight is a way to avoid arousing suspicion by the police or neighbors in a city where homosexual practices are officially forbidden. These gendered norms in the nightlife scene get extended into the professional sphere—two very closely linked worlds in Dubai, since it is common to indulge in professional networking at a nightclub.

DUBAI'S HEDONISM AS A TEMPORARY PHASE

Most of the single Western passport holders that I interviewed, once they had been in Dubai for at least a year, identified two phases since their arrival. In the first, they checked out the nightspots, feeling a bit disoriented by the jet-set atmosphere and the number of ephemeral encounters. In the second phase, they wanted to "settle down," tightening their social circle into a group of close friends, or moving in together as a couple, and in certain cases, getting married and "starting a family." Sabrina, 26, a manager who had lived in Dubai for four years, and Marion, 28, an architect who had arrived five years earlier, both considered themselves in the second phase, as these interview extracts reveal.

"For the first six months, it was basically all about discovering Dubai, going out, meeting people, partying. It was essentially what people do in Dubai, I imagine, at least during the first year. . . . You are introduced into a completely different world, where it's all luxury and glitter, parties, things we don't even tell our girlfriends [back in France] because they wouldn't believe it, or it would be like we were showing off or something. But here, it's the way everybody lives, every day. And it was pretty nice at first, I must admit. . . . We had a great time, I was single—I mean, those were the days, in a way. Then after a year or so, I settled down. I met someone, the person I'm with now. We live together, etc. So, you get tired pretty quickly of these very superficial people that you meet at a party. . . . It lets you see more clearly, to take stock of who you are, who you'd like to be, and with whom, especially. . . . I was in that sort of frivolous world, let's say, with frivolous people. And then I soon realized that it's not my life, it's not what I want. But I don't regret a thing, absolutely not. I met . . . most of my current friends, the ones I still hang out with, during that early period." [Sabrina]

"It's so different, so bling, so surreal, in fact, that I loved it because I felt like I was in a movie. I loved my little crazy year, going out all the time, drinking a lot with friends. . . . I really enjoyed those years because I was constantly meeting new people, and we'd then get together in these huge gangs. We went to parties on boats in Abu Dhabi . . . There was truly no limit back then! It wasn't expensive at all. We all managed to live this life of luxury, insane, and without spending that much. . . . I was still in my post-student phase and wanted to keep partying. And afterward . . . , well, I'd just had enough of it. It wasn't that I suddenly found it lame—not at all. The whole bling thing, that's fun for a while, but there comes a time when you say: 'I have absolutely nothing in common with those people, I have no idea what I'm doing here.' . . . After a while, age catches up with you, too. I realized that I wasn't 24 anymore and that I was hanging out with a lot of younger people. . . . I didn't have the same kind of life they did. . . . I had a steady job, and I had a lot of friends older than me, married people with kids. So, all that made me totally want to settle down in Dubai. To live a different sort of life, in fact.

(*Later in the interview*) "We [she and her future husband, whom she met in Dubai] are certainly not going to stay. . . . We already hope to have a family, we want to get married soon, so we know we don't want to have children here in Dubai. When they're infants, fine, that works well. But still, we're living in a very, very materialistic world." [Marion]

These women, who were living unmarried with men they met here, describe the luxurious singles life in Dubai as a phase, one worth living, though the important thing is to eventually "settle down." This normative vision of life stages—marriage and family following a youthful period of living it up—pertains to the construction of distinctive subjectivities, since the majority of Dubai's inhabitants have no access to the hedonistic lifestyle that the city offers its wealthier residents. For many Westerners, Dubai is a place where young people live—as seen through all the stereotypes that apply, such as going out at night, drinking a lot, serial one-night stands—which contrasts sharply for some with their background, rural or working-class, which does not necessarily offer such opportunities. During an informal discussion, Ahmed, a sports coach, 27, told me he was bored in the little French town where he grew up. For him, Dubai represents, above all, the possibility to go out with his group of friends to nice places. For others like Juliette, the lifestyle adopted in Dubai was a continuation of the hedonistic practices she had adopted at business school, but it took on a new dimension thanks to her income and the luxuriousness of the venues she was frequenting.

Sabrina and Marion, like others, stepped back from what they called the city's "bling" style, the luxury offered by a city in a non-hegemonic country, seen as nouveau riche in a way. These young women cast an exoticizing, sometimes condescending gaze on their surroundings. They said they were experiencing the Dubai lifestyle, notably the nightlife, as an adventure, almost like an extended vacation. Although they admitted they enjoyed it, they made a point of distancing themselves from it, notably through the age gap, but also nationality and class: the figure of the nouveau riche, associated with superficiality and bling, acted as a kind of foil. What really mattered was finding the right partner, someone respectable, and in certain ways at least, who resembled them.

The second phase, then, consists of "settling down"—that is, moving in together as a heterosexual couple and eventually having a family. In this respect, Marion's story, like Juliette's, echoes those of many married people with children: they consider Dubai as a positive setting for "enjoyment" but not so good for raising children once they are old enough to become aware of its "values," or its "materialism." Both women therefore hoped to limit their stay in Dubai to a few years: they could live there as a couple or with young children, but they would have to leave soon after.

Among the residents with unmarried migration status that I questioned, fifteen, including Sabrina and Marion, were living as a heterosexual couple with a partner they met in Dubai through close friends or through work, almost never in Dubai's bars or clubs. Only four were living with a person of the same nationality. Several women were involved with partners who did not hold a Western passport, but all were at a professional level equivalent to or higher than theirs. Conjugal relations could thus move beyond certain borders, notably Western and non-Western. The biopolitics of Dubai tend to reconfigure forms of racialization, the delineation of groups, and the boundaries shaped among them, as we shall see at the end of this chapter. Gender configurations tend to respect a certain order: in the majority of couples, the man occupied a professional position at least as high as the woman's.

NEGOTIATING INTIMATE RELATIONS

The city was often described by my interviewees as a place conducive to fleeting encounters and superficial relationships, whether professional, friendly, or sexual, but where it was difficult to experience a "serious" relationship. The neoliberal ideology playing out in Dubai, the temporary status of the great majority of its inhabitants, as well as the multiple hierarchies that structure this urban society seem to shape people's affective lives, according to the narratives of unmarried persons dissatisfied by the type of relationship developed in the city. Their narratives showed once again a need to distinguish oneself from a society deemed too materialistic, where relationships lack authenticity.

Self-distinction from sexual consumerism

Several interviewees, male and female, emphasized how hard it was to meet serious partners and attributed this difficulty to the context of the transient city and to consumerism: people do not stay long, so they try to take maximum "advantage." This connects back to Katie Walsh's analyses of the intimate experiences of male and female single British residents in Dubai, whose performances of migrant heterosexuality featured an avowed quest for play, freedom, and sexual pleasure, while being shaped by gender relations.[7] Among my interviewees, the notion of play, however, almost never came up as a matter of choice. The lack of stable relationships in the city and particularly the difficulty in finding a conjugal partner were identified as problematic. Only Anis's narrative, where he fully assumed his refusal to get involved, diverged from this general tone. He introduced a theme brought up by other males: the connection between sex and money.

> "Here, it's more complicated because . . . though with me, it's different because I don't have very high social status yet. But I watch my buddy, my flat mate. He earns €6,000 [$7,800] a month. . . . When he meets someone, he . . . has to make sure that the girl isn't coming on to him just for his money. . . . And there are people, there are girls who are there for just that. . . . That's why you have to be really careful; it's not always obvious. I like to say jokingly that with me, they're barking up the wrong tree. . . . Okay . . . so I haven't found the girl I wanted, [and even though] I'm 30, I'm still having a good time. So you see, I don't overthink it. Not for now, anyway."

Anis's refusal to get involved dated back to his late adolescence. Living in Dubai added a further layer of complexity, he felt, to many people's purpose for relocating there—that of "making a lot of money." How could one be sure of a woman's sincerity in such a context? This was a question also raised by Mike, an American in his 50s, divorced. He explained that most of the women he knew were married, and his few encounters had proven inconclusive: "No one wants to commit here. Everybody thinks they're gonna leave. So they don't want to commit in a relationship. . . . I'd have a few drinks, I would start talking to a woman and then she would ask me for money. There are so many prostitutes here. It's depressing. So I stopped drinking." In his case, the connection between sex and money seemed at cross purposes with the search for sincere and authentic feelings.

The figure of the money-hungry female, whether through sex work defined as such or some more implicit sex-for-money exchange, is ubiquitous in the narratives of single males as soon as the topic of intimate relations arises. Their stories recall the figure of the "hustler woman" analyzed by Magdalena Brand with regard to French male expatriates in Bangui.[8] The fear some of them feel in encountering a woman who wants their money is the corollary of their privileged position in the labor market where, as men holding Western passports, they earn higher salaries than others from the start—especially compared to women not holding Western passports. However, their narratives conceal social hierarchies; they self-present as virtuous men threatened by greedy women. Their subjectivities are constructed not only by the legitimizing of the structural advantages they enjoy (rendered invisible by the expression of their vulnerability to these women), but also by their quest for relationships conceived of as authentic, not based on money. None reported having paid for sex from a prostitute—perhaps because these men, identifying with the most valued model of masculinity, see themselves as "necessarily desirable."[9] The opposition between sexual relations construed as mutual and egalitarian and those described as unequal and material contributes to shaping distinctive Western subjectivities.[10] Once again, it is by defining oneself as egalitarian, engaged in sincere, horizontal, and disinterested exchanges rather than economic-sexual ones[11] that they identify with the distinctive status of Westerner.

Single heterosexual women also emphasized how hard it was to enter into relationships in Dubai, which they blamed on material matters; their narratives, however, divulged another version of men's behavior, suggesting a re-actualization of gender hierarchies within the group. Several women, all in their 30s, asserted that many men were looking for sex without involvement, an attitude they attributed to the sexual availability of a large proportion of the women, as suggested by Kate, a manager and Australian national, quoted earlier. "What's great is that there are more men than women, but at my company," she said, "there are all these gorgeous young women, of every origin, and all single." Explanations such as this and the following ones transpose to the sphere of sexual and affective relationships a neoliberal reasoning in terms of market, of supply and demand.

"You can't take these guys seriously, I think. Unfortunately, there are girls here who are pretty easy, so for these guys, they have no trouble getting girls. So that's how it is: they enjoy life, until what age I'm not sure, but in my age bracket, 35, you can't take them seriously." [Sarah, 30, manager, has been in Dubai for five years]

"Here, my impression is that certain men, if they're looking to get laid on a given night, they can get it. Prostitution, there's a lot of it around here, too. You see in a hotel, for example, . . . a guy goes up to a bar, he gets hustled by three chicks, African or Moroccan. . . . Okay, let's go up to the room. He pays, and that's that. So why would he bother getting involved with someone, when he can get everything on the side? Though I don't paint them all with the same brush, I think there are also some good guys. . . . Well, anyway, it's pretty tricky." [Nadia, 35, head of logistics, has been in Dubai for four years]

Several were nearly ready to leave Dubai when they turned thirty, after having lived there a couple of years, convinced they would never find anyone there to start a serious relationship with. Amy, a white American in her 30s, was on the verge of leaving Dubai for that reason when she met her partner. Figuring that she had pretty much "done the rounds" professionally, she had gotten married and hoped to devote herself to her future children over the coming years. Others told me about departures among their acquaintances for the same reason.

"As a woman, I figure: 'If I don't find anyone, I'll have to go back to France, because I want to have children.' And I have a woman friend and a guy friend who went back because they didn't find anybody. She was 36 and had been living in Dubai for fifteen years without managing to find someone, so she figured . . . And one of my British buddies, he went back because he wanted to be with an English girl, not with an Arab, an Iranian, or some half-and-half type. He was English and he wanted someone English, who had the same culture. . . . So at some point I figured: 'If you don't find anybody . . .' Thank God I met someone. . . . It's a subject that comes up constantly when you're in a group, this issue of being unmarried." [Hanane, 34, has been in Dubai for seven years]

These women's stories reproduce the widespread tendency to standardize gender identities in the field of love and sex according to a binary heteronormative pattern: men are looking for sex only, and women want a long-term relationship.[12] Beyond the law of supply and demand they invoke, these women are referring to an intrinsically consumerist masculinity, sexually speaking.

Though some do acknowledge having once been in a state of mind where "having fun" was important, they say they quickly tired of it. Several compare themselves to women cast into a non-Western "elsewhere," all in the same "market" but where the women are younger, prettier, and have less constraining expectations with regard to men. Their stories set up a continuum between "prostitutes" and "women attracted by money . . . each one more

beautiful than the next," from whom they distance themselves without for-
mulating any judgment. By naming this category, they set themselves apart,
nevertheless, as selfless and sincere, in search of authentic relationships that
they feel are hard to come by in Dubai.

In all the narratives, I had the impression that the men do the choosing,
that the ball is always in their court, that they call the shots. Some seemed
to develop strategies for meeting a woman of this or that nationality and
racial identity, like Hanane's friend, who she says was seeking to preserve a
"culture" through homogamy, which is why he returned to Great Britain to
find a partner—white like him, one assumes. Others as well, now married
with families, went back to their country after a few years of life abroad for
the specific purpose of living as a couple, and then left again. These men distinguish two periods: one marked by consumption, in all meanings of the
word—conspicuous spending, sexual experimentation—and another period
of building a hetero-parental family, based on the principle of homogamy.

Thus, single men and women merge in their representations of Dubai
as a city conducive to sexual consumerism, from which nearly all claim to
distance themselves in their search for authentic relationships. Although the
women's testimony points out that men do not always practice what they
preach, other examples invite more nuanced, less binary representations
than those tending to essentialize gender. Three single men told me they left
Dubai, among other reasons, because of the affective vacuum they felt there.
Marwan was one of them:

> "The main thing that made me go back home was being so far away from family,
> which weighed on me quite a bit, on the one hand, and on the other, the fact
> that over there, especially when it comes to family, . . . to put it simply, a wife and
> child—over there everything is very mobile, dynamic, people always coming
> and going, so that in the long run, it gets a little complicated to stay there with
> such loose, unstable ties. At any rate, that's how I felt about it."
>
> "And now, do you feel like leaving again for some other place?"
>
> "Not right away. . . . I wouldn't be so concerned once I'm . . . once I have a
> more structured family core than I do now [laughs]." [Marwan, 28]

These interview extracts reveal how deeply normative married life and
family are among the group of Westerners, creating a kind of melancholy
for those who do not achieve them. This desire to meet someone, to "settle

down" and have a hetero-parental family contrasts with the trajectories of certain "unmarried" residents from other regions, who are fleeing family pressure experienced in their home country. Youssef, a young man from Lebanon, who had lived in France and the United States and who called himself "very liberal," said he chose to live in Dubai because "you can have the life you want to lead, but nothing clings to you. It's the only place in the region like that," referring in particular to the absence of pressure to get married. Another interviewee, in his 40s, of Saudi nationality and who had lived several years in Europe, explained that in Saudi Arabia, as a bachelor, his life was confined, and that conversely, "the freedom this country offers is really nice: there are no limits—if I respect myself and respect others, I am respected." Sami, of Lebanese nationality, explained:

> "I don't think I prefer the family structure . . . I don't see myself in that position, not currently at least and I do not see it in my future. . . . I don't think I would be okay with the idea of having children. So . . . which is of course difficult, you know, for someone from the Middle East because the expectation always is to get married and have kids."
>
> "That's not that specific to the Middle East . . ."
>
> "Well, but you know I have always been different. Ideologically, philosophically, religiously, socially, culturally . . . so I don't fit the Middle Eastern standard."

For these men, Dubai offers the freedom to escape the dominant family norm they attribute to the "Middle East" or to particular countries. For other interviewees, it is also about being able to live a minority sexuality more freely. A flight attendant, self-defining as gay, describes most of his male coworkers as gays who prefer to be based in Dubai and travel around the world for this job rather than staying in their own home country, in Asia most notably. One young woman of Egyptian nationality, who self-defines as lesbian, speaks of Dubai as her default location to flee both country and family, having failed to obtain a visa for a European Union country as she would have wished.

These persons often spend several years in Dubai, and some identify with it as a city where they have forged strong affective bonds. Even though homosexual practices are officially banned there, Dubai has occasional parties or even clubs that have been described to me as "gay friendly," and specialized internet sites also represent a meeting place, though some have been censured, requiring users to create their own private virtual networks. The distinctive heteronormativity expressed by most Western residents contrasts with the norm-defying lifestyles of one part of the residents of other nationalities, even beyond those who self-define as gay or lesbian.

Escaping the couple standard

A few Western passport holders do somewhat transgress, though not explicitly, the prevailing heteronormativity among Western residents, even when they have made blatantly binary statements elsewhere regarding attitudes of men and women. In conjunction with the singles lifestyle turned toward luxury leisure and experienced as temporary, in anticipation of "having a family," they create lives for themselves in Dubai that elude the dominant models. They value friendship first of all, where they invest all the more since their family and friends back home are so far away.

Several single French women spoke of their tight friendships with persons like them in Dubai—with whom they sometimes shared an apartment—referring to them as they would to a family member.

"Elodie—that's my amazing little story from when I first got here, and it's still continuing. . . . As soon as I contacted her, we got together maybe two or three times. . . . She suggested that I move in with her. At first, we had a one-bedroom plus a big living-room. . . . Then later on, we saw that we got along really, really well. And that was it, she has become my family, and I've become her family in Dubai, so we got a much larger apartment, directly opposite. . . . I feel a little bit privileged to have been so lucky, meeting her. So that's really wonderful—it's something I would wish on everyone, in any country. It helps a lot." [Ilham, 30, marketing manager, had been in Dubai for two years]

"Like most of us here, we don't have any family. Our friends become our family, so we end up spending a lot of time together."

"So how does that work? You have a little group of friends, or what?"

"Let's say I have three separate groups of friends, which I don't mix much and which each brings me something different, with whom I don't have the same activities. . . . The first group is kind of Frenchie, very informal. We're always at each other's apartments having drinks in the evening. I can do just about anything with that group. Then I have a group of just ladies. They come from all over the place but we're really a group of girls, so what we do mostly is to go out together. And then I have a third group that is mostly couples. We mostly do fun restaurants together, don't stay out too late, some desert parties, weekends together on the other side of the country . . . stuff that's more leisurely, I guess." [Agathe, 28, entrepreneur, had been in Dubai for four years]

At other moments, these women expressed their desire to get together with someone as a couple. The ambivalence of these affirmations is undoubtedly reinforced by social norms that make it particularly difficult for women to imagine "a life of one's own," without husband or children.[13] Some made clear, however, that it was not their priority; others, like Nadia, who was aware that she had restrictive expectations, explained it by the fact that they saw themselves in the future as "alone"—that is, single—but with lots of close friends in their life.

"I'm kind of a special case. I'm frank. I want absolutely no connection with Franco-Maghrebis. . . . And at the same time, I know very well that the person I'd like to settle down with, in a love relationship, I mean—I want him to be Muslim, so I'll be looking again to Arabs. But the problem is that there is a culture gap, you see [laughs]. On the one hand, we have a common base, the Arabic-speaking culture, let's call it, but you've got to make the distinction between Maghreb culture and Arabic-speaking culture. Because we're different, after all. And then at the same time, as a woman, . . . the fact that you're single, living in your own place, that you're set up nicely in a foreign country, that has a kind of castrating effect. Where the guy, in everything I just described, has no place."

(Later in the interview) "So when I project into the future, I'm staying single. I don't know how else to say it. I've always done things by myself."

Without claiming it as such, these women defended a certain independence. This did not prevent them from feeling a kind of melancholia with regard to the norms, or more exactly, the nonconformity to certain norms.[14] Nadia's narrative was also steeped in a melancholia linked to a social displacement: she rejected both community life in her Parisian working-class suburb and Franco-Maghrebis as a whole, and yet, she aspired to meet someone who shares her "culture." Her yearning for moments of complicity with such a person, while distancing herself from the place of her upbringing, was realized somehow in the deep friendships and solidarities she had forged with her "Franco-Maghrebi girlfriends" living in Dubai, with life paths comparable to hers.

The heteronormativity of Dubai's group of Westerners might seem for some less pronounced than in their home milieu.

> "I mean, here's the thing. I'm 30. When I go back to France, to my city, and I see my girlfriends I went to school with and worked with . . . , they're all married with kids, they've bought a house, the whole deal. So when I go back to France, it really hits me hard, I feel way behind, I look like a spinster, in fact. While in Dubai, being 30 and single is completely normal." [Inès]

This observation, which echoes Katie Walsh's (2007), whereby Dubai can be envisioned by singles as an escape from the norm of couples and family, depends on their social background before migration. In this regard, Dubai is like most large cities where professional careers are valued as such.

AFFECTIVE DISTANCING

The subjectivities of my interviewees, whether single or living as a family, tended most often to reinforce a distinctive heteronormativity. For instance, although certain persons with single status constructed conjugal relations with persons of similar professional positions but without Western passports, they still strived to establish and maintain affective distance with regard to others whom they imagined as somehow deviant and unmodern. Sabrina, for example, explained her indifference toward service personnel by pointing to differences that struck her as insurmountable:

> "It's funny, you know, because there are so many differences in everything! In Europe, you go out to have a drink, you flirt a little with the waiter or waitress, you meet up with them later at a club—no big deal. Here there is such a gap between social classes . . . that you barely even say hello to a server. And it's not like you're ever going to swap phone numbers with a Filipino or Indian server who's there in front of you."

While Sabrina stressed the differences between Dubai and France, her perception of these differences betrayed how she turned her position into a class issue: in France, her parents belong to the working class; in Dubai, thanks to her passport and her managerial position, she belongs to the upper classes. When she alluded to this boundary with the service staff, however, she also referred to their nationality. In her explanation, the explicitly noted difference in social class was matched by a more implicit racial assignment to once again delineate the "strangers" with whom no affective bond was possible.[15] My interviewees often distanced themselves from those who represented the "strangers," notably during our informal conversations outside the interview format. Once, while we were talking about networking groups, one French passport holder advised me not to join one expatriate network where, he felt, there were "a lot of Indians" whose intentions he considered extra-professional. Another one, while we were out walking, advised me to cover myself when we passed by construction workers, a reference to their stereotyped sexual frustration.

These projections touching on intimacy cast certain persons into an intractable difference. While the theme of sexual frustration mostly referred to Indians, single Western residents, not unlike married persons, sought more broadly to differentiate themselves from "others" whose practices, when it comes to gender and sexuality, were associated with abnormality and deviance. In doing so, they fashioned a distinctive heteronormativity. During my study, several white men reported the precautions they take so as not to be perceived as gay in a context where the line between heterosexuality and homosexuality seems less clear-cut—a fact that they stigmatized in their statements. Other interviewees placed a clear divide between a normal and abnormal way to be single. Charlotte, 27, a salaried professional, migrant-status unmarried but living with a partner she met in Dubai, spoke of the "frustration" of her boss at work, an Emirati woman:

> "Emirati women . . . feel a little frustrated because they can't show themselves, and her in particular, at 37 and not married yet, so I think she's looking for a husband, which is not trivial, I think, from a psychological standpoint, for her to see girls strutting around, flaunting their beauty."

Although Charlotte presented her boss as an exception, her discourse focused on the woman's frustration via what she was wearing ('abaya and veil), suggested by the phrase "they can't show themselves," which did not correspond to her liberal vision of female emancipation and sexual freedom. The heteronormative hedonism that many single Western women and men promote is also a way of distinguishing themselves from these "others" considered less modern, less liberated. By pointing to the opposing figures of female frustration, on the one hand, and the "prostitute" or the "gold-digger" on the other, the interviewed women portrayed a respectable hedonistic sexuality, with which they identified.

Numerous practices aim to distance persons perceived as other and to stay in one's enclave described as Western, as revealed by (American) Amy's narrative about various co-workers:

> "I mean, I would never see an Egyptian Arab man outside work. . . . So, number one, having other Westerners is a huge determinant of whether or not there was a possibility of a relationship outside the office. And number two, it depends on whether we're talking about women or men. In the first company [where I worked], I was with all Arabs, or it was all Indians, and . . . Indian women are so culturally different from me, it didn't make sense for us to communicate outside the office. We had nothing in common, I guess."

Amy defined herself here as Western and justified her aloofness toward other categories of persons according to certain criteria: "Arab" men were described as womanizers and harassers, and she saw "Indian" women as too different from her. This kind of generalizing about one category or another did not keep her, elsewhere in the interview, from denouncing the racism of Dubai society. Like Amy, several interviewees admitted to having only Western friends, or "Western-type"—that is, "educated in the West," to quote John, an American male.

The practices meant to reinforce the boundaries of this affective enclave are numerous. On the internet, meet-up groups among Dubai residents define their communities as "Western singles" or "European singles."[16] A gay white man explained that, on the meet-up applications, he looked for a "white" physical type. The Western clubbing set moves to a different establishment once there are "too many Indians" at their current one.[17]

Nationality and racial assignment interact in an unstable manner depending on sociability groups. It is this kind of distancing, including in intimate life, that Tony experienced and that motivated his decision to leave Dubai:

> "Basically, it's a transient city, a city that's all about appearances, all about the bling, and all that. Obviously, it's great to take advantage of it all, to have an extraordinary quality of life. For me, it just wasn't reality, that's all. . . . Physically, I look Indian, so when it comes to assessing beauty, I fall to the bottom in the hierarchy of nations . . ."

"You felt that . . ."

"Oh yes, clearly. . . . So, when it comes to my love life, it was a little complicated, let's put it that way."

Certain nonwhite Western passport holders, like Tony, can in certain situations be interpreted as subalterns and therefore rendered invisible and kept at a distance affectively. As for nightlife, which most Western residents praise for its accessibility, it is therefore a site where race hierarchies are reinforced. The affective distancing of non-Western, nonwhite "others" who get cast into subaltern status always impacts the hierarchies shaped within the group of Westerners as well.

Among French singles, whites seem to have contrasting attitudes toward people of color. Networks of relatively inclusive solidarity have developed. For example, certain francophone Facebook groups allow for mutual assistance, notably in the search for internships and jobs. On a smaller scale, certain apartment shares, which bring together white and nonwhite French persons (and sometimes persons of other nationalities), represent networks of sociability and solidarity. Whiteness does remain a key category, nevertheless, in hierarchizing within the group. For many white interviewees, the linkage between French status and whiteness is taken for granted, including in Dubai. Marion, for instance, a white single French woman, who said she grew up in "expatriation" with parents whose profile came close to matching that of white, well-to-do French couples living in Dubai, expressed a certain anxiety with regard to the particular definition of the French in the Dubai job market, to the extent that it may include nonwhiteness. Although she had never lived in France, she considered herself more French than the "second-generation, third-generation immigrants," in her words.

Several more routine, less vehement conversations attested that, among the white, well-to-do French, many spontaneously associate Frenchness and whiteness, predictably so, given their socialization in France in majority-white milieus. For instance, during a conversation following our interview, Mathilde told how she once took offense at being mistaken for an Algerian carrying a false French passport at the Dubai airport:

"When I got to customs, they mistook me for an Algerian. They kept me for half an hour, saying that I was lying."

"Despite your passport . . ."

"Despite my passport, despite how I look! I have blue eyes, fair skin. Unless you're Kabyle, there's a chance in a thousand! Single Maghrebi women are a big problem here. They're often prostitutes."

Her rationale, built on the evidence of physical difference, affirmed between the lines that either you are French or you are Algerian, and that the two categories correspond to two quite distinct physical types ("unless you're Kabyle"). Her indignant tone suggested that she was offended not only because her Frenchness and her whiteness (the same thing, in her view) had not been acknowledged, but also because she had been mistaken for a "Maghrebi woman"—in other words, a "prostitute." In her statements, clearly couched in biological terms, the conviction that she belongs to a race was intrinsically linked to the claim of sexual normality and respectability as a white woman.

*   *   *

Dubai offers Western singles a lavish nightlife in venues described as luxurious. Nightlife is often described as accessible despite the associated costs: to be able to frequent such luxurious spaces, even if it means going into debt, is among Dubai's many pleasures, or more to the point, the pleasures of being a Westerner in Dubai and belonging to an advantaged group. Within this sociability, however, they feel consumerism pervades every dimension of their affective lives. For many men, intimate relationships initiated in Dubai are felt to be tainted by motives of material gain that diminish their authenticity. In their narratives, they attempted to distance themselves from sex in exchange for money, underscoring their yearning for mutual, egalitarian, and disinterested relationships. For their part, women often deplored a supposed unfair competition with "other" women, sometimes associated with non-Western nationalities, who they believed were seeking no commitment from the men. These strongly differentiated narratives between men and women do have one point in common: the nearly unanimous yearning to "settle down" as a couple or a family, the hedonistic nightlife being deemed a necessarily temporary phase. Even though fifteen of my single interviewees met their partner in Dubai, the group as a whole regularly declared that this city made it impossible to commit to a true conjugal relationship based in a reciprocal, disinterested spirit. By describing Dubai as inauthentic and materialistic, these persons thereby associated sincere love with the West, to the point where some wanted to leave the city for that very reason. To perceive themselves as authentic, serious-minded, modern, and desirable partners was key to their identification with a distinctive Westernness.

This aspiration to form a respectable couple based on an authentic, egalitarian relationship contrasts with the apparently less heteronormative lifestyles of certain residents of other nationalities. Affective and sexual relationships, at the heart of Western subjectivities, contribute to their distinction vis-à-vis those they construct as "others," frustrated, deviant, and/or unmodern. Nightlife is a space of hierarchical reinforcement of gender, but also of race, via the othering of all the service personnel who work in that space, cast into an intractable difference, and of anyone else likened to them.

CHAPTER 7

WESTERN PRIVILEGE AND WHITE PRIVILEGE

"This is the safest country in the world! I don't have to worry about my black husband being racially profiled, or being shot for simply being who we are. Life here is stress free." [Janelle, US American professor self-defined as Black][1]

"I'd say I'm actually treated better as a Black person out here than I was back in the UK; it's interesting not to be in the 'underprivileged' or 'disadvantaged' categories for once. . . . It doesn't really matter how you 'identify' or what subcategory you belong to when filling out forms back home. Here, it depends on your passport. . . . I feel as though the systemic racism embedded in most Western societies doesn't affect me here." [blogger Helen Debrah-Ampofo][2]

AS THESE SELF-ANALYSES SUGGEST, living in the Arab Emirates compels many persons to compare their social position there to their previous one, in the country where they used to live. Yet, narratives of past and present, here and there, self and others, the categories employed and judgments declared all vary according to the person's position in a social hierarchy, especially when it comes to race. The way one defines security or inhabits a privileged position—with or without accustomed ease—is situated, as is the very extent of the privilege experienced. This chapter delves first of all into the analysis of the discrepancy between the ways white and nonwhite Western passport holders experience Western privilege in Dubai. Based on contrasting narratives, this analysis will explore the extent to which the perception of Dubai social order differs depending on the person's racial position, interlocked with gender and class, and according to the individual's trajectory. This chapter then shows that whiteness, in practice, does remain a privileged position among Western passport holders. In other words, the hierarchies among nationalities hardly overshadow race, gender, and class, as some might believe at first glance, and this intensifies in the medium term.

Based mainly on the experiences of French people and put into perspective with those of other Western passport holders, this chapter analyzes how residents reflect their place in this society, often referring to the social structure they used to experience. Race constitutes an important dimension of the social hierarchies in the different societies in question, though obeying different modalities and shaped by singular histories. The point here is not to compare them but to begin from the viewpoint of persons moving from one society to another to better understand how migration and the experience of a new social position transform the ways people define themselves and others and the extent to which racial hierarchies constructed elsewhere are questioned and/or reinvented in the Dubai context.

To reflect on these categorizations, I drew partly on the concept of "racial schemas" posited by Wendy Roth in her book *Race Migration*,[3] focused on Latin American migrants in the United States. Racial schemas cover "the bundle of racial categories and the set of rules for what they mean, how they are ordered and how to apply them to oneself and others."[4] Although the schemas vary from one society to the next, people may use several at the same time, notably when they are on the move. Put differently, having been socialized within a certain "racial schema" influences the way people categorize their interlocutors in another context. This cognitive approach to race, however, must be combined with the perspective focused on the social hierarchies, including structural racism, that governs this book. Because of this focus, the interviews I conducted bear not on the categorizations themselves but on the personal experience that points to forms of hierarchizing, exclusion, and discrimination. As we shall see, the stories of French men and women most often reflect a racial schema marked by the majority/minority binary opposition in France and either by the multiculturalism or "caste society" (depending on the speaker) in Dubai. The shift from one to the other involves forms of transformation and reinvention of what it means to be French in Dubai, for whites as well as for people of color.

ELUDING RACISM?

On the city of Dubai's official website, it is portrayed as "tolerant and cosmopolitan."[5] Many French people of color echoed these words in the interviews and described Dubai as a multicultural city, in contrast most notably with their earlier experiences in France. Urban Dubai society, made up of various groups, is noteworthy in their view for types of cultural hybridity and tolerance that are widely commended, though the hierarchy among racialized national groups, meanwhile, gets overshadowed. They then appropriate a neoliberal discourse on multiculturalism, asserting the chance for success offered to each and every one without distinction, a discourse that has become hegemonic today in a variety of settings.[6]

From France to Dubai

Praise for Dubai's multiculturalism is constructed by comparison to racism and discrimination experienced in the home country, which several people mention as one of the reasons they left.[7] The French people of color that I interviewed in Dubai were mostly experiencing upward social mobility. Most were on a linear career path (or presented it as such), from their college degrees to a series of internships that eventually led them to Dubai. Others put forward a more uneven trajectory, with a series of jobs considered either seasonal or temporary that were unrelated to their college degree. Many had other experiences abroad before coming to Dubai, either in some formal program (an exchange year with an American university, for example) or not, like Amin, who went on his own to New York "with a thousand euros in my pocket" to learn English and spent a year there after graduating from college.

Many raised the issue of hiring discrimination in France or of forms of oppression at the workplace that weighed in their decision to leave. Hiring discrimination was mentioned in several interviews as a reason for leaving, which resonates with higher rates of unemployment among people of color.[8] Despite their university degrees, several had trouble finding their first job. This was the case of Devi, 30, with a double master's degree, living in a working class Paris suburb before leaving for Dubai.

"At an early stage, I first tried to job-search in France, for personal reasons, because I wanted to stay here, but the professional opportunities I had after getting my degree were either very low quality, a fixed-term contract (CDD), very poorly paid, or nothing at all. I could not find any open-ended contract (CDI). So in the end, having a string of academic titles, an American degree, etc. is not worth much in France, and that's when I thought it might be a good idea to try for something abroad. . . ."

"And the fact that you had so few opportunities and all that, you ascribe that to the economic downturn?" (*I am returning to a topic that she brought up earlier.*)

"Yes, to the financial crisis, or at least mainly. Because even during one of the CDDs that I was able to get, I was in the pre-hiring phase, and during my six-month CDD, the company got into real trouble and had to let go people who had been there for twenty-five years, so naturally, what they called pre-hiring turned into "we're not renewing your CDD." . . . And for a little pessimistic note, I'm not sure if what I'm saying is true, but . . . some of it has to do with racism. Not necessarily racism, let's just say favoritism toward the white population, unfortunately. . . . I mean, it's pretty flagrant, because when you arrive in one of those huge open spaces, you see perfectly well that you're the only person of color. . . . And then, frankly, it's just an idea. . . . I don't know if it's just in the companies where I happened to find myself, with very few people of color, or not. . . . I'd rather not venture any further on the subject, but it's true that . . . in any case, it's not an advantage to have been a person of color."

Amin, 33, also spoke of how hard it was to find a job in France in the communications sector.

"It was a real struggle to find a job, to get hired. Even though I already had plenty of experience and expertise . . . , it's an uphill battle in France because, well, there are very few slots and people aren't going to let go of what they have . . . I don't know. I'm not going to go back to specific details in connection with my being a descendent of immigrants, but it does matter and makes things a bit harder. It didn't help me much in France. In the United States, believe it or not, it was just the opposite. People want to work with you because you have a double culture. You're someone different, unconventional, so they want to work with you. For them it's interesting, it's a plus. In France, much less so. They still haven't figured that out, but it'll come someday. It's moving forward slowly. I'm very optimistic for France, in spite of it all."

Devi and Amin had trouble finding jobs that matched their degrees, or any job at all. Both blamed the economic downturn but also pointed out the extra difficulty encountered in France as a person "of color" or "being a descendent of immigrants," to quote them. Their careful wording—both addressed the issue of racism euphemistically, suggesting doubt—could mean that they perceived it potentially as a question I might dismiss, unless they have gotten into the habit of minimizing its importance. Several persons with graduate degrees admitted that they did not believe that discrimination was real until they themselves came up against repeated unsuccessful job searches—or jobs that lacked any kind of security—in contrast to others in their graduating class who were able to find satisfying employment. While white French men and women were also in search of professional opportunities, they would often work with a CDI-type contract—secure and open-ended—before leaving France. Very few left because they could not find work at all.

Certain nonwhite persons, however, wished to leave even though they had careers in France, mainly due to the ordinary racism in the professional workplace, as explained by Sana, 30, who had moved to Dubai with her husband shortly before our interview:

"I really liked my job, to be honest. I was pretty well-paid. But I was sick of Paris, and of France generally. . . . Let's say I was sick and tired of the mentality in Paris. I feel like people are very closed. . . . I see it clearly in my everyday dealings at work: people don't mix much, firstly, and then, they're always making the same comments. . . . When I dress really nicely . . . , people wonder where I come from . . . , because I have a first name that's not very common, and my last name . . . they don't know it, they can't place it . . . . They don't suspect right away that I'm Maghrebi, in fact, or maybe not at all. When I tell them, they're a bit surprised. But when there are special occasions—religious holidays, for instance—I always hear the same remarks. I'm fed up. Well, I mean, I'm talking about my own experience, my own circle, because we have friends from all over, and in my family or with friends, we never have this kind of problem, but it's really the work scene that upsets me. . . .

"I'm telling you how it is, frankly, even though I've worked with people . . . who have been to the most prestigious schools . . . , but the way they looked at me was oppressive. I always felt stressed and anxious at the idea of answering their questions. In fact that's what I found so disturbing, to always be asked, 'Where are you from? What are you?' The way they ask it . . . I don't know how to explain it. You have to experience it to know what I'm talking about. I'm not saying it's racism or anything like that, but it's always the same questions that keep coming back. It gets you down after a while."

Sana had been achieving a certain professional success in France. She gives evidence here of a specific form of oppression: being constantly subjected to people trying to place her in a racial category without knowing which to use. This form of oppression can be compared to the "dissection" analyzed by Haritaworn[9] with regard to multi-racialized persons besieged with incessant questions and remarks about the "origin" of their name or about certain parts of their body. For Sana, being confronted with "dissection" combined with the experience of Islamophobia as soon as she mentioned her second nationality or her religious affiliation.

The experiences Sana described in the rest of the interview (in particular, her co-workers' remarks during the month of Ramadan) took place mainly in her professional environment, but not exclusively. She noted in particular the time she and her husband were turned down as potential tenants, even though their application "was at the top of the list." At least in Dubai, she said, as long as you can pay, you can rent an apartment. Among her arguments for explaining her departure, the second most important was her frustration at not being able to buy an apartment in the Paris region despite their double income, combined with the feeling that their taxes were too high. Sana's neoliberal vision of the world came up against forms of discrimination and oppression in practice, ones that even her flawless school record and high-income management position in the private sector in France could not erase. Her departure for Dubai was motivated by the hope of not encountering these same obstacles. It was to make her story known, one she suspected was widespread among Maghrebis, that she volunteered for the interview:

"When I saw your message, I absolutely wanted to report my experience because I am Maghrebi. In fact, I'm French, but for many, I'm considered more Arab than French.... I feel more French than anything else, and I left France for all those reasons.... And honestly, 80 percent of my friends are doing exactly the same. So, it's too bad.... Our parents came to France to have a better life, and we're leaving France to have a better life."

Mehdi, 30, who was working in France as an educator in the public sector for a modest salary, relates a slightly different form of workplace oppression: that of being identified as a go-between. In the working-class neighborhood in southern France where he grew up and worked for several years, he had always been seen by the "French French—who had problems with young people's attitude issues—as an educator who is Franco-Maghrebi but always respectful, who lives like a decent person, and who is capable of handling these little monsters." He was "worn out" from always being assigned the role of go-between, from constantly being reminded of his "difference" by "French

French people." The lack of advancement possibilities, together with this difficult and degrading position, made him feel like trying his luck in Dubai. Despite the considerable job insecurity, he felt better there.

Whether the issues they raised had to do with getting a job or putting up with workplace oppression, these interviewees sounded generally very cautious and nuanced in their formulation of the problem, favoring alternatives to the term *racism* and constantly questioning their own interpretations. When it was a matter of France, the majority/minority schema still structured the narratives, however, whether it was about "white population" versus "persons of color," or "mono-nationals" versus "bi-nationals," or "French French" versus "Franco-Maghrebis," or about exposing forms of oppression and discrimination suffered as a "Maghrebi" or a "descendant of immigrants" or "having a double culture." In all these stories, the most often-used categorizations were those referring to nationality. Although their administrative existence legitimizes their use, they also reflect racial categories, depending on how they are deployed, especially with reference to "French French" or "mono-nationals" (i.e., whites, a word that is used only by Devi). Most of the interviewees, however, placed more emphasis on the acts they endured than on the persons performing them—perhaps to avoid hurting my feelings as a white person. Though the categories used to talk about France might well apply to Dubai, the way they were paired and matched—the way they related to each other—was thought of differently; they were not positioned and hierarchized the same way in the two contexts.

Self-reconstruction in Dubai

For these persons, relocating to Dubai meant, in the first instance, gaining access to an easier professional and personal life, not only thanks to the advantages of being French but also because they were given a chance, according to Nassima, 30, living in Dubai for five years:

> "In Dubai, something you don't find in France, you are given real responsibilities.... As soon as we arrive, we're made responsible for something, we're given a project, asked to track it and follow through, whatever it costs, and it's our responsibility. That's what's so great about this place."

What Nassima says here makes no reference to a specific affiliation or prior experience of discrimination: she had never applied for a job in France. At the time of the interview, she defined herself simply as "a recent graduate." Like many of the interviewees, she adopted a self-narrative as an autonomous individual, unaffiliated, and whose success depended solely on her ability to accomplish projects. Naturally, this discourse overlooks the unequal access to this type of career path in Dubai. Aside from a couple exceptions, such as Khaled,[10] the interviewees generally attributed their professional position and salary to the fair assessment of their skills rather than to a structurally advantageous treatment due to their Western passport.

Beyond the job market, many said the reason they felt good in Dubai was the "cosmopolitan" dimension of the social spheres that mingle there. The relief they felt was not reducible to an improvement in their class position; it also resulted from the fact that they no longer felt underestimated or stigmatized. Those who identified as having a "double culture" underlined that it was seen either as an asset, an enrichment, or as something ordinary. The multicultural schema of Dubai enabled them to reconcile their plural affiliations and to live them fully, free of any particular tension: they could define themselves in Dubai as "French" or as "bi-cultural." While French people of color praised Dubai's multiculturalism as opposed to French "monoculturalism" or universalist republicanism (even if nobody described it in such a direct way), many nonwhite residents coming from countries where political authorities also promote multiculturalism (like the UK or the US) often found that Dubai was more multicultural and that whiteness was less hegemonic there than in their home countries.[11]

If living in a "Muslim country" results in practical advantages for practicing Muslims (availability of a large range of halal consumer products, Fridays off work, shortened work hours during Ramadan, etc.), it was especially the city's reputation for religious freedom that persons identifying as Muslims commended, whether practicing or not. In that respect, Dubai was often compared to other large cities such as London. Several cited the uncomplicated mingling of "the Russian woman in mini-shorts" and "the Emirati in a niqab" as living proof of religious "tolerance," contrasting it with the "atmosphere" in France. This was Khaled's case. When he arrived seven years ago, he quickly realized that the Dubai job for which he resigned from his steady employment (CDI) in France did not correspond to the way it had been described to him prior to his departure. It was the "freedom" that made him want to stay in Dubai despite this early setback, and to seek another job.

"The point is it was the surprise factor that made me love Dubai right away. I met lots of people in no time; I made close friends with certain people here; and so, I found the country very free, though a lot of people don't think of it that way.... For me, I think it's a very free country, in the sense that it's packed with paradoxes and contradictions but . . . if someone wants to dress in very short clothes, she can, or if somebody wants to wear—and I'm not saying I'm in favor of it—to wear a burqa, she can do that, too. So that's the way I see true freedom. And it doesn't bother either of them, in fact, when they pass by each other at the mall or somewhere. So that's my view."

Linda, 30, had been living in Dubai for four years and drew a more explicit comparison between this religious freedom and the way she was confronted by Islamophobia in France.

"What I love about Dubai, more than all the materialistic and superficial aspects, all the comfort you have here, is the fact that I've never seen anywhere else, or at any rate not in France.... For example, when you go to JBR (a partially pedestrian zone bordering the beach in an upscale residential and commercial neighborhood), you can see, walking practically side by side, a Russian woman in mini-shorts and a tank top . . . and an Emirati woman completely covered by her burqa. And nobody is going to stare; nobody's going to criticize; you do whatever you want; you wear whatever you want—and frankly I find that . . . In France today, that's what's really missing.... In France, everything's always a bit of a struggle. Personally, I had co-workers, when I was observing the Ramadan fast, right up until the last day, the twenty-ninth day of Ramadan, they would still be asking me every morning if I'd like some coffee.... In Dubai, it's my impression that this kind of thing could never happen.... You dress however you like. If you don't drink alcohol, . . . they aren't going to pressure you to drink.... They really respect your religion."

Neither Khaled nor Linda wore any outward sign of their religious practice and therefore could not have been discriminated against for that reason in Dubai.[12] The choice to juxtapose mini-shorts and burqas as a sign of a cosmopolitan and tolerant society is significant. The use of the term *burqa*, commonly heard in the French media when speaking of Afghani women and during the controversy over the 2011 French law banning face veiling in public spaces in France, reveals how much the discourse on Dubai is constructed as an inverse mirror image of Islamophobia as experienced by these individuals in France. In the Emirates, the piece of fabric at issue is generally called a niqab. These two interviews took place a few weeks after the attacks of 7 January 2015 in France and the numerous Islamophobic acts that followed—including the implicit demand incumbent upon all people perceived as Muslim to take a position on the events. This context most likely brought the theme of religious tolerance to the forefront during the interviews, echoing the situation in France. Dubai, in contrast, was seen as a place that allows mingling and healing. Neha Vora analyzed similar discourses among some Pakistani-American and Arab-American university professors living and working in Qatar, who feel excluded and concerned about racism and mounting Islamophobia in the United States.[13]

In this society perceived as "cosmopolitan," not only were encounters with forms of discrimination and/or racism much rarer, but they were less likely to affect the persons concerned, which allowed them more latitude to leverage their affiliations and make strategic use of the impressions they produced on others. Mehdi explained it thus:

"Here, I'm going to say I'm French . . . because here, there's passport discrimination. So, your instinct is to say you're French, but in any case, I myself am actually French because I was born in France, I lived in France, I'm steeped in French culture. Even if I have a double culture. But in France, when people would ask, I would say I'm Franco-Moroccan."

Although Mehdi felt the need to claim his double affiliation in France, where, as he explained elsewhere, he often suffered from not being acknowledged as fully French, he did not feel the same need in Dubai, where the categorizations did not involve him in the same way. He felt relieved, he said, to take this time-out, to step back a bit from France's political debates and issues. Getting away for a while, living outside his own country, adopting a more consumerist lifestyle, and finding his place in a society experienced as new, where he thought of his presence as something temporary, offered him a little respite.

Life in Dubai is conducive to an attitude put forward in several interviews: the drive to succeed without focusing on problems. Hence, in the professional sphere as elsewhere, many tended to downplay discrimination they experienced in Dubai when based on appearance or name. Anecdotes related in a neutral tone reveal the dissonances that are at the heart of these experiences, such as the one reported by Nawel, 21:

"When I was apartment hunting, . . . I had an unpleasant surprise. I called the owner about an apartment, . . . and on the phone, he asks, 'Right, where are you from originally?' So I tell him 'I'm French.' . . . So I get there, and the guy is Egyptian. . . . I introduce myself, . . . and he says, '[Your first name] is Arab.' I say, 'Well, yes, I'm of Moroccan origin.' He says, 'Well, I'm sorry, I can't rent to you.' At that point I say, 'What do you mean, you can't?' And he says, 'I don't rent to Moroccan women or Russian women or Rumanian women.' So that was it. Because apparently, there's a lot of prostitution today in the Emirates. . . . But I've forgotten all that, in fact. I had such a great time while I was there that. . . . In the end, all those little things, it's all in the past . . . I found something better. . . . I found a super apartment and great flat mates. We all got along really well. We would eat together, cook together, . . . exactly what I was looking for, in fact."

The tacit assumption of prostitution, which many nonwhite women I interviewed complained about, is gendered and racialized in the sense that it especially impacts women of certain nationalities, or those liable to be categorized as such.[14] Beyond this case, several real estate developments use the whiteness of their residents as their branding image, which results in a selection based on this criterion: several nonwhite French women and men reported this type of experience. Despite this episode, Nawel repeated throughout the interview how fulfilling and enriching her year in Dubai was, both professionally, where she leveraged her "double culture" (she speaks, reads, and writes Arabic) and socially, in her leisure hours. Like Nawel, many of my interviewees tended to downplay the "unpleasant surprises" linked to structural racism in Dubai society. Although their status was unstable in Dubai, it differed from the constantly minoritized status they experienced in France. Beyond the advantages of salary and lifestyle, Dubai's multinational, multicultural schema, which values religious freedom and cultural hybridity most notably, was experienced as emancipating compared to what their lives were like in France.

Their relative upward social mobility, however, did compel many interviewees to question their advantageous position in a society whose non-egalitarian structure was obvious to them. What made them worthy of inclusion while others were excluded?[15] Some called into question the multicultural-multinational schema of tolerance and hybridizing. Of all the interviewees, Tony was the one who spoke the most about diverse forms of racism and discrimination in Dubai, even though he made clear that he was trying not to focus on it, "except when it jumps out at me." He left Dubai for

home notably because he could not abide the forms of hierarchy that structure Dubai society, but also because a professional opportunity arose.

"Once again, when you're from an Asian or Bangladeshi background, you
feel more like you're in an Indian country than an Arab one, because . . .
there is . . . a huge majority from India, Bangladesh, Sri Lanka. And I saw
myself reflected a little bit, in the end. And seeing their working conditions, their pay scale, the separation from their families back home, knowing that in Asia, notably in India and Sri Lanka, the family is sacred . . .—so
knowing all of that, and through a certain closeness I have with them due
to my origins, it's something that really struck me, that really jumped out
at me. To see these super-wealthy people in luxurious vehicles, Maseratis,
Lamborghinis, and so on, and right next to them, busses so crammed you
think they're going to fall to pieces, with all those Indian and Pakistani
laborers, and I know what their living conditions are like and how much
they're paid—it's violent."

Tony was one of the rare French interviewees to identify with the Indian
subcontinental residents working at so-called unskilled jobs, and he found
intolerable the sight of such blatant inequality in Dubai society. Several
elements can explain his particular position: he himself was subjected to different forms of racism in Dubai (at the hands of the French community at
Mass, during his apartment search, in his affective life). His parents in France
hold so-called unskilled jobs—let us note that others whose parents worked
in comparable jobs, including some of subcontinental Indian background,
did not adopt a similar rhetoric. And lastly, his language skills allowed him to
communicate with persons at the low rung of the professional ladder, such as
the teaboy (the paid employee in charge of bringing beverages to others) in
the company where he worked. He told me that he sought out contacts of this
type, a rare initiative among the interviewees.

Although expressions of indignation over the treatment of "Indians" (the
racializing term that many interviewees used to designate persons assumed to
be such, regardless of their nationality) often emerged during the interviews,
the stigmatizing remarks aimed at this population were as commonplace
among the French, both white and nonwhite, as they were among the Dubai
residents in general. Such statements appeared not only utterable and acceptable, but even unexceptional, and many French men and women contributed

to perpetuating this local norm. Indeed, this form of racist discourse was the most widespread and the least socially stigmatizing, as Mehdi explained:

"Personally, this is what I hold against a lot of my friends . . . , French Maghrebis who say to you: 'Man, those Indians, I can't stand them. . . .' So I say, maybe a bit harshly, 'Don't forget that you're Indian . . . In France, you're the Indian.' . . . But it's true that, unconsciously . . . Let me give you a simple example. . . . You see how people drive here, right? Well, here, you can't afford to have problems with the locals. . . . Unconsciously . . . , you realize that when you drive, you'll allow yourself to shout at somebody depending on what he looks like. . . . When you see that it's an Indian, you'll say, 'Okay, I won't get into any trouble with him.'"

This interview extract directly compares two societies and applies the majority/minority schema to urban Dubai society. It provides an example of how migrant persons can transpose different racial schemas in order to interpret the societies they currently inhabit. The parallel drawn by Mehdi between "French Maghrebis" and "Dubai Indians" suggests the ambivalence of the social shift performed by French people of color who move to Dubai. They are able to a certain extent—but only to a certain extent—to free themselves from the minority, subaltern condition experienced by their parents and themselves in France, and even earlier, by their ancestors in the colonial context. But although they do manage to navigate more or less successfully the complex interlocking of national and racial hierarchies in Dubai, they still come up against constraints, having to adapt to restrictive expectations and, in certain situations, experiencing forms of rejection and exclusion. The ambivalent gaze that many cast upon the Dubai social order—between denunciation of the job market's structural inequalities and the incorporation of the most locally admissible forms of racist speech—seems somehow to respond to the uncertainty, instability, and ambivalence inherent to their status in this neoliberal urban society. It also reveals the extent to which the logic of racial hierarchizing in Dubai is composite, aggregating the elements of an essentializing Emirati national culture, of white supremacy, Western hegemony, multiculturalism, and the racializing of nationalities.

WHITE GAZES

Throughout the interviews, white French individuals never used the word *white*—nor did I ever prompt them to, as none of my questions bore directly on racial identifications or categories. Every time I asked them to specify the social milieu where they were raised, they would mention the place, sometimes their class, and more rarely, a political affiliation. The only person to self-define as white was a US American. This characteristic silence among majority persons in a society structured in terms of majority and minority[16] is itself inherent to white subjectivities. It stands in flagrant contrast with the use of racial categories and references to forms of structural racism in nearly all the interviews with nonwhite French persons with respect to France, even though I was using exactly the same lead-ins in all cases.

Concerning their experiences in Dubai, however, the narratives of white persons provide a wealth of categorizations, both national and racial. Studies on expatriation have shown that relocation to non-hegemonic countries often comes with a racialization of whiteness, in the sense that it gives rise to an awareness of the particularity of this status for the persons concerned, numerically in the minority and therefore noticeable as such.[17] Racialization of whiteness, as well as the essentializing of nationalities, takes on forms that have their specificities in Dubai; more broadly, the configuration of racial categories does not correspond to the majority/minority schema to which white persons are accustomed in France. The following paragraphs deal with the way whites comprehend the forms of hierarchy that structure Dubai society and how they represent their own position there. At some point during their interview, many valorized Dubai's "cosmopolitanism," but at other moments, they regretted how hard it was to meet Emiratis or how rigid the boundaries between different groups were.

Most people who move to Dubai did not choose this city, and many harbored a negative bias, denouncing the inequality so commonly associated with this urban society before they had even arrived. The choice of Dubai did not satisfy their exoticizing desire for authenticity, an important dimension in certain white migrations.[18] Few were fond of the recently constructed buildings supposed to stereotypically represent the Emirati culture, like Madinat Jumayra, a commercial and hotel complex that houses Belgian beer bars and pizzerias, among others, in the alleyways designed to evoke traditional Middle Eastern marketplaces. The city was often described as "fake": "It's all fake, but it's fun." "Everything is fake, but you can find your niche as a European." Such assessments, frequent among white people, implicitly construct Europe as the reference in terms of culture, history, and authenticity, opposed to the Emirates as too modern to meet their orientalist expectations.[19] In this regard, certain nonwhite interviewees who sought to get closer to the Arab, Indian, and/or Muslim cultures with which they identified manifested a different attitude, for they found in Dubai an opportunity to meet many Arabic speakers, Indians, and/or Muslims. Like those persons who left their home country for reasons of racial discrimination or other forms of oppression, this often led them to praise the "multiculturalism" rather than to criticize the "fake." Asha, manager in the hotel business who described herself in the interview as British of Indian origin, said she rather liked Dubai "because it looks a lot like an Indian city, and at other times, it looks a lot like London." This way of highlighting the cultural richness of Dubai was most often denied by white interviewees.

A caste society?

The white people I interviewed rarely considered Dubai as a multicultural city. Some, like Véronique, made statements denouncing a social order she saw as segregated and non-egalitarian, divided, she said, into several relatively impervious pan-national groups.

> "There are three separate worlds in Dubai. The native population, the Emiratis, to which I think we can add all people of the Gulf, . . . along with the regular [impatriés][20] Arabs in Dubai—i.e., the Palestinians, the Jordanians—they all make up the first group, who live among themselves, in the Muslim way, with the women and men socializing separately from one another. So that's the first world. . . . The smallest number, about 15 percent, are the native Emiratis. Then the second population bracket, which is also pretty small, the one I belong to, are the expatriates who have the right to come as a family. You have to earn above a certain amount to have the right to come as a family. They're called Westerners, but in fact, not all of them are Western. . . . There are people of all nationalities, but they're wealthy, and most of the time are on salary. . . . Then there's the third category, the most numerous: those who come to Dubai for work and don't have the right to bring their families. They account for about 70 percent of the population. This 70 percent is made up of mostly people from the subcontinent, Indians and Pakistanis, but also from eastern Africa, Sudan, and Somalia, that type, or from Nepal or the Philippines. They make up the vast majority. These three worlds don't mingle, don't socialize together."

Mathilde, 28, raised in France among the upper classes, and who had previously lived in London, described the Dubai social order thus:

> "It's not really multicultural here, not like London or New York. It's a caste society: the groups are well delineated. There are the locals, the expats and the workers. These three groups never mix. Each conforms to the place it's allotted."

When white French persons use a category to define themselves within the Dubai social framework, it is most often "expat"—regardless of the type of contract—followed by "Western." To describe Dubai society, Véronique and Mathilde portrayed slightly different groups. Véronique referred more explicitly to racial boundaries when she included "Arabs" in the "locals" and assigned them a shared culture: her use of a neologism, *impatriés* (as opposed to "expatriates"), to describe them conveyed her perception that "Arabs" make up a civilization with homogenous practices, overdetermined by Islam; their migrations from one "Arab" country to the next are finally nothing but movements within a unified whole. She used a second criterion to delineate the two other groups, the "Westerners" and "those who come to Dubai for work": the right to bring your family, or not. Mathilde, meanwhile, identified three groups which she equated to "castes," blending the nationality criterion and status in the working world (expat, worker). This reading was shared by John, American, who spelled out the advantageous position of Westerners, while later denying that he is privileged. After describing what he called a "caste system," I asked him: "And how do you experience this?"

> "What . . . where I am in the social caste system?"
> "Yeah . . ."
> "Hmm . . . no, I don't feel I am privileged."
> "You don't feel privileged?"
> "No. I'm just one of . . . one of the group. I mean Americans are only . . . we are only a few thousand, a very small percentage."

Note that Mathilde made London and New York the standard of multiculturalism, associating it with not only very large cities but very large cities located in Western countries, purportedly more open and egalitarian. These descriptions depict Dubai society as exceptionally non-egalitarian and segregated by implicitly or explicitly presenting Western cities as models of egalitarianism and/or multiculturalism. This sort of reading contrasted sharply with statements by many nonwhite interviewees who, as we have seen, most often analogized the two societies without raising up one, the French one, as a model and considering the other, Dubai, as the exception.

The exceptionalist reading of Dubai conveyed by many white female residents resonates with the way their friends and family back in France judge their lifestyle. To a certain extent, the stereotypes about Dubai, the basis of their distinction as Western women, backfire. These persons are challenged over their supposed materialism to the detriment of "culture," over the hiring of domestic workers considered as an unfair and outdated practice, over the use of facilities deemed particularly polluting and/or showy, unlike what is defined as "tasteful" in France. One woman, married and raising children, expressed relief that her sisters, whom she sees every summer in France, had never shown any desire to come visit her in Dubai: she would have felt embarrassed if her sisters had seen her house in Dubai, she said. This sense of discrepancy or, for some, even guilt suggests that in the eyes of their friends and family, the consumerist lifestyle typical of Westerners in Dubai would somehow violate the moral code and values of their place of origin. The decision to leave for Dubai is often labeled opportunistic. It earns a particularly negative reputation among the upper classes with high cultural capital, few of whose members relocate to this city.

This opposition by one's circle to a move to Dubai was particularly developed by a female resident, French, 34, formerly a civil servant in Bordeaux, recently married to a Malian businessman who had been living in France for several years. She spoke of a genuine "culture shock," both because of her family's opposition (left-voting civil servants, she said) to the neoliberal entrepreneurial cultural and their vision of Dubai as a place where women's rights were flouted. Matters were made worse when she left for Dubai with a Muslim husband, raising anxiety among her loved ones who imagined a *Not Without My Daughter* scenario,[21] she told me. Even she researched the situation in Dubai before accepting the proposal, having at first associated this city with Saudi Arabia. Based on the interviewees' experiences in France, the confusion between Dubai and Saudi Arabia appeared to be more common in the upper classes than in the working classes, where the "Dubai dream" conjures up more accurate images that don't liken it to Saudi Arabia.

While most of the white interviewees criticized how "communitarian" and "closed" Dubai is, regretting what they perceived as an absence of mixing among different population groups, those persons living as a couple with a spouse of another nationality and/or nonwhite tended to praise Dubai's "cosmopolitanism" and "multiculturalism" more. On this point, they agreed in part with the statements made by nonwhite French men and women, though raising only the aspects connected to their children's lives, without addressing the issues of discrimination or Islamophobia. Marie, 46, living as a couple with a British man of Indian descent, whose daughter, she emphasized, only has friends of "double nationality" or of "mixed color," concluded her narrative thus:

> "We're like everyone else, in the end. It's in Europe that it's different, isn't it? Here, we go rather unnoticed, I think. At any rate, for us, it's never been a problem. Not one that I'm conscious of, at any rate."

Christophe, 35, married to a woman of Filipino nationality that he met in Manama a few years previously, praised how little judgment there is in Dubai of "multinational" couples.

> "In our six-unit section of the apartment complex right now . . . , there's Maria and me, Franco-Filipinos; our neighbor across the way is German; and the couple next to us are a Turkish husband and a New Zealander wife; . . . for another couple, he's Spanish and she's Ukrainian; and the neighbors are Algerian. So when our daughter was born, in the same wing, there were three babies in twelve days, six nationalities [*laughs*]. So, that's how it is, no one here judges any of that. They don't judge a couple for that, and things are just great. It's really quite wonderful."

This statement matches the discourse that emphasizes Dubai's cosmopolitanism and the possibility to live a "double culture" undisturbed. The reference to Europe gets inverted here: Dubai is more cosmopolitan than France or Great Britain, and these individuals feel it is easier for a multinational couple to live there and raise children.

A frustrating quest for exoticism

Some narratives reveal a quest for authenticity and exoticism, and the disappointment experienced in Dubai in this regard. For instance, several whites, married, with middle- to upper-class backgrounds, who had already lived in several other countries, declared how frustrated they were about being unable to make friends among Emiratis, perceiving this lack of contact with the "locals" as a failed "expatriate" experience. Two women spontaneously mentioned their relationships or lack thereof with Emiratis, assuming that this question was necessarily at the core of my research. Claudine, in her 40s, spoke of her friendship with an Emirati woman:

> "I feel I was incredibly lucky . . . to have had an Emirati woman friend. It's very difficult. I don't know anybody else who . . . Men can have work friends or go over to someone's house, have someone over, but I don't have a single other woman friend who had an Emirati friend. I was the only one. We'd do all kinds of things together. . . . I went to meet her family. . . . It was extraordinary for me to have access to the Emirati middle class, to Emirati culture . . . , to see how wrong all those clichés are about Emiratis being super-rich, not working, never having any problems, all living in palaces. No, it was a working couple who lived in a little apartment."

For Véronique, 50, who had experienced a number of "expatriations," not being able to meet Emiratis came as a surprise:

> "I know it's a question you're going to ask, and I had a very typical expatriate life in Dubai, meaning I met tons of people, cosmopolitans, but extremely few Emiratis, extremely few people from any of the Gulf countries."
>
> "And did that come as a disappointment for you?"
>
> "Let's say it was something of a surprise because in all the other countries where I've lived, I always got to know the locals. That was part of the charm of living abroad, to get to know the folks who live there, I've had quite a few total immersion experiences. For example, in Hong Kong, where [in the company I worked for] I was the only Westerner, everyone around me was Chinese. . . . So when I arrived in Dubai . . . , you also have to admit that the Emiratis, people from the Gulf, represent only 15 percent of the population who actually live here, who are native. So I guess it's normal that you have a hard time meeting them.
>
> (*Later in the interview*) "I met a few women . . . who spoke Arabic, for different reasons, . . . so they were able to get into contact with Emirati women, and they had a totally different experience, which would be much more interesting for you. I was just part of the classic expat set, who live among other expats. It's not very interesting, but . . . [*laughs*] it's a typical experience, I'd say. With a husband on salary at a company, the most typical scenario, I'd say."

By crediting this narrative, these persons were endorsing the Emirati state ideology by restricting their definition of "locals" to persons of Emirati nationality, excluding, among others, persons born and raised in the Emirates but not having Emirati nationality. The wish to meet Emiratis, even when unfulfilled, reveals how these persons exoticized Emiratis, who became the fetishized other, and how they essentialized national affiliation: meeting Emiratis would be by definition interesting and enriching; having a certain nationality would automatically render someone attractive.

This phantasmagorical construction of exoticism fits into a particular way of being in the world; it corresponds somehow to the "imperial eyes"[22] whereby non-Western societies must be authentic, coherent, and different from the "West." This desire to meet Emiratis is so strong that the tourist industry (hotels, museums, sightseeing tours, etc.) hires them for this reason: "It's a good thing to have Emiratis working in the hotel. Guests often want to take pictures of us," I was told by one Emirati national in charge of security at Hotel A. This echoes statements made by young female Emiratis that Jane Bristol-Rhys met in Abu Dhabi; they told her they avoided hotels because tourists would boldly stare at them and take pictures, making them feel like "freaks on display."[23]

Organized desert excursions or trips to Oman are often ways to fulfill this quest for exoticism.[24] For instance, one of the classic Dubai excursions involves a cruise in a dhow (a wooden boat used in trade between Gulf cities and the Indian Ocean) into the Musandam fjords, an impressive landscape spread over an Omani coastal enclave in the Emirates, near Dubai. When I took this side trip in the company of British residents and members of their family who had come to the Gulf to visit, our dhow was captained by an Omani man. I observed the way my fellow dhow-mates were taking photos of him and selfies with him—this staging of himself as a local was undoubtedly part of his job description.

Several interviewees of a particular profile (white married women belonging to the upper class) claimed they would be uninteresting for my study because they lacked exotic appeal compared to the "locals"—or even to "Saudi women," one of them offered, in response to a mention of my previous book. While this attitude matches a widespread tendency among women socialized as such, especially if they are not engaged in a professional career, to think of themselves as uninteresting, this type of statement ("I am/my husband and I are like everyone else," "I lack exotic appeal") amounts to a reaffirmation of normality—white and heterosexual. These women wondered why I was studying them, since they thought they represented the norm: white women married to white men working in companies with a "classic" status of expatriate. Between the lines of these admissions of normality lies a tacit definition of whiteness: to consider oneself the opposite of exotic.

This reading of the world on the basis of authenticity and exoticism coexists, however, with another discourse, structured by the opposition between Muslim and non-Muslim, prevalent among the whites I interviewed, as well as in many of the books and brochures intended for expatriates, considered tacitly as non-Muslim. Islam is thus associated with the "locals"—a discourse that conforms to Emirati state ideology. For instance, in the *Time Out Residents Guide 2013*, a handbook published by a magazine that lists all the places to go out in Dubai, one of the first articles, entitled "Culture Shock,"[25] featured two photographs on opposite pages, one of a mosque (left-hand page) and the other of the entrance to a mosque (right-hand page), along with a text explaining that Emiratis live in extended families, that there are five prayers per day, that the weekend does not coincide with the same days in Europe, that apparel is different, and that women do not "yet" have the same rights as men.

This stereotypical discourse depicting Emirati culture as overdetermined by religion was used at times during the interviews to describe Emiratis, women in particular, who were pictured as oppressed: whiteness was thus defined between the lines by a distancing of Islam, cast into an unsurpassable otherness, especially when it comes to male-female relations. Two women in particular—white, in their 20s, migrant status single (one of them living as a couple with a white Frenchman she met in Dubai)—both said they were disturbed by the place of religion, deemed excessive, in Dubai. One cited the call to prayer, the other Ramadan, during which it is forbidden to eat in public, and both felt that the country was "too" Muslim. Still, such outright rejections of Islam were in the minority: several interviewees told me, on the contrary, how living in the Arab Emirates enabled them to deconstruct certain prejudices regarding Islam.[26]

A further type of discourse about Islam is prevalent in the Emirates, and more broadly in the Gulf. Certain persons denounce the "hypocrisy" with reference to what they perceive as the dissonance between social practices and Islamic precepts—for instance, between the official ban on alcohol (until 2020) and the accompanying crackdown on public drunkenness and the fact that alcohol is served in bars and clubs in Dubai. These statements define the subject uttering them as Western and white, both by the distancing of an "other," expected to be authentic and coherent, and by the assertion of an oversight position authorizing the subject to pass judgment on the coherence of this other's practices.

Despite their depiction of Dubai society's negative aspects, in terms of fake versus (Western) authenticity, exploitation versus (Western) equality, or Islam versus (Western) secularism, most white interviewees described themselves as happy in Dubai, which they associated with comfort and security.

SITUATED EXPERIENCES OF HAPPINESS

The government of Dubai promotes an ideology of happiness aimed at the most privileged residents (see chapter 1). Many interviewees made this ideology their own, linking happiness to certain characteristics of their lives in Dubai. Notions of happiness and wellness came up in many interviews, directly or indirectly, as soon as the topic shifted to the "quality of life," "security," and "feelings of success" that life in Dubai inspires. As feminist scholar Sara Ahmed has done most notably, it is possible to adopt a critical stance with regard to the social and political uses of emotions in general, and happiness in particular. For Ahmed, "feelings might be how structures get under our skins."[27] She stresses the relation between widespread representations of happiness and privilege and suggests that "attributions of happiness might be how social norms and ideals become affective, as if relative proximity of those norms and ideals creates happiness."[28] I will be analyzing here the emotions that the interviewees positively associated with Dubai and the way these emotions are situated: quality of life or security finally reflect different definitions and modalities depending on the background of the persons discussing them in terms of race, class, and gender.

Apart from the multiculturalism mentioned by some of the interviewees, happiness and quality of life, in the statements I compiled, were associated with living in spacious accommodations, being served, enjoying a natural environment that matches the stereotypical vacation setting (sun, sea, etc.), and being driven by a "sense of success." These statements almost always contained, implicitly or explicitly, mentions and assessments of the social order of Dubai and revealed various ways of inhabiting a structurally advantaged status. However, at closer inspection, the statements made by persons of middle- and working-class backgrounds, most often people of color, differed somewhat from those by upper-class whites. In other words, happiness was defined in different ways depending on the interviewees' trajectories and previous experience.

Residents with middle- and working-class backgrounds

The remarks by persons of middle- and working-class backgrounds often connected happiness to the sense of belonging to an advantaged group. For instance, Miguel, 28, whose parents belonged to the middle class of one of the French Caribbean islands, known for its high rates of poverty and unemployment, and who had been living in Dubai for nearly a year, after several years in Paris, told me:

> "Meeting people, networking, going out with co-workers, after-works—all of that is much easier here than in Paris. Barriers are lifted; it's very stimulating. You have a sense of success, beautiful cars, a comfortable life. You're challenged. And you feel somehow attracted by this social success. You feel like joining the club."

It's noteworthy that Miguel used the word *sense*. Success is thus a sensorial experience for him: consuming sophisticated food and drink; moving through immaculately clean, elaborately decorated spaces; mingling with well-dressed, fragrantly perfumed people; riding in luxury cars owned by acquaintances, and so on. These are the kinds of sensations that Dubai offers many of its Western residents.

Nawel, 21, whose parents belonged to France's lower middle class, and who had lived for a year in Dubai, put forward the idea that happiness might be more widespread in Dubai, while pointing out its selectivity.

> "People are much happier. But then again, people who are in Dubai are people who are working, so they necessarily have money, whereas in France, money problems are always there. . . . I've noticed that in France, people are pretty depressed, always down, but the reason they're down is that they always have financial problems, that they're unemployed, that . . . It's a vicious circle. But in Dubai, if you aren't working, you can't stay, so . . . People have money, money to go out, to discover, to live. If you want to go out to a restaurant, everyone's OK with it. . . . Over there, it really favors happiness."

Nawel liked being surrounded by people who are working, earning money, and spending it. She was not the only one to make these kinds of comments. They refer to the requirement of a work contract in order to live in Dubai—and therefore the relative absence of unemployed among foreign residents. Mingling with people who are earning money as she was, not having to face people in financial trouble, contributed to the happiness she felt in the city. Nawel specified further on that residents unable to adopt the hedonistic lifestyle were also present in the spaces she frequented; these, however—designated as "Indians," "Filipinos," "servers," and "working class"—were not part of her affective entourage.

A certain clique of successful individuals seems comforting, soothing: it allows especially French persons from middle- and working-class backgrounds to experience a form of upward social mobility without having to face persons they grew up with who may not have experienced this same mobility. Geographical remoteness would appear to create a certain carefreeness. Miguel's narrative matches Nawel's: the "sense of success" he referred to resulted from being surrounded by wealthy people. Nawel expressed both her desire to belong to the upper class and her happiness at feeling it was possible to be included.

For Western residents, unlike other nationalities, it is easier to adopt a lifestyle coded as typical of the upper classes and to develop an insider's network than it would be in other national contexts. Within spaces frequented by the upper classes, the distinction between "old money" and "nouveau riche" would seem less of an issue, though it can still remain pertinent within the group of French residents. Beyond their national group, people socialized in Western countries who experience a rapid rise in social status are unlikely to be dismissed for not knowing the codes of the bourgeoisie. Some express value judgments, comparing what is done in Dubai with what is done in their own country, as when the French complain that service in restaurants, even the high-end ones, is too fast as compared to how it's done in France. These narratives construct Dubai as a space of imitation, or even faking "good" bourgeois manners. As Westerners, these individuals from middle- to working-class backgrounds feel mostly legitimate not only for patronizing luxury venues, to which they were unaccustomed prior to arriving in Dubai, but also for judging what goes on there.

A further source of comfort has to do with not being confronted on a daily basis by the discrepancy with one's community of origin. Certain persons of working-class background concealed their new living conditions from their family and friends back home. This was the case of 32-year-old Vincent, who grew up in a housing project and whose parents, a clerk and a cashier, still live there today.

> "It's like day and night. I would never tell them how much I pay for rent. I'd probably get slapped! I could pay the whole family's rent!"

Linda, 30, who grew up in a medium-sized town, also attempted to conceal certain elements of her new lifestyle from her circle of friends back in France.

> "I'm the one who feels the gap now. . . . I'm careful not to shock folks back in France. . . . I mean, the life we live, the amenities we have. I don't dare talk about my problems here, because compared to their real problems in France, well, there's no comparison. I don't have to think about having to do laundry on weekends or being stuck at home. All those little things . . . having to live in a 300-square-foot studio just to be able to live in central Paris and go out at night without all the transport problems involved, or else take subway and be careful not to have my phone stolen, not wear my diamond rings, which I wear naturally when I'm here [in Dubai]. When I'm in France I take off my diamonds, all my jewelry. I dress completely differently. I don't carry a designer bag; I'd be really afraid to . . . That's the gap I'm talking about. And even the things we talk about, it's totally different. They're just not open to the world. They're still asking me questions—what I said a moment ago, about how women here live, that kind of thing . . . Unfortunately, they've never left the country, . . . so they don't have any experience with different kinds of people."

To describe the gap with her home community, Linda contrasted security, comfort, and quality of life, features of her daily existence in Dubai, with fear, household chores, and being stuck at home on weekends, all of which she associated with France. In her view, she stood apart from her group of friends left behind in France, whose supposed ignorance she deplored and to whom she displayed a kind of condescension: she mustn't "shock" them.

Various strategies for concealing their Dubai lifestyle from folks back home came up during our conversations. For instance, a French couple who met in Dubai organized two weddings, one in Dubai and one in France, with different guest lists, so that persons from the home community and those they knew in Dubai would not mix. Keeping distant from acquaintances envious of one's success is another strategy, mentioned by Javed. He says he felt used on several occasions, notably by acquaintances from France whom he hosted when they first arrived in Dubai and who then never made contact again once they were on their feet. Javed stressed how much effort he and his parents had made to overcome obstacles. He included his Dubai experience in his parents' ongoing efforts and felt all the closer to them. On the other hand, the same experience distanced him from his friends back in France, who were "jealous." When he first got to Dubai, he let several of them stay with him while they were trying their luck in Dubai, but later he refused to house anyone who wasn't a family member. This relationship with the home milieu—fitting into the continuity of his parents' migratory path but breaking with his friends and acquaintances—pervaded the narratives of several individuals of working-class background whose parents moved to France as adults.

The individuals I interviewed had a range of incomes, and yet nearly all of them adopted a lifestyle of luxury consumption, even if it meant they had to stop saving, or for some, start going into debt. Upon arriving in Dubai, most chose to live in expensive neighborhoods and high-end residential housing developments, including those whose earnings hardly warranted it, even when it meant sharing a room with a housemate—none of them moved into the neighborhoods seen as "Indian," for example. On my first trip, I was able to observe people's astonished reactions when I said I was living in Deira, in "old Dubai." Access to luxury residential neighborhoods and recreational venues is facilitated by high salaries, but also more directly by the status of Westerner. The chance to be welcomed into these spaces and treated with deference, even when a person does not earn a commensurate salary or is living on credit, constitutes, in a way, the "wages of Westernness" in Dubai. These wages of Westernness, by analogy with the notion of "the wages of whiteness,"[29] allow access to certain advantages thanks to a dominant position in (racialized) relations of nationality, irrespective of real income. This desire for "quality of life" and the possibility of achieving it despite income diversity differentiates Westerners from other categories of inhabitants: other national groups, like Indians, adopt highly contrasted living modes, more modulated by even more disparate income levels.[30]

Among a number of residents who had lived for several years in Dubai, the city tended to create a reframing of the past and future marked by material frustration. Even those who never used to aspire to such a lifestyle, after a few years in the city, deemed these consumer practices necessary for their well-being and anticipated the hardship of no longer having access to them. Only a few persons told me they had overcome their desire to consume, often after several years, so that they could start setting some money aside to plan for the future and to escape what one of the interviewees described as the "Dubai trap," which basically amounts to the habit of privilege and the fear of losing it by leaving the city.

Upper-class residents

Happiness as conceived by people of upper-class background involves a social order described as pacified and non-conflictual. Marc, 44, a white entrepreneur whose wife is under expatriate contract, said he was happy to be living in a "bubble":

> "Before experiencing this life myself, whenever anyone said 'expat in Dubai,' this is exactly how I imagined it could be. Huge house, huge car, sun, sea, swimming pool, friends . . . lots of barbecues, and then, bingo, here we are! . . . We're not exactly dying to get back to France. Because here, we really are in a bubble, everything is done for us. Going back to France will mean having to do things for ourselves again."

The terms "easy" and "convenient" were often used by persons in this class position, like Patricia, 45:

> "Whenever we go back home to France, we're glad but after about two days, there are strikes, demonstrations, mass transit problems, rain. Here, there are a lot of conveniences."

For Patricia and Marc, who belonged to the French upper class, happiness was, apart from the sunny climate, earning a lot of money, not having to do anything for yourself, with everything easy and relaxing, without contingency. It also meant not being confronted with social grievances or other forms of discontent that would call into question the structural advantages that members of the upper class enjoy. In Dubai, and more broadly in the Emirates, upper-class Westerners face no direct challenge to their advantages.

The wealthiest individuals I interviewed were pleased to be able to display their wealth without fear. Stéphanie, a former member of the Parisian upper class, told me:

"And [in France] there's a kind of mood . . . like an anti-rich mood, without even knowing what it means to be rich, which is serious. Your cars get keyed . . . Here, people's taste is always a bit dubious. I mean, they drive around in, like, gold-plated cars . . . They like to show off, but it would never occur to anyone to go key somebody's car just because it's nice, thinking, 'Yeah, that guy has an expensive car and I don't.' But in France, you really get the feeling that . . . people are out to get each other instead of being . . . instead of working together toward a common goal."

For Stéphanie, security was what sheltered the well-to-do from conflicts: without questioning the basic inequity, she sang the praises of a pacified social order in which the rich can safely display their wealth, which further contributes to their well-being—even if Stéphanie was careful, in passing, to note the "dubious taste" of the wealthy in Dubai. The upper class is indeed free to parade its wealth outside the boundaries of their enclave in the high-end neighborhoods of Dubai and even beyond.

Dubai is not, in fact, an enclave for the super-rich, since persons earning very low salaries are present in all the spaces they frequent. The sight of la-borers often causes the rich to feel sorry for them and even to verbalize their moral judgment in pathos-laden tones, but only rarely will it result in a ques-tioning of their own lifestyles. On the one hand, the laborers are cast into an intractable difference, an absolute alterity, and on the other, many Western-ers see themselves as outsiders to Dubai's social order, as we saw in earlier chapters.

Selective security

Within the notion of happiness, well-being, and comfort as experienced in Dubai, security holds an important place next to social success, as we have seen in Stéphanie's statements. Where people from countries at war tend to associate security with peace, for Western residents it implies first and foremost respect for private property—that is, protection from robbery or damage to one's personal possessions, and this attitude cuts across a broad range of income brackets. The same examples often recur: you can put your smartphone on a table in a fast-food restaurant in order to reserve it, then go off to order, or leave your car unlocked trouble-free. This is supposed to relieve you of certain worries and let you relax, not feel fearful, not refrain from certain activities due to this fear. Security, as with respect for private property, reinforces a certain class order, allowing advantaged persons to live without fear.

Security can also assume other dimensions, like feeling safe from police harassment or other infringements of one's integrity and dignity. Several online narratives by British and American women self-identified as black mention the security of not fearing the police or of not feeling "followed" (by security personnel) in shops.[31] These narratives echo statements by a French male during an informal conversation, mentioning the respectful treatment by the police, deliberately overstating the situation:

> "Even the police, when you go to the station, they welcome you, serve you coffee, tea, totally different from France. People here treat you well so long as you're in the right. But if you ever make one false move, you can be put on a plane within the hour."

In France, the police are liable to interpret his long beard and short djellaba as signs of "radicalization," a basis on which a considerable number of people have been singled out as suspects to be monitored.[32] Of course, other residents of Dubai, on the contrary, do feel threatened by the police. Security is differently perceived depending on a person's social position, but it still occupies a key place in the shaping of social order in the city, and Western passport holders often mask its selectiveness. As in other places, the designation of people to be protected as opposed to people associated with danger participates in constructing privilege.

Further connotations of security in terms of gender were mentioned in the interviews, with various modalities and ramifications. For instance, several women of French nationality developed a gendered definition of the feeling of security, no longer referring to the protection of private property but rather to their personal integrity. This was notably the case with Delphine, 26, a flight attendant, and with Deborah, 26, a sales manager.

> "What I used to feel when out and about in Paris, for example, in the street, I don't feel at all here. And it's really nice."
>
> "By that, you mean . . ."
>
> "With regard to men in France who always have to be . . . ogling you, whistling at you, trying to chat you up and, well . . . it's exhausting, isn't it? I'd got so tired of it in France, and here, it's something I've never had to deal with, ever. There's real respect here, I think." [Delphine]

"It's just so nice to be able to walk anywhere I want, or at least in the Marina, at any hour of the day or night, by myself, and not have to keep looking over my shoulder. I'm never afraid that something's going to happen. We feel so secure here in Dubai." [Deborah]

This sense of security relies upon a policy of protection of middle- and upper-class women. In Dubai, street harassment is forbidden, as are insults. This rarity of street harassment has caused women to develop a unique relationship to public space in the city, since, unlike what takes place in many cities,[33] they are present, at times alone, and at all hours in a variety of neighborhoods that I visited or lived in during my various stays in Dubai. A female hotel manager of Indian nationality, born in Mumbai, also stressed how much she appreciated the security situation, which allowed her to live and move about on her own in the city without fear, echoing what the Indian women expressed in Abu Dhabi, in interviews with Bristol-Rhys and Osella.[34] This security policy in public spaces relies nevertheless on a definition of security that excludes a large portion of working-class women in Dubai, notably those who are domestic workers, confined in their employer's homes and exposed to police checks, should they ever escape.[35] The security policy thus differentiates between certain women constructed paternalistically as vulnerable subjects and others who are always objects of suspicion (notably of prostitution), but the dividing line is fuzzy, and scrutiny of behavior in public space can be turned against almost any woman.

The security policy also distinguishes dichotomously between a potentially dangerous exterior space that needs to be monitored by the authorities and a domestic space represented as safer for women. In other words, as in other contexts where security policies are put in place,[36] the danger is identified as exclusively exterior and foreign. This has two noteworthy effects on social order. On the one hand, security policy and especially the outlawing of street harassment tend to reinforce the disciplinary supervision of certain men cast into otherness and subaltern status, constructed as dangerous for women, notably those who work in construction and live together exclusively among other men. On the other, the sanctification of domestic space reinforces the invisibility of multifaceted violence that can take place inside the home.

Security policy combines with other legislation that frequently backfires on female Dubai inhabitants, especially migration policy, the ban on sexual relations outside marriage, nonintervention in marital relations, and the ubiquitous nature of the police.

Firstly, the prohibition of sexual harassment does not generally affect the professional world for foreign women, given how hard it is, as we have seen, to lodge a complaint, because of migration policy that links residency rights to the work contract. Thus, a nonnational female harassed by her hierarchical superior would have a hard time filing a claim—I came across such a case during my study. Secondly, in a setting where the law strongly restricts authorized sex acts, rape cases sometimes end up in court where the victim gets accused of prostitution or drunkenness—these reversals have given rise to scandals especially when the victim is a Western passport holder and is backed by the embassy of her home country.[37] Thirdly, rape is not recognized within a married couple: the marital home is conceived as a protective space and not as a possible site of violence. As for nonmarried couples, because that is itself illegal, any attempt to file charges is not only vain but counterproductive.[38] And fourthly, the omnipresence of the police can prove threatening for certain categories of women. Residents of Asian nationalities, especially sex workers, are often subjected to rape at the hands of the police, as in many other contexts.[39]

Despite its limits, most women I interviewed described Dubai as an especially "safe" place for them as women, thereby ratifying a certain selective definition of security: that of being able to go out unmolested in urban spaces. While such a definition is significant of their unequal access to public spaces in their home cities, it has the effect of erasing what this feeling of security in Dubai owes to their position in class, race, and nationality hierarchies. Only one type of experience was able to result in a reversal of this discourse. Several Western passport holders had spent one or two days in jail, for a variety of charges: the employer had not renewed the company license for one, which meant that her visa was automatically annulled, and her presence in the Emirates rendered illegal without her knowledge; another had lent someone her access badge at an event despite strict security guidelines; a man was arrested for a check refused by the bank of the recipient because of a signature deemed confusing. All these individuals were quickly released, thanks to the networks and resources available to residents from Western countries. This short stint in jail, however, transformed their trust in Dubai security. The risk of being jailed—real though of short duration for these individuals—is now thought to be the "price" of happiness when adopting a privileged mode of living.

AN EPHEMERAL OR SUSTAINABLE PRIVILEGE

What happens to the feeling of happiness and to the experience of privilege after a few years of living in Dubai, or when one leaves the city? The final phase of the study, in 2019, when I interviewed people I had met in Dubai between 2012 and 2015, identifies three elements that update in the medium term the interlocking hierarchies of gender, class, and race among French passport holders: access or not to mobility, stability or precariousness of the position achieved, and the differentiated consequences of stereotypes about life in the Gulf in the event of a return to the country of origin.[40]

Remaining in Dubai, a constrained choice?

The persons I interviewed do not all have the same potential for mobility, depending on their position in hierarchies of gender, class, and race. White males under expatriate contract, to a large extent, can decide to stay, go home to their country of origin, or apply for jobs in other countries. For instance, Louis, 43, who went from being in charge of southern France for a specific activity in his company to heading up "a region called Africa and the Middle East" when he moved to Dubai, signed an expatriate contract for two years, renewable one further year for as long as he wants; he said he can return home at his convenience after the end of the initial contract. White males under expatriate contract interviewed between 2012 and 2015 and recontacted in 2019 have generally relocated elsewhere or gone back to France: having worked in Dubai does not foreordain that a person remain in the city. During the interviews, several had compared their "expat experiences" in various countries. If they stayed in Dubai, it was because they decided to, as did some who resigned from their company to find a local contract with an equivalent or better package. Conversely, many under local contracts considered Dubai as a relatively constrained choice, and some felt stuck there. Amin, who reported the trouble he had in France finding a job despite his university degrees, felt he had no choice but to leave, for reasons of discrimination:

> "I love France more than you can imagine, but it's just that I never really got the chance to show what I was capable of, to accomplish great things. So I was obliged to leave."

He fit his departure into the pattern of upward social mobility of parents who themselves had left their birth country in order to attain a better standard of living.[41] Several persons spoke of parents who had "sacrificed," notably in order for their children to achieve academic success. Success is thus understood as all the more well-deserved in that it resulted from effort exerted over several generations and was insufficiently rewarded in France. In this way, the Dubai experience is a culmination of family destiny. The persons concerned often stressed the importance of their relationship with their parents: despite the geographical distance, they stayed in touch via regular visits and sometimes sent part of their earnings to help them out or even to lift them out of their subaltern condition in France. Amin related:

> "I help out my family quite a bit, in fact, I send money to France to help out my parents. . . . I grew up in the housing projects, a low-rent apartment, the whole working-class suburb scene. My parents are just factory workers, so I send them quite a lot of money. . . . A good third goes to France. It's funny, you don't pay taxes, but I guess . . . it's my way of paying taxes. All of that goes to France."

Those who leave France for this reason experience their departure as a choice in a constrained context, by default. Although these persons can critique Dubai's social order, they do not idealize the social order of their home context as meritocratic. Their statements do not pit the non-egalitarian Dubai social order against a social order idealized as egalitarian in France, unlike the viewpoints of the nanny employers for example: both social orders are seen through critical eyes. Still, their success in Dubai enables them, to a certain extent, to compensate for hardships experienced in France, by their professional position, salary, and/or lifestyle. It is a kind of revenge after years, even decades, of "hassle," to use Javed's term.

Javed also spoke of how much he wanted to help out and relieve the burden of his parents, who sacrificed all their lives, as well as of how he was confronted with forms of structural racism in France. After a year and a half of internships without any possibility of getting hired, he wished to leave. He chose Dubai because members of his extended family were already there. He left France without finding a job beforehand and gave himself three months to search. When we met, he had been working for two years on the small Dubai team of a multinational. Pleased with the prevailing atmosphere, he was thinking about looking for another job: "Basically, I don't see any possibility for advancement." He intended to remain outside France for several years before going home not only because he enjoys travel, but also because he believed he wouldn't find a job commensurate with his ambitions in France if he returned after only two years abroad. Nor could he abide the forms of racism that he sensed, even from afar, were intensifying in France. The interview took place in early 2015:

> "South Africa, . . . or the United States . . . Those are more tempting countries than France right now. Especially at this time, with what's going on in France. I'm talking about the economic downturn, but even more about, let's say, the noxious atmosphere you feel there. A kind of racism, or an identity that France is searching for.
>
> (*Later in the interview*) "There's a lot I love about France. . . . I love French culture, French food, French history. And I love the multiculturalism you find in France. . . . But . . . I just don't see myself there. It's not the France I used to know, I guess. . . . There's a double standard that's taking over. . . . People feel victimized, the hyphenated French, of some other supposed origin, because we have the impression that there is a certain social class that is privileged, unlike all the others. And that's when . . . France starts heading downhill."

Javed was paid about $4,500 a month, in sharp contrast with the situation of his parents back in France, whom he wanted to help out. He hoped to arrange things so that his father, a janitor who "has been washing windows in France for twenty-five years now," might quit his job. For the moment, he was helping his parents financially by covering all his mother's expenses when she came to Dubai.

For persons like Amin and Javed, the choice to move to Dubai and then to stay on was experienced as relatively constrained. The social success experienced in Dubai would appear difficult to "repatriate" back to France. Sustaining it implies most often remaining in the city. After several years of life in Dubai, a number of interviewees did not associate Dubai with happiness anymore. They wished to leave for a variety of reasons (too much work and pressure on the job, health problems, cost of living too high to raise children, affective void, lack of green landscapes, remoteness from family), but most expressed how hard it was to actually leave.[42] Some individuals feared a downgrade in terms of salary and living conditions if they were to leave, though they were fully conscious that low charges and taxes were offset by the absence of social rights. Others were staying because they were a bi-national couple and would have trouble finding another city where both partners could pursue their professional careers. For a consultant who wore the hijab, returning to France would have amounted to ending her career. Several struggled to project themselves into France's professional culture: they feared its slow work pace and career advancement, its hostility toward profiles and career paths that diverge from a certain mono-national, mono-lingual norm, and its inflexibility and backwardness in terms of procedures (to quote their explanations). Many planned to relocate elsewhere, without going back to France: the destinations envisioned were Singapore, the United States, Canada, Great Britain, New Zealand, Switzerland, Australia, and Thailand. But several persons felt a bit stuck in Dubai, among other reasons, because they dreaded the experience of discrimination once back in France. Thus, even though a Western passport does represent an undeniable advantage in the global job market, not all holders have the same range of options in practice. Just as relocation to Dubai can be experienced as a constrained choice due to racial discrimination in the job market in France, staying also amounts to a constrained choice for certain persons, in particular for nonwhites fearing they will be unable to find a job that matches their qualifications once back home.

For women whose residence depends on their husband's job, the latitude of choice, whether for coming[43] or for staying, can also be tenuous. Marie, 46, outlined her feelings on the matter four years after our first interview, reflecting from the standpoint of family, so much so that she had trouble expressing a desire that was wholly her own. Should they stay in Dubai when the husband is enjoying the work less than before but still finds the projects more stimulating and the salary higher than it would be for an engineer in Europe? And when their teenage children keep saying they would like to "go back" to Europe—where they have never lived? Given the cost of higher education, it seemed to Marie and her husband, however, that it would be better to stay in Dubai and save as much as possible. These are "the calculations we've been doing for some time now," she declared. In all that, Marie defined herself as a "dependent": "I gave up my career to follow my husband. There's been positive and negative. I try to see the positive." Later in the interview, she said she had a hard time knowing what was best for her children and added that "it's so independent of what I want for myself."

Precariousness versus stability

Conducting interviews with the same persons at intervals of a few years allowed me to identify situational reversals that affected, among my interviewees, only women of color, revealing the precariousness of the professional positions they had achieved. For instance, four out of the six nonwhite women I interviewed both in 2015 and 2019 had to deal with an abrupt worsening of their living standard subsequent to health problems, a pregnancy (Lina), an unlawful action by her employer (Sandy), and emotional harassment from a superior. I am presenting here the cases of Lina and Sandy. I did not encounter a comparable case among the white female interviewees. After a rapid professional rise, on the "jump career" model in Dubai, Lina was still in the trial period for a position that matched "the job of her dreams" when she started living with a partner and got pregnant. When the company found out, it ended her contract. Although this practice is not exceptional in Dubai, the three other women with French nationality who were single professionals when I first met them and had experienced pregnancies when I interviewed them again in 2019, perhaps because they worked in sectors where women are in the majority, benefitted from a more flexible attitude on the part of their employer. One, for example, was granted unpaid leave, allowing her to double her legally mandated forty-five-day maternity leave. Lina, however, ended up jobless and without insurance coverage. After giving birth in France, she went back to Dubai, where she found a job far below her previous one. Her husband then got a job offer in Tunisia and the couple decided to relocate. At the time of the interview, Lina had been looking for work for a year.

Sandy, a consultant for a multinational, employed by a subcontractor, lost her job when the multinational broke with the subcontracting company over an issue of fraud. The subcontractor, having confiscated her passport, attempted for several weeks to blackmail her into signing a letter of resignation. Meanwhile, the same multinational offered Sandy a job at its Qatar subsidiary, which she accepted. She went on holiday, waiting for her work visa to be processed. Months went by, and the visa application was finally rejected, probably due to bilateral relations between the two countries. Sandy decided to head back to France, while expanding her job search to other countries: she was afraid she'd come up empty-handed, as she had as a young graduate a few years back. In the end, she found a job easily but at a very low salary, as if she were starting all over again. Disappointed at the low standard of living she had been forced into (after ten years of professional experience in finance, she was living in a studio apartment), she was planning to leave France once again.

Although I did interview nonwhite French women whose success in Dubai is ongoing, one a CEO, the other in the luxury goods business, the stories of Lina, Sandy, and the two other interviewees mentioned suggest that women of color are overrepresented in the most unpredictable and precarious positions. They seem structurally more exposed to situations such as landing in a company that is running deficits or in one where unlawful business practices develop. "Jump careers" are thus nowhere near as advantageous as expatriate contracts, in both the short and medium terms. For these women, the experience of Western privilege seems fleeting or even reversible.

The differential consequences of stereotypes about the Gulf

Among the persons who returned to France after having been in Dubai on local contract or in an international internship program (in French law, an expatriate contract with relatively low pay and fixed duration, where candidates must be under 28 years of age), some stayed with the same organization: these were mostly young graduates (in particular, among my interviewees, males from working-class and minority backgrounds in France's class/race spectrum) who garnered favorable notice in Dubai and whose bosses recommended them for positions in France. Their experience in Dubai thus appears to have been acknowledged.

Others had to resign from their jobs in Dubai and look for work in France. In that regard, the prevailing negative stereotypes surrounding the Gulf seem to benefit whites returning from this region, while they disadvantage, at least in the short term, those assigned an Arab or Muslim identity, as revealed by the contrasting narratives of Adel and Claire.

Adel, with a double master's degree from France and the United States, returned from Dubai in 2014 after two years in the city. Initially, he resumed the job he was working as a student, considered as an unskilled position. He then found a job in his sector, transport, but with fewer responsibilities and for half the salary he had been earning in Dubai. This was how he worked for a year before getting hired by a client looking for someone capable of working in English and with clients and collaborators from many countries. He explained that once back from the Emirates, "the Dubai experience was not an asset," that people at job interviews were wary and would ask if he was thinking about going back. He felt like he was "starting from scratch." It was only recently, at his current job, that he used the linguistic and relational skills he honed in Dubai: several years later, it was experience in France, in his view, that allowed the expertise accumulated in Dubai to be valorized.

The widespread image of Dubai as an Eldorado where easy money can be earned undermines the person concerned—in Adel's case, notably by virtue of the ubiquitous narrative in the media about "Maghrebis/Muslims who make a fortune in the Gulf." According to this narrative, the "Maghrebis of France" or the "Muslims of France" (terms often used interchangeably) supposedly leave France for specific reasons, particularly hiring discrimination, and are greeted with open arms by the Gulf countries, where they purportedly make their fortune, a success sometimes ascribed to the presumed cultural-religious (and, implicitly, racial) similarity.[44] Several aspects of this narrative stereotype were contested by these persons, who especially refuted the determinism that purportedly explains their behavior and life choices by casting them into a unidimensional identity of "Maghrebi" or "Muslim." Several hastened to point out the diverse and complex causes of their relocation to Dubai; they did not specifically choose an "Arab" or "Muslim" country. The Eldorado narrative obscures the effort it takes to migrate and the work performed in Dubai, or its legal forty-five-hour workweek; the narrative reinforces the idea of a cultural or religious continuity that would facilitate success, while disregarding the fact that the advantages many French people enjoy in the Gulf are linked mainly to their passport. If a short-term "international experience" seems valued for the "signal of adaptability" it emits,[45] the frequent conflation of "Maghrebis" and "Gulf," a reflex of ordinary racism, also tends to blur it. The success in the Gulf of persons consigned to their Maghrebi identity gets construed as dubiously acquired or too easily and quickly obtained. It precludes their triumphant return to France with an aura of prestige. It remains circumscribed—that is, associated with a geographical location, an elsewhere perceived as foreign and remote, or even unjust and slaveholding, according to the dominant neo-orientalist image of the Gulf countries in the French media. These particular career paths are implicitly contrasted with other forms of upward mobility more associated with meritocracy. Adel's case suggests that a set of stereotypes does harm to persons assigned to Maghrebi identity when returning to France, although it would take a larger number of cases to confirm this, since the majority of my interviewees avoided this experience by not planning to return, despite their desire to leave Dubai.

Adel's experience contrasts with Claire's. After working for five years in Dubai in human resources (her area of training), she followed her partner, whom she met locally, after he was transferred to Qatar. There, she opened a job recruitment consultancy. After a few months, she was lured away by a multinational that promoted her to a position (a local contract, but with bonuses and perks) that she deemed unlikely for her age and experience. She stayed there for three years. She believed that the international experience made all the difference on her CV once back in France—she quickly found a job commensurate with her ambitions. Even if the experience in a second country, perhaps deemed more difficult than the first, is in some way signifi- cant, it seems, compared to other cases, that a professional experience in the Gulf for a white woman, especially given the sexist stereotype so commonly associated with these countries, would be more easily valorized profession- ally in France. Claire believed that this unconventional experience attracted attention on her CV and was interpreted as proof of a strong sense of pur- pose. This valorizing figure of adventuresome whiteness contrasts with that of the otherness, which aroused various suspicions that were projected onto Adel by virtue of his stay in the Gulf. Stereotypes about the Gulf seem in this way to benefit or harm the people in search of employment, depending on the gender and race category projected upon them.

*   *   *

The neoliberal discourse trending among Dubai authorities and other global elites promotes the unaffiliated individual assessed on his or her merits alone. This discourse coexists with salary scales varying according to nationalities and countries where degrees are earned; furthermore, the pressure to per- form a stereotypical Westernness weighs on persons holding skilled jobs, especially if they are not white, as we have seen. Yet, persons from France's racial minorities generally experience their position in the Dubai social order as an improvement. Even if accessing better jobs, salaries, and consumer patterns remains key, this improvement cannot be reduced to those factors

alone: no longer being constantly confronted with the forms of structural racism experienced in their home country also greatly contributes. And based on
blog articles and interviews quoted in this chapter, this echoes experiences of
Westerners socialized as nonwhite in other European and North American
contexts, even though structural racism has a different history and singular
characteristics in each society.

The experience of Dubai's social order differs depending on a person's
racial position. The persons I interviewed seemed more inclined to appropriate the neoliberal multicultural discourse celebrating Dubai as a city offering
equal opportunity to all if they had previously been subjected to forms of
oppression and discrimination. In Dubai, their status was complex, often
dissonant: they experienced structural advantages in the job market, linked
to colonial and imperial history, while at the same time feeling excluded in
various interactions due to racial projections.[46] Bandana Purkayastha[47] has
shown how university educated South-Asian Americans simultaneously
experience forms of privilege (with regard to their parents' society of origin) and marginalization (with regard to their own society in the United
States) that constitute their transnational existence; for this reason, in her
view, the intersectionality paradigm is still too often envisioned within the
nation-state, while many people's experience is far from mono-national. This
observation can be further complicated if we focus on the case of nonwhite
persons migrating out of a society structured along majority/minority lines
and into a global city that brings together numerous nationalities and where
whiteness is not predominantly thought of as a neutral status. Indeed, not
only do these persons experience, transnationally, situations of both structural advantage (in Dubai, as Westerners) and marginalization (in France,
as members of a racial minority), but in Dubai, they also have simultaneously dissonant experiences, depending on their situation and location.
Whites—who do not define themselves as such—more rarely appropriate
the discourse of Dubai as multicultural society. Although some whites might
applaud multiculturalism, most don't consider Dubai as a truly multicultural
city, unlike London or New York, but as an Emirati city, "too Muslim," or as a
caste society. This is how, by distancing and differentiating themselves from
this society, deemed exceptional, they construct themselves as Westerners,
often by implicitly excluding the nonwhites from this status, regardless of
their nationality.

For all these persons, quality of life, presented as particularly accessible, instantly provides a sense of success and makes tangible on a daily basis an upward mobility that is nevertheless hard to "repatriate," to retrieve and assert once back home. This sense of success pertains to most Westerners in Dubai, living in upscale neighborhoods and consuming luxury goods and services. It constitutes the "wages of Westernness": the possibility of being admitted into lavish spaces and being treated with deference, regardless of income. Thanks to this lifestyle, Western residents contribute to shaping a kind of equivalency in Dubai society between Westernness and affluence, even if it means living on credit. The access to luxury goods and services contributes to the construction of Western privilege and is a widely shared experience among the group. Many interviewees associate such a lifestyle with happiness.

The feeling of happiness expressed by many interviewees in Dubai, however, takes on different aspects and meanings depending on the interviewees' trajectories and backgrounds. Members of the upper class enjoy in particular the standard of service in Dubai and the absence of conflict and violation of property: nothing seems to delegitimize their wealth. Those of working-class background appreciate the potential for social mobility as compared to the position they occupied in their home country; some attempt to conceal aspects of their lifestyle from their home community, while others consider this social success as the legitimate result of their parents' and their own striving, underappreciated and insufficiently rewarded in France due to structural discrimination. Security also takes on different meanings depending on race and gender.

While Western privilege does cover different material and subjective conditions, shaped by each person's position in the hierarchy of gender, race, and class, the discrepancy among the interviewees had widened overall by the time I recontacted them in 2019. The most ample upward mobility, in terms of both conditions (salary, position, etc.) and freedom to choose where to live, applied to white males. Conversely, many persons, notably nonwhites, remained in Dubai for want of an alternative. While expatriate contracts had benefitted mainly the white males among my interviewees, to the exclusion of other social categories, the second model of upward professional mobility, which I call "jump careers," had fallen far short of providing the same benefits. Several persons, notably women of color, ended up in difficult situations, after several years of steady but precarious career progress. Furthermore, these experiences were difficult to valorize outside Dubai, especially in France where they seem to be interpreted differently depending on whether the person is white or nonwhite.

Through these trajectories, this chapter has also suggested that not all women benefit from Western privilege to the same extent. Their situations are even more diverse than men's. The racial dimension is combined with marital and parental status, and with the model of emphatic femininity analyzed in chapter 2. Women who came as a "dependent" of a white man and were raising children suffered from structural discrimination on the job market but benefitted from a very privileged lifestyle through their husband's contract. White women with no kids, while they did not have access to the most advantageous contracts (expatriate contracts, family packages), benefitted from a particular aspect of white privilege in the medium term: having worked in the Gulf, especially for a white woman, may be interpreted as proof of strong will in Western professional contexts, while for a person of color, such experience may reinforce white employers' perception of them as other/stranger. Interviewing the same women at different moments in their careers also suggested that their contracts were in general more precarious than men's and that maternity, as well as health problems, were not easy to negotiate in a job market that valorizes both total availability of workers and the performance of a stereotyped, sexualized model of femininity.

The point of showing how heterogeneous the category of Westerner is in Dubai is not to minimize Western privilege but rather to spotlight how Westernness and whiteness interact between themselves and with other dimensions of social hierarchy, especially gender and class: certain persons, mainly white males, enjoy ongoing structural advantages, while for others, whose life path leads them through several national spaces, the privileged position proves short-lived or confined to a particular social context.

CONCLUSION

THREE IN THE MORNING. An alarm, mingling with the noisy commotion of a loudspeaker, wakes me out of a deep sleep. Wondering whether this is a drill or a real fire, I slip into my flip-flops and hastily head down the emergency staircase, the thirteen floors separating me from the ground. At street level, firemen and police wave me over to join the other high-rise dwellers gathering on the opposite sidewalk. Heads raised, all are watching the spectacle of flames licking this glitzy structure from the fiftieth floor on up—the building, called The Torch (!), is a seventy-story tower. The images will be seen all over the world, as happens every time a Dubai skyscraper catches fire.

Some residents managed to fill a suitcase before making their way down. One woman, who I imagine works as a nanny, is holding an empty stroller; a couple, an infant cuddled in their arms, have their backs turned to her. All I took with me was my phone, and I'm starting to worry about my passport, which I left along with all my things in the room I am renting. My return flight is tomorrow: what will happen if the whole building burns to the ground, or if access is prohibited?

The next morning, I finally reach my landlord by phone, a Frenchman who rents the room in his two-room apartment through Airbnb; he didn't come home last night. He tells me he will handle everything and asks that I not speak directly to the authorities, since he is renting to me illegally. In the meantime, he's going to drive over and take me out to breakfast. I warn him that I'm in my pajamas (in fact, a black tee-shirt and jogging pants). "You're dressed just right for Bur Dubai [a neighborhood perceived as "Indian"]," he replied. As we walk to his car, passing by some men who are cleaning the sidewalk, he nevertheless offers me his jacket to wear over my top: "There are Indians," he says.

On the ten-lane highway that cuts through Dubai, this man who I'd guessed was in his late 30s, employed by a tobacco company, fair skin accentuated by his shaved head, is driving his massive white SUV at full throttle while chatting on his smartphone, ranting against "Indian" and "Paki" drivers. "Here, the driving instructors are Indians and Pakis who don't even know how to drive themselves, so you can imagine," he proclaims condescendingly, sure of my complicit approval. In an attempt to relax after my ordeal, I ask him a few questions about his previous experiences with life abroad. He has lived in South Africa, and he tells me that "the problem there is that there is no brain; they have to bring in brains from Europe and North America." For a short while, he was in Iraq, "to show that you're prepared to go to places where no one wants to go. It's good for your CV." He concludes: "At any rate, here in Dubai, you have to take what's there for the taking, the cash, and get the hell out."

These scenes echo various elements of the analysis presented in this book. The key role played by the passport, which makes its loss particularly nerve-racking; the palpable affective distance between employers and domestic employee despite their co-presence in all circumstances; class dominance, flagrantly on display, here as elsewhere, through the kind of vehicle one drives; the construction of distinctive Western subjectivities in areas as diverse as driving, sexuality, and the professional field. All three of these themes are touched on by my landlord in his remarks about "Indians," his ranting at the wheel, and his references to previous expatriations.

Conducting this sort of study presupposed that I would be getting involved with persons whose convictions I find offensive, that I would be assimilated in spite of myself into situations of complicity—which I have called the epistemology of unease. The attitudes of most of the people with whom I came into contact, however, proved far more ambivalent than my landlord's. Although they did coincide at times on certain basic notions, at other times, my interviewees questioned the social order and the resulting forms of injustice, whether in Dubai or elsewhere. Some of their discourses, which we may qualify as exceptionalist,[1] territorialize non-egalitarianism as something peculiar to Dubai and contrast it with other societies and with Western values. Others refute this vision by comparing different societies.

Statements of an ethical nature made by my interviewees, combined with their lifestyles and practices, played an important role in how I analyzed their forms of distinction as Westerners. Many asserted their commitment to egalitarianism in the areas of professional, conjugal, and domestic relations, while adopting practices that often, though not always, failed to coincide with this value. The moral discourse asserting egalitarian values constituted a shared element within the group of the structurally advantaged. It was through this discursive egalitarianism that members of this fluidly bounded group identified themselves and set themselves apart from *others*.

This assertion of distinctive egalitarianism did not prevent most of them from believing they were *objectively* more competent, with this competence legitimizing in their view the structural advantages they enjoyed in the job market. In the intimate sphere, they also thought of themselves as more advanced, though often more implicitly. What characterized this group, in addition to the advantageous socioeconomic positions its members occupied, was therefore an egalitarian discourse matched by the conviction of being more advanced and/or having greater skills by virtue of being a Westerner. The persons I interviewed saw egalitarianism as one of the values that set the West apart as one of the most advanced zones in the world. This discursive egalitarianism contributed to producing and justifying hierarchy-generating differences via the construction of a non-egalitarian, and thus backward-looking, Other.

This book has sought to shed light on the formation of a group that, although diverse in many respects, is privileged in the urban society of Dubai. To describe this group, I had to bring to light the different co-constructed dimensions of social hierarchies. Thus, gender, class, race, and nationality are shaped by processes working in concert: because skills have for a long time been essentialized as Western, racialized nationalities are hierarchized in the job market by salary level, as well as by contracts and differentiated professional positions. This has far-reaching effects because salary levels and work contracts directly determine whether or not one can sponsor "dependents" and bring up children in the urban space of Dubai. Among white upper-class couples raising children, the identification with a distinctive Westernness is interlinked with a specific form of heteronormativity. These couples, despite a sharply accentuated division of labor, claimed they shared work more horizontally, in partnership, and were more egalitarian than the "locals," whose domestic relationships were associated with (conjugal) sexism and slavery (of their live-in employees). The male and female single residents of Dubai described their lifestyle in Dubai as hedonistic, but they experienced this moment in their lives as a passing phase before settling down with a serious partner: many believed that establishing a sincere and disinterested relationship was particularly difficult in Dubai. Relationships of this type are often presented as the purview of Western societies. Most of the singles thus deployed projections of conjugal and familial respectability that coincided with those of the married couples. These projected self-images contributed to their distinction as Westerners who believed they were more egalitarian in the professional, conjugal, familial, and domestic spheres.

Such moral discourses play a role in establishing distinctions and boundaries within the middle and upper classes of Dubai.[2] Even when their primary socialization had not necessarily prepared them for it, the persons socialized in Western countries tended to behave like a member of these classes, perceiving themselves as more virtuous and more advanced than other members of the upper classes. These moral discourses tended to shape distinctive subjectivities, sociabilities, and solidarities. This distinction, however, was not necessarily transferable to the subject's context of origin, and the social mobility enabled by the move to Dubai may well be confined to that territory. Indeed, for certain persons, especially people of color, the experience of privilege proved ephemeral.

*   *   *

Taking into account the social structures of each society involves a contextualized approach to race. This book has looked at the way persons relocating from one society to another position themselves in the hierarchies of race and class in interaction with the status they have been assigned. Thus, persons assigned to minority status in their home country, such as that of "Maghrebi" in France, experience a status just as complex but more socially advantageous in Dubai: that of French and/or Arab, Franco-Tunisian, Franco-Moroccan, or Franco-Algerian. Likewise, whiteness in France and whiteness in Dubai do not cover exactly the same self-representations and definitions of alterity, and even though this status rests upon structural advantages in both cases, the latter differ from one context to another.

By choosing to extend the study's frame beyond white people, my intention is by no means to invalidate the concept of whiteness. On the contrary, this framework has enabled me to compare the structural advantages and subjectivities of white and nonwhite Western passport holders. Among whites, Westernness can be a way to attribute positive content to their status, which they did not conceive as specific when living in a white majority society. They use this content to legitimize a hegemony defended as more just than that of nonwhite elites, a hegemony that allows them to live in advantageous conditions as white Westerners.

For Western passport holders socialized as people of color in majority-white societies, Westernness in Dubai represents a valorizing status with permeable borders and a promise of inclusion that nevertheless can always be called into question. Although they benefit from a certain number of advantages thanks to their passport and stereotypes linked to their nationality, they do not enjoy the same privileges as whites and can at any moment be cast into subaltern status. Although Dubai's postcolonial neoliberalism can deliver a promise of inclusion for persons with the right passport but who are nevertheless treated as subalterns in certain respects, this promise comes with major normative constraints in terms of behavior and self-presentation. This study of Dubai allowed me to problematize forms of hierarchizing and racializing of nationalities that structure the job market, sociabilities, and social positions in the global city.

*   *   *

This book provides an uncustomary consideration of theoretical questionings regarding Western hegemony by showing what Westernness actually does today in practice, in a global city of a non-hegemonic country. Westernness is mobilized by a set of people in order to rank, hierarchize, legitimate, justify, regroup, and set boundaries. It can represent a high-speed asset for crossing not only national borders but social frontiers as well and for adopting practices coded as specific to the upper class. Studying Westernness in Dubai in effect involves focusing on a fraction of the middle and upper classes whose behaviors are neither totally different nor totally identical to those observed elsewhere. The terms of access to these privileged lifestyles derive from a combination of postcoloniality and neoliberalism; they shape an urban society that is patently non-egalitarian while boasting an apparently peaceful multiculturalism as deployed in the city's highly surveilled public spaces. Unequal as it is, this social order allows successful professional careers for people who were discriminated against in their home countries. It can be experienced as open, even liberating, because for Western passport holders, neither whiteness nor socialization in the upper class is a prerequisite for gaining access to relatively privileged positions, even if those remain conditions for accessing the most privileged positions. Nonwhite Westerners' experiences invite us to put into perspective unequal social orders in different contexts, rather than exceptionalize Dubai's unequal social order.

Ultimately, this work has shown that persons structurally advantaged via their passport are not outsiders in Dubai society. From the moment they arrive, most adapt at remarkable speed to the dominant position that is theirs in Dubai. Despite the sharply different trajectories and living conditions of the persons I interviewed, nearly all of them got caught up in the game of luxurious nightlife and inexpensive consumer services relative to their income. These practices gave them the impression that their lives had become easy. The idea of a temporary stay made it possible both to step back from the local social order and to disavow any responsibility for it by claiming outsider status. And yet, by adopting this kind of lifestyle, these persons actually did play a role in perpetuating the social order that structurally favors Western passport holders, the ranking criterion that remains key despite the continual turnover of residents.

* * *

This concludes a thought process spanning several years, one that has led me to challenge some misconceptions strongly rooted in exceptionalist representations of Dubai. Various encounters with academics and with some interviewees, in Dubai and elsewhere, helped me become aware of these preconceived notions and to move beyond them throughout the field research, analysis, and the writing itself. One of my objectives at the outset was to study what the belief in the superiority of the West does sociologically—that is, how this belief materializes in the social structures of a global city. At each stage of my project, I found I had to deconstruct my own sometimes exceptionalist and demonizing vision of Dubai, broadly shared among France's intellectual professionals, by acknowledging what it also owes to the implicit belief in Western superiority. Moreover, this process also helped me to question inequalities I had become used to in France—for instance, between different categories of workers in universities. Obviously, we can criticize Dubai's social order, provided we look beyond the most widespread exceptionalist and exoticizing images that prevail in much of today's media. Thus, this book has demonstrated how complex and ambivalent trajectories and subjectivities, marked by an identification with the West seen as progressive, and by a willingness to disassociate from the presence of exploitation, contribute to shaping and reinforcing the hierarchies that structure Dubai's social order.

Notes

INTRODUCTION

1. Stoler (2002) 2013.
2. Ong 1999: 21.
3. Kanna 2011.
4. Said (1978) 2003; Said 2000; Mohanty 1984.
5. Hall 1996: 186.
6. Fechter and Walsh 2010: 1200.
7. See also Patterson 1997.
8. Fechter and Walsh 2010.
9. Le Renard 2014a; Le Renard 2019.
10. Ahmed 2000: 11.
11. Hanieh 2011; Kanna 2014.
12. Hanieh 2011.
13. Davis 2007.
14. Sassen 1998.
15. Mignolo 2001; Mignolo 2012.
16. Connell 2014.
17. Hooks 1992; Kebabza 2006; Cervulle 2013.
18. Vest 2013.
19. Coles and Walsh 2010.
20. Frankenberg 1993: 1.
21. Ahmed 2004b.
22. McWhorter 2005: 536.

23. Fechter 2005; Knowles and Harper 2009; Fechter and Walsh 2010; Leonard 2010; Lundström 2014.

24. Especially works by Katie Walsh, Catherine Lundström, Brenda Yeoh, and Pauline Leonard, quoted throughout the book.

25. Leonard and Walsh 2019.

26. Melamed 2011; Haritaworn 2012.

27. The notion of transnational spaces and expatriates "living in a bubble" is developed in Fechter 2007.

28. Walsh 2007; Walsh 2008; Kanna 2014; Vora 2012; Vora 2014; Vora 2018; Cosquer 2018; Kanna, Le Renard, and Vora 2020. There are numerous studies on construction workers in the Gulf (Gardner 2010; Bruslé 2015; Buckley 2015), on women hired as nannies or maids (Brochmann 1993; Gamburd 2000; Shah 2004; Sabban 2004; Percot 2006; Nagy 2008; Fernandez and Regt 2014; Debonneville 2015; Mahdavi 2016; Ahmad 2017), on sex workers (Mahdavi 2011), and on such national groups as Indians, Iranians, and Egyptians (Vora, 2013; Moghadam 2013; Pagès-El Karoui 2016). But work on the place of Westerners in these societies is still in its early stages (Walsh 2007; Walsh 2008; Kanna 2014; Vora 2014; Cosquer 2018), as is work on the value and uses of the so-called Western passport (Camelin 2013).

29. Hill Collins (2000) 2010; Ehrenreich and Hochschild 2003.

30. Leonard 2010: 19–34.

31. Acker 2006.

32. Holvino 2010.

33. Holvino 2010.

34. Ong 2006.

35. Ong 2006: 155; Kanna 2011.

36. Melamed 2011: xxi.

37. Haritaworn 2012.

38. Haritaworn 2012.

39. Hill Collins (2000) 2010; Stoler 2013.

40. Stoler 2013.

41. Pratt and Rosner 2006; Wilson 2012.

42. Ahmed 2000.

43. Vitalis 2007.

44. Seccombe and Lawless 1986: 569. See also AlShehabi 2019.

45. Abu Lughod 1998.

46. Le Renard 2014a; Kanna, Le Renard, and Vora 2020: 55–79.

47. For more details, see Kanna, Le Renard, and Vora 2020: 42–49.

48. Works on other segments of the middle and upper class include, for instance, Kanna 2011; Moghadam 2013; Vora 2013.

49. http://www.bqdoha.com/2015/04/uae-population-by-nationality (accessed 20 April 2015).

50. "Every day, three new French people move to Dubai," *La Tribune*, 6 January 2014.

51. El-Tayeb 2011.

52. Bleich 2000; Guénif-Souilamas 2000; Guénif-Souilamas 2006; Fassin and Fassin 2006; Ndiaye 2009; Mazouz 2017.

53. Amiraux and Simon 2006; Simon 2014.

54. Three mentioned they had double nationality. I did not ask this question systematically, however.

55. I was unable to find out anything about thirteen of my original interviewees. I had not anticipated this second round of interviews and had failed to archive my contacts in any systematic way. To protect privacy, I had often omitted noting the family name of the interviewees.

56. Leonard and Walsh 2019.

57. See chapter 4.

58. Wagner 1998; Colombi 2016.

59. Lundström 2014.

60. See also Croucher 2012; Kunz 2016.

61. Leonard and Walsh 2019.

62. Kofman and Raghuram 2005.

63. Benson and O'Reilly 2009; Benson and Osbaldiston 2014.

64. Nagy 2010; Vora 2013.

65. Lundström 2010.

66. Tissot 2011.

67. Avanza 2008.

68. Boukir 2016; Quashie 2017.

69. Heteronormativity among "expatriates" is analyzed by Walsh 2007; and Lundström 2014. More recently, in French, three dissertations feature it as a central concept (Brand 2016; Duplan 2016; Cosquer 2018).

70. Kanna, Le Renard, and Vora 2020.

71. Vora 2013: 11.

72. See also Bristol-Rhys and Osella 2018: 4.

CHAPTER 1: THE CONSTRUCTION OF SKILLS

1. Mignolo 2001; Mignolo 2012; Quijano 2007; Sanna and Varikas 2011.

2. Mignolo 2001: 57.

3. The categories used by historical works, which I am using here, would be worth discussing on the basis of period sources.

4. Kanna 2011.

5. Kanna 2011: 48.

6. Kanna 2011: 24, 59.

7. Davidson 2008; Kanna 2011.

8. Onley 2007: 34.

9. AlShehabi 2015: 5–6.

10. Vora 2013: 208.

11. Heard-Bey 1982.

12. Said Zahlan 1978: 11.

13. Al-Sayegh 1998.

14. Kanna 2011: 50–51.

15. Davidson 2008.

16. Abdulla 1984: 96–97.

17. Abdulla 1984; Kanna 2011: 54.

18. Assaf 2017.

19. Vora 2013.

20. Moghadam 2013.

21. Kanna 2011.

22. Kanna 2011.

23. Kanna 2011.

24. Ong 2006; Kanna 2011.

25. Kanna 2011.

26. Cosquer 2018.

27. Coles and Walsh 2010.

28. In 2008, many residents left the city during the economic crisis. Still, by the time I began my field research in 2012, everyone felt that the city had become attractive once again.

29. A company need not have an Emirati partner in order to create a company there, which is not the case outside such zones.

30. Al Maktoum 2014 ("The Brain Regain," *Project Syndicate*, https:// www.project-syndicate.org/commentary/mohammed-bin-rashid-al-maktoum-highlights-the-success-of-some-developing-countries-in-reversing-the-outflow-of-their-most-talented-people?barrier=accesspaylog).

31. Davidson 2008.

32. Thiollet 2016.

33. AlShehabi 2015: 6–7.

34. Beaugé and Büttner 1991; Thiollet 2016.

35. Kanna 2012.

36. Louer 2012: 17; Vora 2012; Vora 2014; Vora 2015.

37. The list of relevant countries in 2015: the twenty-eight countries of the European Union, Switzerland, the United States, Canada, Australia, New Zealand, South Korea, Croatia.

38. Dubai Statistics Center, "Employed (15 Years and Over) by Occupation and Nationality Groups," 2011.

39. Fechter and Walsh 2010: 1204.

40. Munif (1984) 2013.

41. Vitalis 2007.

42. Seccombe 1983; Seccombe and Lawless 1986.

43. AlShehabi 2015: 6–7.

44. Al-Shirawi 2005, cited in AlShehabi 2015: 5–6.

45. Seccombe and Lawless 1986. This disparity in treatment might be comparable to the situation prevailing in the French colonial empire.

46. Heard-Bey 1997: 119.

47. Heard-Bey 1982: 310.

48. See chapter 2.

49. Dubai Statistics Center 2011.

50. Vora 2014.

51. Al Maktoum 2014 ("The Brain Regain," *Project Syndicate*, https://www.project-syndicate.org/commentary/mohammed-bin-rashid-al-maktoum-highlights-the-success-of-some-developing-countries-in-reversing-the-outflow-of-their-most-talented-people?barrier=accesspaylog).

52. Visit Dubai (http://www.visitdubai.com/fr/articles/working-in-dubai, accessed 15 January 2017).

53. Several governments over recent decades have put forward happiness as one of their main objectives, notably Bhutan and Venezuela. Beyond these cases, the notion of happiness, though not central in international politics, has nevertheless gained recognition. A report commissioned by the United Nations on "world happiness" ranks the UAE twenty-eighth in terms of happiness. World Happiness Report, http://worldhappiness.report/.

54. Paul 2017.

55. Smith 2010.

56. Kanna 2012.

57. In 2020, the government created a renewable five-year retiree visa for people over 55 years of age, conditioned on high material resources. This recent measure, which is beyond the scope of this study, opens the possibility to stay in Dubai without a job contract, which is an important change.

58. Five individuals were there in connection with a volunteer internship in a business program, a contract under French law for one year, once renewable,

available to persons under 28 years of age who would like to work in French companies abroad.

59. See chapter 4.

60. Sayad 1999.

61. Vora 2013.

62. Vora 2014.

63. Ong 1999.

64. Boussard 2013.

65. See chapter 5.

CHAPTER 2: STRUCTURAL ADVANTAGES IN THE JOB MARKET

1. Jack et al. 2011.

2. See Acker 2006; Holvino 2010.

3. Pitti 2005.

4. According to available data, Europeans and North Americans earn more on average than any other national group, including the Emiratis. Dubai Statistics Center, 2011, "Employed (15 Years and Over) by Monthly and Annual Income and Nationality Groups." The most recent statistics I could find distinguish only two groups, Emirati and non-Emirati.

5. Vora 2013.

6. Cortéséro et al. 2013.

7. Mitchell 2002.

8. Bonilla-Silva 2014.

9. Walsh 2012.

10. Ewers and Dicce 2016. See also "Percentage Distribution of Employed 15 Years and Over by Occupation and Nationality Groups—Emirate of Dubai 2015," https://www.dsc.gov.ae/en-us/Programs-Statistical-Surveys/Pages/Statistical-Project-details.aspx?ProjectId=21#DSC_Tab2.

11. Kunz 2016.

12. Jounin 2008; Leonard 2010.

13. Ngai 2005.

14. Roediger and Esch 2012.

15. Montigny 2002: 219.

16. Camelin 2013; Moghadam 2013.

17. Hajjat 2010: 452; Fassin and Mazouz 2007.

18. Domestic workers, for instance. See Paul 2017.

19. Sayad 1993: 29.

20. Ong 1999: 112.

21. El Tayeb 2011; Ndiaye 2009.

CHAPTER 3: PERFORMING STEREOTYPICAL WESTERNNESS

1. Hidri 2007.
2. Hochschild 1979.
3. McDowell 1995; McDowell 1997.
4. McDowell 1995: 68.
5. Skeggs 2009.
6. Kanna 2011.
7. Kanna 2011; Vora 2013.
8. Melamed 2011; Haritaworn 2012.
9. Dubar 1996; Buscatto 2006.
10. Wagner 2007: 85–100.
11. Some of the following paragraphs have been previously published in "'Ici, il y a les Français français et les Français avec origines.' Reconfigurations raciales autour d'expériences de Dubaï," *Tracés*, no. 30 (2016): 55–57.
12. Hajjat and Mohammed 2013; Asal 2014.
13. Haritaworn 2012.
14. Discussion posted on 13 July 2011, under pseudonyms. "UK Indian in UAE," BritishExpats.com, https://britishexpats.com/forum/middle-east-60/uk-indian-uae-724535/.
15. Vora 2014: 190.
16. Souilamas 2000: 127.
17. S. Soto, *Black Living in Dubai: My Experience*, 4 March 2017, https://www.youtube.com/watch?v=z6OH9LExurU.
18. Vora 2014.
19. Cousin and Chauvin 2014.
20. See chapter 7.
21. Connell 2014.
22. Lan 2011.
23. McDowell 1995; McDowell 1997.
24. See chapter 2.
25. Hochschild 1979.
26. Vora 2013.

CHAPTER 4: THE HETERONORMATIVITY OF "GUEST FAMILIES"

1. V. Bentley, "Benefits of Moving Your Family to Dubai," *Time Out Dubai*, 15 October 2015, https://www.timeoutdubai.com/kids/features/66713-benefits-of-moving-your-family-to-dubai.
2. Mahdavi 2016.
3. A shorter version of the ideas presented in these three chapters has been

published as "Multiple Yet Normative: Heterosexual Subjectivities and Western Distinction in Neoliberal Dubai," in S. Sehlikoglu and F. Kariokis, *The Everyday Makings of Heteronormativity* (Lanham, MD: Lexington Books, 2019), 121–36.

4. Kofman and Raghuram 2005; Yeoh and Willis 2005.

5. Pochic 2005.

6. Coles and Fechter 2012: 1.

7. Walsh 2008.

8. Arieli 2013.

9. Manalansan 2006.

10. Walsh, Shen, and Willis 2008: 576.

11. Duplan 2016.

12. Fechter and Walsh 2010; Fechter 2010; Lundström 2014; Brand 2016; Cosquer 2018.

13. Stoler 2013.

14. Hasso 2010; Inhorn 2015.

15. Bristol-Rhys 2007; Bristol-Rhys 2016.

16. Carvalho Pinto 2012; Assaf 2017.

17. Babar and Gardner 2016.

18. Buckley 2015: 134.

19. Lori 2011; Buckley 2015.

20. Bristol-Rhys and Osella 2016.

21. Mahdavi 2011.

22. Bruslé 2015; Mahdavi 2016.

23. Ahmad 2017.

24. See chapter 7.

25. Yeoh, Huang, and Willis 2000.

26. Boussard 2013.

27. Ibos 2012.

28. Ong 1999: 20, 112.

29. Connell and Wood 2005.

30. See also Walsh, 2008.

31. Abu Lughod 1998.

32. Bristol-Rhys and Osella 2016; Cosquer 2018.

33. Mahdavi 2011: 71.

34. Coles and Fechter 2012.

35. Yeoh and Khoo 1998; Fechter 2010.

36. Arieli 2013.

37. Cosquer 2018.

38. See also Cosquer 2018.

39. Duplan 2016: 314.

40. Stoler 2002: 61.

41. Many of the larger hotels offer brunch buffets with unlimited food and alcohol.

CHAPTER 5: RELATIONS WITH DOMESTIC EMPLOYEES

This chapter has been adapted from an article first published as "Petits arrangements avec l'égalitarisme: Les Françaises de Dubaï et les employées domestiques," *Genèses: Sciences sociales et histoire*, no. 109 (2017): 118–38.

1. Brochmann 1993; Gamburd 2000; Sabban 2004; Shah 2004; Fernandez and de Regt 2014; Mahdavi 2016; Ahmad 2017.

2. Rollins 1987; Huang and Yeoh 1998; Ibos 2012; Lundström 2013.

3. Rollins 1987: 33.

4. Stoler 2013.

5. Cervulle 2012.

6. See, for instance, Ibos 2012.

7. Ibos 2012: 229.

8. Meuret-Campfort 2017.

9. Pinçon and Pinçon-Charlot 2007.

10. Memmi 2008.

11. Parreñas 2001; Ehrenreich and Hochschild 2003; Falquet et al. 2010.

12. Williams et al. 2009.

13. R. Ruiz, "Filipina Maids Shunned in UAE over Minimum Wage Demands," *The National*, 13 February 2013, http://www.thenational.ae/news/uae-news/filipina-maids-shunned-in-uae-over-minumum-wage-demands.

14. *Time Out Dubai* 2013.

15. Ibos 2012.

16. Ibos 2012: 108.

17. Ibos 2008.

18. Walsh, Shen, and Willis 2008.

19. Arieli 2013.

20. See chapter 4.

21. Fabian (1983) 2006; Bentouhami-Molino 2015.

22. Moujoud 2012.

23. Gavanas 2010.

24. Rollins 1987.

25. Ahmed 2000.

26. Ibos 2012.

27. Posted to Facebook group "Francodubai," 21 July 2015.

28. Stoler 2013.

29. J. Talbot, "Living in Dubai: Enjoy the Spoils, But Don't Get Spoilt!" *Sassy Mama*, 11 August 2016, https://www.sassymamadubai.com/living-dubai-luxury-spoilt/.

30. Inspired by the title of Sara Ahmed's essay (2004), "Declarations of Whiteness: The Non-Performativity of Anti-Racism."

31. Ibos 2012.

CHAPTER 6: HEDONISTIC LIFESTYLES

1. Vora 2013: 78.

2. See chapter 7.

3. Vora 2013.

4. This notion gets further developed in chapter 7; it draws on the notion of "the wages of whiteness" (Du Bois 1977; Roediger 1991).

5. World Bank, "Population, femmes (% du total), 1960–2019," http://donnees.banquemondiale.org/indicateur/SP.POP.TOTL.FE.ZS.

6. Walsh 2007: 512–13.

7. Walsh 2007.

8. Brand 2016.

9. Brand 2016.

10. Mai and King 2009; Brand 2016.

11. Tabet 2005.

12. Clair 2007.

13. Flahault 2009.

14. I draw freely here on Butler's notion (2002) of melancholia: for this author, there is melancholia in giving up everything that does not conform to gendered and sexual norms. The interviews I conducted among women reveal conversely a melancholia when stepping outside those norms, renouncing socially gratifying conformity, and notably married life.

15. Ahmed 2015.

16. Groups at the site Meet Up, which existed in 2013.

17. Walsh 2007.

CHAPTER 7: WESTERN PRIVILEGE AND WHITE PRIVILEGE

1. Interviewed in "The Black Expat: Living In Abu Dhabi As a Black Woman Has Been 'Amazing,'" 24 October 2018, https://travelnoire.com/the-black-expat-my-life-in-the-uae-is-amazing. (She was living in Abu Dhabi, not Dubai.)

2. Helen Debrah-Ampofo, "Black Expat in the UAE," 9 October 2019, https://helendebrahampofo.com/black-expat-in-the-uae/. (This blogger lives in Abu Dhabi, not Dubai.)

3. Roth 2012.

4. Roth 2012: 12.

5. Smart Dubai, http://www.dubai.ae/en/Lists/Articles/DispForm.aspx?ID=133&event=Planning%20to%20visit%20Dubai&category=Visitors.

6. Grewal 2005; Melamed 2011; Haritaworn 2012.

7. See also Lestra and Settoul 2018.

8. Meurs and Pailhé 2008; Safi and Simon 2013; Beauchemin, Hamel, and Simon 2016.

9. Haritaworn 2012.

10. See chapter 2.

11. Based on the interviews and blogs quoted in this chapter.

12. See chapter 3.

13. Vora 2018: 150–53.

14. Arab and Moujoud 2018.

15. On selective inclusions, see Haritaworn 2012: 46.

16. Guillaumin (1972) 2002.

17. Fechter and Walsh 2010.

18. Korpela 2010; Quashie 2016.

19. Cosquer 2018.

20. In the French, the interview coins the neologism "impatriés," which might be interpreted, at first glance, as "stateless" in English, which for many Palestinians is actually the case. But this is not what she means, as I will explain a bit further on.

21. This American film, that was based on a novel and came out in 1990, has contributed to representing Muslim men as violently sexist and Muslim majority countries as prisons for women.

22. Pratt (1992) 2008.

23. Bristol-Rhys 2016: 93.

24. Coles and Walsh 2010.

25. *Time Out Residents Guide 2013*, 12–13.

26. See also Cosquer 2018.

27. Ahmed 2010: 216.

28. Ahmed 2010 : 11.

29. Du Bois 1977; Roediger 1991.

30. Vora 2013.

31. See chapter 7 epigraph and Helen Debrah Ampofo, "Why It's Better Being Black in the UAE vs UK," 31 October 2019, https://helendebrahampofo.com/why-its-better-being-black-in-the-uae-vs-uk/.

32. Hergon 2019.

33. Liebe 2008; Le Renard 2011; Le Renard 2014c.

34. Bristol-Rhys and Osella 2018.

35. Mahdavi 2016.

36. Grewal 2016; Amar 2011.

37. See, for example, "Dubai Sentences Norwegian Woman Who Reported Rape," BBC News, 20 July 2013, http://www.bbc.com/news/world-middle-east-23381448; A. Molloy, "Austrian Rape Victim Returns from Dubai," *Independent*, 1 February 2014, http://www.independent.co.uk/news/world/middle-east/austrian-rape-victim-returns-from-dubai-but-may-still-face-charges-of-having-sex-outside-marriage-9101465.html.

38. At least until 2020.

39. Mahdavi 2016.

40. A previous version of this subsection has been published in the article "Approche intersectionnelle et postcoloniale d'un privilège: Occidentalité et blanchité sur le marché du travail de Dubaï," *Travail, genre et sociétés*, no. 44 (2020): 89–108.

41. Santelli 2001.

42. Among the seventeen interviews conducted in 2019 with persons I met between 2012 and 2015, seven persons out of ten who stayed in Dubai wished to leave the city but were having trouble doing so.

43. Cosquer 2018.

44. See, for example, "Cette jeunesse musulmane qui veut quitter la France pour Dubai," *Le Journal du Dimanche*, 15 March 2010, http://www.lejdd.fr/Economie/Cette-jeunesse-musulmane-qui-veut-s-expatrier-a-Dubai-722926# ; "Bienvenus à Dubaï," *Compléments d'enquête* (France 2), 2013, https://www.youtube.com/watch?v=bECw7Xc_8z0; "Muslims Leave France for UAE Dream," *The National*, 29 March 2015; "Le nouvel Eldorado des beurs" (about Qatar), *Envoyé spécial*, 2010, https://www.youtube.com/watch?v=yg4gJl_soLU.

45. Colombi 2016.

46. See chapter 3.

47. Purkayastha 2010.

CONCLUSION

1. Kanna, Le Renard, and Vora 2020.

2. On the moral boundaries of the upper class, see Lamont 1995; Tissot 2011.

Bibliography

Abdulla, A. K. 1984. "Political Dependency: The Case of the United Arab Emirates." PhD diss., Georgetown University.

Abu Lughod, L. 1998. *Remaking Women: Feminism and Modernity in the Middle East.* Princeton, NJ: Princeton University Press.

Acker, J. 2006. "Inequality Regimes: Gender, Class, and Race in Organizations." *Gender & Society* 20, no. 4: 441–64.

Ahmad, A. 2017. *Everyday Conversions: Islam, Domestic Work, and South Asian Migrant Women in Kuwait.* Durham, NC: Duke University Press.

Ahmed, S. 2000. *Strange Encounters: Embodied Others in Post-Coloniality.* London: Routledge.

———. 2004a. "Affective Economies." *Social Text* 22, no. 2: 117–39.

———. 2004b. "Declarations of Whiteness: The Non-Performativity of Anti-Racism." *Borderlands* 3, no. 2.

———. 2010. *The Promise of Happiness.* Durham, NC: Duke University Press.

Ali, S. 2010. *Dubai: Gilded Cage.* New Haven, CT: Yale University Press.

Al-Sayegh, F. 1998. "Merchants' Role in a Changing Society: The Case of Dubai, 1900–90." *Middle Eastern Studies* 34, no.1: 87–102.

AlShehabi, O. 2015. "Histories of Migration to the Gulf." In *Transit States: Labour, Migration and Citizenship in the Gulf,* ed. O. AlShehabi, A. Hanieh, and A. Khalaf, 3–38. London: Pluto Press.

———. 2019. "Policing Labour in Empire: The Modern Origins of the Kafala Sponsorship System in the Gulf Arab States," *British Journal of Middle East Studies,* DOI: 10.1080/13530194.2019.1580183

Al-Shirawi, A. 2005. *Working Papers* (in Arabic). Beirut: Dar Al-Kunuz Al-Adabiyya.

Amar, P. 2011. "Turning the Gendered Politics of the Security State Inside Out?" *International Feminist Journal of Politics* 13, no. 3: 299–328.

Amiraux, V., and P. Simon. 2006. "There Are No Minorities Here: Cultures of Scholarship and Public Debate on Immigrants and Integration in France." *International Journal of Comparative Sociology* 47, nos. 3–4: 191–215.

Arab, C., and N. Moujoud. 2018. "Le stigmate de 'Marocaine' à Dubaï: Les résistances des migrantes à l'épreuve de l'intersectionnalité." *Migrations Société* 173, no. 3: 99–114.

Arieli, D. 2013. "The Task of Being Content: Expatriate Wives in Beijing, Emotional Work and Patriarchal Bargain." *Journal of International Women's Studies* 8, no. 4: 18–31.

Asal, H. 2014. "Islamophobie: La fabrique d'un nouveau concept." *Sociologie* 5, no. 1. http://sociologie.revues.org/2185.

Assaf, L. 2017. "Jeunesses arabes d'Abu Dhabi (Émirats arabes unis): Catégories statutaires, sociabilités urbaines et modes de subjectivation." PhD diss., Université Paris Nanterre.

Avanza, M. 2008. "Comment faire de l'ethnographie quand on n'aime pas 'ses indigènes'? Une enquête au sein d'un mouvement xénophobe." In *Les Politiques de l'enquête, épreuves ethnographiques*, ed. D. Fassin and A. Bensa, 41–58. Paris: La Découverte.

Babar, Z., and A. Gardner. 2016. "Circular Migration and the Gulf States." In *Impact of Circular Migration on Human, Political and Civil Rights: A Global Perspective*, ed. C. Solé, S. Parella, T. Sordé, and S. Nita, 45–62. Switzerland: Springer International.

Bacchetta, P. 2015. "Décoloniser le féminisme: Intersectionnalité, assemblages, co-formations, co-productions." *Les Cahiers du Cedref* 20. http://cedref.revues.org/833.

Beauchemin, C., C. Hamel, and P. Simon, eds. 2016. *Trajectoires et origines: Enquête sur la diversité des populations en France*. Paris: INED.

Beaugé, G., and F. Büttner, 1991. *Les migrations dans le monde arabe*. Paris: CNRS.

Beaugrand, C. 2010. "Politiques de non-intégration dans les monarchies du Golfe." *Transcontinentales: Sociétés, idéologies, système mondial* 8–9. http://transcontinentales.revues.org/793.

Benson, M., and K. O'Reilly 2009. *Lifestyle Migration: Expectations, Aspirations and Experiences*. Farnham: Ashgate.

Benson, M., and N. Osbaldiston. 2014. *Understanding Lifestyle Migrations: Theoretical Approaches to Migration and the Quest for a Better Way of Life*. London: Palgrave Macmillan.

Bentouhami-Molino, H. 2015. *Race, cultures, identités: Une approche féministe et post-coloniale.* Paris: PUF.

Bernard, L. 2016. "Des ascensions sociales par un métier commercial: Le cas des agents immobiliers." *Politix* 29, no. 114: 73–98.

Bessis, S. 2003. *L'Occident et les autres.* Paris: La Découverte.

Bleich, E. 2000. "Antiracism without Races: Politics and Policy in a 'Color-Blind' State." *French Politics, Culture & Society* 18, no. 3: 48–74.

Bonnett, A. 2004. *The Idea of the West: Culture, Politics, and History.* New York: Palgrave Macmillan.

Bonilla-Silva, E. 2014. *Racism without Racists: Color-Blind Racism and the Persistence of Racial Inequality in America.* 4th ed. Lanham, MD: Rowman & Littlefield.

Boukir, K. 2016. "'Les Maghrébins seront Maltais': L'ethnographe à la merci de ses 'origines.'" *Tracés: Revue de sciences humaines* 30: 147–62.

Boussard, V. 2013. *Injonction de mobilité et différenciation de carrière pour les cadres: Le cas de la mobilité géographique.* IRES/CFE-CGC Report.

Brand, M. 2016. "Boxer Bangui: Les femmes libres aux frontières des politiques sexuelles de l'expatriation française en Centrafrique." Thesis in Social Sciences, Université de Paris 8 Vincennes-Saint-Denis.

Bristol-Rhys, J. 2007. "Wedding, Marriage and Money in the United Arab Emirates." *Anthropology of the Middle East* 2, no. 1: 20–36.

———. (2010) 2016. *Emirati Women: Generations of Change.* Reprint, London: Hurst.

Bristol-Rhys, J., and C. Osella. 2016. "Neutralized Bachelors, Infantilized Arabs: Between Migrant and Host Gendered and Sexual Stereotypes in Abu Dhabi." In *Masculinities under Neoliberalism,* ed. A. Cornwall, 111–24. London: Zed Books.

———. 2018. "Contexts of Respectability and Freedom: Sexual Stereotyping in Abu Dhabi." *New Diversities* 20, no. 2: 1–20.

Brochmann, G. 1993. *Middle East Avenue: Female Migration from Sri Lanka to the Gulf.* Boulder: Westview Press.

Bruslé, T. 2015. "Habiter un camp de travailleurs: Appropriation, usages et valeurs du dortoir en milieu contraint." *Annales de géographie* 702, no. 3: 48–74.

Buckley, M. 2015. "Construction Work, 'Bachelor' Builders and the Intersectional Politics of Urbanization in Dubai." In *Transit States: Labour, Migration and Citizenship in the Gulf,* ed. O. AlShehabi, A. Hanieh, and A. Khalaf, 132–50. London: Pluto Press.

Buscatto, M. 2006. "Introduction: Quand la qualification fait débat(s)." *Revue française de sciences sociales* 96: 5–10.

Butler, J. 2002. *La vie psychique du pouvoir: L'assujettissement en théories.* Paris: Léo Scheer.

Camelin, S. 2013. "Des itinéraires dans le temps et dans l'espace: Stratégies de mobilités de femmes arabes diplômées à Abu Dhabi." *Arabian Humanities* 1. http://cy.revues. org/1912

Carvalho Pinto, V. 2012. *Nation-Building, State and the Genderframing of Women's Rights in the United Arab Emirates (1971–2009)*. Reading, UK: Ithaca Press.

Cervulle, M. 2012. "La conscience dominante: Rapports sociaux de race et subjectivation." *Cahiers du genre* 53: 37–54.

———. 2013. *Dans le blanc des yeux: Diversité, racisme et médias*. Paris: Amsterdam.

Clair, I. 2007. "La division genrée de l'expérience amoureuse: Enquête dans des cités d'habitat social." *Sociétés & Représentations* 24: 145–60.

———. 2011. "La découverte de l'ennui conjugal." *Sociétés contemporaines* 83: 59–81.

Cognet, M., and E. Mireille. 2013. "Composer avec le racisme: postures stratégiques de jeunes adultes descendants de migrants." *Migrations Société* 147–48: 221–34.

Coles, A., and A.-M. Fechter. 2012. *Gender and Family among Transnational Professionals*. London: Routledge.

Coles, A., and K. Walsh. 2010. "From "Trucial State" to "Postcolonial" City? The Imaginative Geographies of British Expatriates in Dubai." *Journal of Ethnic and Migration Studies* 36, no. 8: 1317–33.

Colombi, D. 2016. "Les usages de la mondialisation: Mobilité sociale et marchés du travail en France." PhD diss., Sciences Po Paris.

Connell, R. W., and J. Wood. 2005. "Globalization and Business Masculinities." *Men and Masculinities* 7, no. 4: 347–64.

Connell, R. 2014. *Masculinités: enjeux sociaux de l'hégémonie*. Paris: Amsterdam.

———. 2015. "Hégémonie, masculinité, colonialité." *Genre, sexualité & société*, printemps 2015. https://doi.org/10.4000/gss.3429.

Cortéséro, R., S. Kerbourc'h, D. Mélo, and A. Poli. 2013. "Recruteurs sous tensions: Discrimination et diversité au prisme de registres argumentaires enchevêtrés." *Sociologie du travail* 55, no. 4: 432–53.

Cosquer, C. 2018. "Faire nation hors les murs: Dynamiques migratoires, construction du groupe national et blanchité dans l'expatriation française à Abu Dhabi." PhD diss., Sciences Po Paris.

Cousin, B., and S. Chauvin. 2014. "Globalizing Forms of Elite Sociability: Varieties of Cosmopolitanism in Paris Social Clubs." *Ethnic and Racial Studies* 37, no. 12: 2209–25.

Croucher, S. 2012. "Privileged Mobility in an Age of Globality." *Societies* 2: 1–13.

Davidson, C. 2008. *Dubai: The Vulnerability of Success*. New York: Columbia University Press.

Davis, A. 1981. *Women, Race, and Class*. New York: Zed Books.

Davis, M. 2007. *Le stade Dubaï du capitalisme*. Paris: Les Prairies ordinaires.

De Rudder, V., C. Poiret, and F. Vourc'h. 2000. *L'inégalité raciste: L'universalité républicaine à l'épreuve*. Paris: PUF.

Debonneville, J. 2015. "Regards croisés sur les récits de vie des femmes philippines dans l'économie mondialisée du travail domestique: Pour une analyse processuelle des carrières migratoire." *Moussons: Recherche en sciences humaines sur l'Asie du Sud-Est* 26: 93–111.

Dornel, L. 1995. "Les usages du racialisme: Le cas de la main-d'œuvre coloniale en France pendant la Première Guerre mondiale." *Genèses* 20: 48–72.

Dubar, C. 1996. "La sociologie du travail face à la qualification et à la compétence." *Sociologie du travail* 38, no. 2: 179–93.

Du Bois, W. E. B. 1977. *Black Reconstruction in the United States 1860–1880*. New York: Free Press.

Duplan, K. 2016. "Devenir 'expat': Pratiques de l'espace du quotidien de femmes en situation de mobilité internationale à Luxembourg." Thesis in Geography, Université Paris 4. http://www.theses.fr/2016PA040057.

Ehrenreich, B., and A. Hochschild. 2003. *Global Woman: Nannies, Maids, and Sex Workers in the New Economy*. New York: Metropolitan Books.

Elsheshtawy, Y. 2010. *Dubai: Behind an Urban Spectacle*. London: Routledge.

El-Tayeb, F. 2011. *European Others: Queering Ethnicity in Postnational Europe*. Minneapolis: University of Minnesota Press.

Ewers, M. C., and D. Ryan. 2016. "Expatriate Labour Markets in Rapidly Globalising Cities: Reproducing the Migrant Division of Labour in Abu Dhabi and Dubai." *Journal of Ethnic and Migration Studies* 42, no. 15: 1–20.

Fabian, J. (1983) 2006. *Le temps et les autres: Comment l'anthropologie construit son objet*. Toulouse: Anacharsis.

Falquet, J., H. Hirata, D. Kergoat, B. Labari, N. Le Feuvre, and F. Sow, eds. 2010. *Le sexe de la mondialisation: Genre, classe, race et nouvelle division du travail*. Paris: Les Presses de Sciences Po.

Fassin, D., and A. Bensa, eds. 2008. *Les politiques de l'enquête, épreuves ethnographiques*. Paris: La Découverte.

Fassin, D., and E. Fassin, eds. 2006. *De la question sociale à la question raciale?* Paris: La Découverte.

Fassin, D., and S. Mazouz. 2007. "Qu'est-ce que devenir français? La naturalisation comme rite d'institution républicain." *Revue française de sociologie* 48, no. 4.

Fechter, A.-M. 2005. "The "Other" Stares Back: Experiencing Whiteness in Jakarta." *Ethnography* 6, no. 1: 87–103.

———. 2007. *Transnational Lives: Expatriates in Indonesia*. London: Routledge.

———. 2010. "Gender, Empire, Global Capitalism: Colonial and Corporate Expatriate Wives." *Journal of Ethnic and Migration Studies* 36, no. 8: 1279–97.

Fechter, A.-M., and K. Walsh. 2010. "Examining 'Expatriate' Continuities: Postcolonial Approaches to Mobile Professionals." *Journal of Ethnic and Migration Studies* 36, no. 8: 1197–210.

Fernandez, B., and M. de Regt, eds. 2014. *Migrant Domestic Workers in the Middle East: The Home and the World.* New York: Palgrave Macmillan.

Flahault, E. 2009. *Une vie à soi: Nouvelles formes de solitude au féminin.* Rennes: Presses universitaires de Rennes.

Foucault, M. 1994. *Histoire de la sexualité.* Tome 1, *La volonté de savoir.* Paris: Gallimard.

Frankenberg, R. 1993. *White Women, Race Matters: The Social Construction of Whiteness.* Minneapolis: University of Minnesota Press.

Gadéa, C., and C. Marry. 2000. "Les pères qui gagnent: Descendance et réussite professionnelle chez les ingénieurs." *Travail, genre et sociétés* 3: 109–35.

Gamburd, M. C. 2000. *The Kitchen Spoon's Handle: Transnationalism and Sri Lanka's Migrant Housemaids.* Ithaca, NY: Cornell University Press.

Gardner, A. M. 2010. *City of Strangers: Gulf Migration and the Indian Community in Bahrain.* Ithaca, NY: Cornell University Press.

Gavanas, A. 2010. "Privileged Irresponsibility, Structural Responsibility and Moral Contradictions among Employers in the EU Domestic Work Sector." In *Gender Equality, Citizenship and Human Rights: Controversies and Challenges in China and the Nordic Countries,* ed. P. Stoltz and M. Svensson, 116–33. London and New York: Routledge.

Gobe, É. 2013. *Les avocats en Tunisie de la colonisation à la révolution (1883–2011): Sociohistoire d'une profession politique.* Paris: Karthala-IRMC.

Grewal, I. 2005. *Transnational America: Feminisms, Diasporas, Neoliberalisms.* Durham, NC: Duke University Press.

———. 2006. "'Security Moms' in the Early Twentieth-Century United States: The Gender of Security in Neoliberalism." *Women's Studies Quarterly* 34, no. 1–2: 25–39.

Grüntz, L. 2013. "Le galérien, le révolté et le yuppie: Trois trajectoires d'immigrés égyptiens à Abu Dhabi." *EchoGéo* 25. https://echogeo.revues.org/13522.

Guénif-Souilamas, N. 2000. *Des "beurettes" aux descendantes d'immigrants nord-africains.* Paris: Grasset.

———, ed. 2006. *La république mise à nu par son immigration.* Paris: La Fabrique.

Guillaume, C., and S. Pochic. 2007. "La fabrication organisationnelle des dirigeants." *Travail, genre et sociétés* 17: 79–103.

Hajjat, A. 2010. "Port du hijab et 'défaut d'assimilation.'" *Sociologie* 1, no. 4. http://sociologie.revues.org/746?lang=en.

———. 2012. *Les frontières de l'identité nationale: L'injonction à l'assimilation en France métropolitaine et coloniale.* Paris: La Découverte.

Hajjat, A., and M. Mohammed. 2013. *Islamophobie: Comment les élites françaises fabriquent le "problème musulman."* Paris: La Découverte.

Hall, S. 1996. "The West and the Rest: Discourse and Power." In *Modernity: An Introduction to Modern Societies,* ed. S. Hall, D. Held, H. Don, and K. Thompson, 184–226. Oxford: Blackwell.

Hanieh, A. 2011. *Capitalism and Class in the Gulf Arab States.* New York: Palgrave Macmillan.

Haritaworn, J. 2012. *The Biopolitics of Mixing: Thai Multiracialities and Haunted Ascendancies.* Farnham: Ashgate.

Hasso, F. 2010. *Consuming Desires: Family Crisis and the State in the Middle East.* Stanford, CA: Stanford University Press.

Heard-Bey, F. 1982. *From Trucial States to United Arab Emirates: A Society in Transition.* London: Longman.

———. 1997. "The Beginning of the Post-Imperial Era for the Trucial States from World War I to the 1960s." In *Perspectives on the United Arab Emirates,* ed. E. Ghareeb. London: Trident Press.

Hergon, F. 2019. "Sociologie des perquisitions et des assignations à résidence de personnes musulmanes dans le cadre de l'état d'urgence en France (2015–2017)." M2 in Sociology, EHESS.

Hidri, O. 2007. "Le 'chassé-croisé' des apparences sexuées: Stratégie d'insertion professionnelle des cadres commerciaux." *Cahiers du genre* 42: 101–19.

Hill Collins, P. 2000. *Black Feminist Thought: Knowledge, Consciousness, and the Politics of Empowerment.* London: Routledge.

Hochschild, A. R. 1979. "Emotion Work, Feeling Rules, and Social Structure." *American Journal of Sociology* 85, no. 3: 551–75.

Holvin, E. 2010. "Intersections: The Simultaneity of Race, Gender and Class in Organization Studies." *Gender, Work & Organization* 17, no. 3: 248–77.

hooks, b. 1992. *Black Looks.* Boston: South End Press.

Huang, S., and B. Yeoh. "Maids and Ma'ams in Singapore: Constructing Gender and Nationality in the Transnationalization of Paid Domestic Work." *Geography Research Forum* 18: 21–48.

Ibos, C. 2008. "Les 'nounous' africaines et leurs employeurs: Une grammaire du mépris social." *Nouvelles questions féministes* 27, no. 2: 25–38.

Inhorn, M. C. 2015. *Cosmopolitan Conceptions: IVF Sojourns in Global Dubai*. Durham, NC: Duke University Press.

Jack, G., R. Westwood, N. Srinivas, and Z. Sardar. 2011. "Deepening, Broadening and Re-asserting a Postcolonial Interrogative Space in Organization Studies." *Organization* 18, no. 3: 275–302.

Jounin, N. 2008. *Chantier interdit au public: Enquête sur les ouvriers du bâtiment*. Paris: La Découverte.

Kanna, A. 2011. *Dubai, the City as Corporation*. Minneapolis: University of Minnesota Press.

———. 2012. "A Politics of Non-Recognition? Biopolitics of Arab Gulf Worker Protests in the Year of Uprisings." *Interface: A Journal for and about Social Movements* 4, no.1: 146–64.

———. 2014. "'A Group of Like-Minded Lads in Heaven': Everydayness and the Production of Dubai Space." *Journal of Urban Affairs* 36, no. 2: 605–20.

Kanna, A., A. Le Renard, and N. Vora. 2020. *Beyond Exception: New Interpretations of the Arabian Peninsula*. Ithaca, NY: Cornell University Press.

Kebabza, H. 2006. "'L'universel lave-t-il plus blanc?': 'Race,' racisme et système de privilèges." *Les Cahiers du Cedref* 14. Online.

Knowles, C., and H. Douglas. 2009. *Hong Kong Migrant Lives, Landscapes, and Journeys*. Chicago: University of Chicago Press.

Kofman, E., and R. Parvati. 2005. "Gender and Skilled Migrants: Into and Beyond the Work Place." *Geoforum* 36, no. 2: 149–54.

Korpela, M. 2010. "A Postcolonial Imagination? Westerners Searching for Authenticity in India." *Journal of Ethnic and Migration Studies* 36, no. 8: 1299–315.

Kunz, Sarah. 2016. "Privileged Mobilities: Locating the Expatriate in Migration Scholarship." *Geography Compass* 10, no. 3: 89–101.

Lamont, M. 1995. *La morale et l'argent: Les valeurs des cadres en France et aux États-Unis*. Paris: Métailié.

Lan, P.-C. 2011. "White Privilege, Language Capital and Cultural Ghettoisation: Western High-Skilled Migrants in Taiwan." *Journal of Ethnic and Migration Studies* 37, no. 10: 1669–93.

Le Renard, A. 2011. *Femmes et espaces publics en Arabie Saoudite*. Paris: Dalloz.

———. 2013. "La nationalisation des emplois au prisme du genre: Les salariées saoudiennes des banques." *Arabian Humanities* 1. http://cy.revues.org/2023.

———. 2014a. "'On n'est pas formatés comme ça en Occident': Masculinités en compétition, normes de genre et hiérarchies entre nationalités dans une multinationale du Golfe." *Sociétés contemporaines* 94: 41–67.

———. 2014b. "The Politics of 'Unveiling Saudi Women': Between Postcolonial

Fantasies and the Surveillance State." *Jadaliyya*. http://www.jadaliyya.com/pages/index/20259/the-politics-of-unveiling-saudi-women_between-post.

———. 2014c. *A Society of Young Women: Opportunities of Place, Power, and Reform in Saudi Arabia*. Stanford, CA: Stanford University Press.

———. 2019. "Vivre dans une communauté fermée en Arabie Saoudite: Du statut ambivalent des 'épouses occidentales.'" In *Les migrations des nords vers les suds*, dir. A. Poli et al. Paris: Karthala.

Leonard, P. 2010. *Expatriate Identities in Postcolonial Organizations*. Farnham: Ashgate.

Leonard, P., and K. Walsh. 2019. *British Migration: Privilege, Diversity and Vulnerability*. London: Routledge.

Lestra, M., and S. Elyamine. 2018. "'Outsiders' in France, 'Westerners' in the Gulf: Motives for Expatriation in the Professional Trajectory of Second-Generation French Graduates of North African Descent." In *Strategies of Knowledge Transfer for Economic Diversification in the Arab States of the Gulf*, ed. R. Gjedssø Bertelsen, N. Noori, and J.-M. Rickli, 205–26. Berlin: Gerlach Press.

Lieber, M. 2008. *Genre, violences et espaces publics: La vulnérabilité des femmes en question*. Paris: Les Presses de Sciences Po.

Longva, A. Nga. 1997. *Walls Built on Sand: Migration, Exclusion, and Society in Kuwait*. Boulder, CO: Westview Press.

Lori, N. 2011. "National Security and the Management of Migrant Labor: A Case Study of the United Arab Emirates." *Asian and Pacific Migration Journal* 20, no. 3–4: 315–37.

Louer, L. 2012. "Les enjeux des réformes des politiques de l'emploi dans les monarchies du Golfe." *Les Études du CERI*, 185. http://www.sciencespo.fr/ceri/sites/sciencespo.fr.ceri/files/Etude185.pdf.

Lundström, C. 2010. "White Ethnography: (Un)comfortable Conveniences and Shared Privileges in Field-Work with Swedish Migrant Women." *NORA—Nordic Journal of Feminist and Gender Research* 18, no. 2: 70–87.

———. 2013. "'Mistresses' and 'Maids' in Transnational 'Contact Zones': Expatriate Wives and the Intersection of Difference and Intimacy in Swedish Domestic Spaces in Singapore." *Women's Studies International Forum* 36: 44–53.

———. 2014. *White Migrations: Gender, Whiteness and Privilege in Transnational Migration*. Basingstoke, UK: Palgrave Macmillan.

Mahdavi, P. 2011. *Gridlock: Labor, Migration and Human Trafficking in Dubai*. Stanford, CA: Stanford University Press.

———. 2016. *Crossing the Gulf: Love and Family in Migrant Lives*. Stanford, CA: Stanford University Press.

Mai, N., and R. King. 2009. "Love, Sexuality and Migration: Mapping the Issue(s)." *Mobilities* 4, no. 3: 295–307.

Manalansan, M. F. 2006. "Queer Intersections: Sexuality and Gender in Migration Studies." *International Migration Review* 40, no. 1: 224–49.

Mazouz, S. 2017. *La république et ses autres: Politiques de l'altérité dans la France des années 2000.* Lyon: Éditions de l'ENS.

McDowell, L. 1995. "Body Work: Heterosexual Gender Performances in City Workplaces." In *Mapping Desire: Geographies of Sexualities*, ed. D. Bell and V. Gill, 75–95. London: Routledge.

McWhorter, L. 2005. "Where Do White People Come From? A Foucaultian Critique of Whiteness Studies." *Philosophy & Social Criticism* 31, no. 5–6: 533–56.

Melamed, J. 2011. *Represent and Destroy: Rationalizing Violence in the New Racial Capitalism.* Minneapolis: University of Minnesota Press.

Memmi, D. 2008. "Mai 68 ou la crise de la domination rapprochée." In *Mai-juin 68*, ed. D. Damamme, B. Gobille, F. Matonti, and B. Pudal, 35–48. Paris: L'Atelier.

Meuret-Campfort, E. 2017. "Il n'est jamais trop tard pour devenir employeur: Les particuliers employeurs âgés et leurs assistantes de vie." *Genèses* 106: 50–71.

Meurs, D., and A. Pailhé. 2008. "Descendantes d'immigrés en France: Une double vulnérabilité sur le marché du travail?" *Travail, genre et sociétés* 20: 87–107.

Mignolo, W. 2001. "Géopolitique de la connaissance, colonialité du pouvoir et différence coloniale." *Multitudes* 6: 56–71.

———. (2000) 2012. *Local Histories/Global Designs: Coloniality, Subaltern Knowledges, and Border Thinking.* Princeton, NJ: Princeton University Press.

Mitchell, T. 2002. *Rule of Experts: Egypt, Techno-Politics, Modernity.* Berkeley: University of California Press.

Moghadam, A. 2013. "De l'Iran imaginé aux nouveaux foyers de l'Iran: Pratiques et espaces transnationaux des Iraniens à Dubaï." *Arabian Humanities* 2. http://cy.revues.org/2556.

Mohanty, C. T. 1984. "Under Western Eyes: Feminist Scholarship and Colonial Discourses." *Boundary* 2: 333–58.

Montigny, A. 2002. "L'Afrique oubliée des noirs du Qatar." *Journal des africanistes* 72, no. 2: 213–25.

Moujoud, N. 2012. "Métiers domestiques, voile et féminisme: Nouveaux objets, nouvelles ruptures." *Hommes & migrations* 1300: 84–94.

Munif, A. R. (1984) 2013. *Villes de sel: L'errance.* Paris: Actes Sud-Sindbad.

Nagy, S. 1998. "'This Time I Think I'll Try a Filipina': Global and Local Influences on Relations between Foreign Household Workers and Their Employers in Doha, Qatar." *City & Society* 10: 83–103.

Nakano Glenn, E. 1992. "From Servitude to Service Work: Historical Continuities in the Racial Division of Paid Reproductive Labor." *Signs* 18, no. 1: 1–43.

Naudet, J. 2012. *Entrer dans l'élite: Parcours de réussite en France, aux États-Unis et en Inde*. Paris: PUF.

Ndiaye, P. 2009. *La condition noire: Essai sur une minorité française*. Paris: Folio.

Ngai, P. 2005. *Made in China: Women Factory Workers in a Global Workplace*. Durham, NC: Duke University Press.

Ong, A. 1999. *Flexible Citizenship: The Cultural Logics of Transnationality*. Durham, NC: Duke University Press.

———. 2007. *Neoliberalism as Exception: Mutations in Citizenship and Sovereignty*. Durham, NC: Duke University Press.

Onley, J. 2007. *The Arabian Frontier of the British Raj: Merchants, Rulers, and the British in the Nineteenth Century Gulf*. Oxford: Oxford University Press.

Pagès-El Karoui, D. 2016. "Égyptiens expatriés aux Émirats arabes unis: Ancrages, connexions transnationales et expériences cosmopolites." *Arabian Humanities* 7. Online.

Parreñas, R. S. 2001. *Servants of Globalization: Women, Migration and Domestic Work*. Stanford, CA: Stanford University Press.

Patterson, T. C. 1997. *Inventing Western Civilization*. New York: Monthly Review Press.

Paul, A. M. 2017. *Multinational Maids: Stepwise Migration in a Global Labor Market*. Cambridge: Cambridge University Press.

Percot, M. 2006. "Indian Nurses in the Gulf: Two Generations of Female Migration." *South Asia Research* 26, no. 1: 41–62.

Pinçon, M., and Pinçon-Charlot, M. 2007. *Sociologie de la bourgeoisie*. Paris: La Découverte.

Pitti, L. 2005. "Catégorisations ethniques au travail: Un instrument de gestion différenciée de la main-d'œuvre." *Histoire & Mesure* 20, no. 3–4: 69–101.

Pochic, S. 2005. "Faire carrière: L'apport d'une approche en termes de genre." *Formation emploi* 91: 75–93.

Pratt, G., and Rosner, V. 2006. "Introduction: The Global and the Intimate." *Women's Studies Quarterly* 34, no. 1–2: 13–24.

Pratt, M. L. (1992) 2008. *Imperial Eyes: Travel Writing and Transculturation*. Milton Park, UK: Routledge.

Puar, J. K. 2007. *Terrorist Assemblages: Homonationalism in Queer Times*. Durham, NC: Duke University Press.

Purkayastha, B. 2010. "Interrogating Intersectionality: Contemporary Globalisation and Racialised Gendering in the Lives of Highly Educated South Asian Americans and Their Children." *Journal of Intercultural Studies* 31, no. 1: 29–47.

Quashie, H. 2016. "Débuter sa carrière professionnelle en Afrique: L'idéal d'insertion sociale des volontaires français à Dakar et Antananarivo (Sénégal, Madagascar)." *Cahiers d'études africaines* 221, no. 1: 53–80.

Quijano, A. 2007. "'Race' et colonialité du pouvoir." *Mouvements* 51: 111–18.

Roediger, D. 1991. *The Wages of Whiteness: Race and the Making of the American Working Class*. London and New York: Verso Books.

Roediger, D., and E. D. Esch. 2012. *The Production of Difference: Race and the Management of Labor in U.S. History*. New York: Oxford University Press.

Rollins, J. 1987. *Between Women: Domestics and Their Employers*. Philadelphia: Temple University Press.

Roth, W. D. 2012. *Race Migrations: Latinos and the Cultural Transformation of Race*. Stanford, CA: Stanford University Press.

Sabban, Rima. 2004. "Women Migrant Domestic Workers in the United Arab Emirates." In *Gender and Migration in Arab States: The Case of Domestic Workers*, ed. S. Esim and B. Smith, 85–107. Beirut: ILO Regional Office for Arab States.

Safi, M., and P. Simon. 2013. "Les discriminations ethniques et raciales dans l'enquête *Trajectoires et Origines*: Représentations, expériences subjectives et situations vécues." *Économie et statistiques* 464–66: 245–75.

Said, E. W. 2003 [1978]. *L'Orientalisme: L'Orient créé par l'Occident*. Paris: Seuil.

———. 2000. *Culture et impérialisme*. Paris: Fayard.

Said Zahlan, R. 1978. *The Origins of the United Arab Emirates: A Political and Social History of the Trucial States*. New York: Macmillan.

Sanna, M. E., and E. Varikas. 2011. "Genre, modernité et 'colonialité' du pouvoir: Penser ensemble des subalternités dissonantes." *Cahiers du genre* 50: 5–15.

Santelli, E. 2001. *La mobilité sociale dans l'immigration: Itinéraires de réussite des enfants de provenance algérienne*. Toulouse: Presses universitaires du Mirail.

Sassen, S. 1998. *Globalization and Its Discontents: Essays on the New Mobility of People and Money*. New York: New Press.

Sayad, A. 1993. "Naturels et naturalisés." *Actes de la recherche en sciences sociales* 99: 26–35.

———. 1999. *La double absence: Des illusions de l'émigré aux souffrances de l'immigré*. Paris: Seuil.

Seccombe, I. J. 1983. "Labour Migration to the Arabian Gulf: Evolution and Characteristics 1920–1950." *Bulletin: British Society for Middle Eastern Studies* 10, no. 1: 3–20.

Seccombe, I. J., and R. I. Lawless. 1986. "Foreign Worker Dependence in the Gulf, and the International Oil Companies: 1910–50." *International Migration Review* 20, no. 3: 548–74.

Shah, N. M. 2004. "Gender and Labour Migration to the Gulf Countries." *Feminist Review* 77: 183–85.

Simon, P. 2014. "La question des statistiques ethniques en France." In *Migrations et mutations de la société française: L'état des savoirs*, ed. M. Poinsot and S. Weber, 297–306. Paris: La Découverte.

Skeggs, B. 2009. "The Moral Economy of Person Production: The Class Relations of Self-Performance on 'Reality' Television." *Sociological Review* 57, no. 4: 626–44.

Smith, B. 2010. "Scared by, of, in, and for Dubai." *Social & Cultural Geography* 11, no. 3: 263–83.

Stoler, A. L. 2002. *Carnal Knowledge and Imperial Power: Race and the Intimate in Colonial Rule*. Berkeley: University of California Press.

Tabet, P. 2005. *La grande arnaque: Sexualité des femmes et échange économico-sexuel*. Paris: L'Harmattan.

Thiollet, H. 2016. "Gérer les migrations, gérer les migrants: Une perspective historique et transnationale sur les migrations dans les monarchies du Golfe." *Arabian Humanities* 7. Online.

Tissot, S. 2011. *De bons voisins: Enquête dans un quartier de la bourgeoisie progressiste*. Paris: Raisons d'agir.

Vest, J. L. 2013. "What Doesn't Kill You: Existential Luck, Postracial Racism, and the Subtle and Not So Subtle Ways the Academy Keeps Women of Color Out." *Seattle Journal for Social Justice* 12, no. 2. http://digitalcommons.law.seattleu. edu/sjsj/vol12/iss2/7.

Vitalis, R. 2007. *America's Kingdom: Mythmaking on the Saudi Oil Frontier*. Stanford, CA: Stanford University Press.

Vora, N. 2012. "Free Speech and Civil Discourse: Producing Expats, Locals, and Migrants in the UAE English-Language Blogosphere." *Journal of the Royal Anthropological Institute* 18, no. 4: 787–807.

———. 2013. *Impossible Citizens: Dubai's Indian Diaspora*. Durham, NC: Duke University Press.

———. 2014. "Expat/Expert Camps: Redefining 'Labour' within Gulf Migration." In *Transit States: Labour, Migration and Citizenship in the Gulf*, ed. O. AlShehabi, A. Hanieh, and A. Khalaf, 170–97. New York: Pluto Press.

———. 2015. "Is the University Universal? Mobile (Re) Constitutions of American Academia in the Gulf Arab States." *Anthropology & Education Quarterly* 46, no. 1: 19–36.

———. 2018. *Teach for Arabia: American Universities, Liberalism, and Transnational Qatar*. Stanford, CA: Stanford University Press.

Vora, N., and N. Koch. 2015. "Everyday Inclusions: Rethinking Ethnocracy, Kafala, and Belonging in the Arabian Peninsula." *Studies in Ethnicity and Nationalism* 15, no. 3: 540–52.

Wagner, A.-C. 1998. *Les nouvelles élites de la mondialisation.* Paris: PUF.

———. 2007. *Les classes sociales dans la mondialisation.* Paris: La Découverte.

Walsh, K. 2006. "'Dad Says I'm Tied to a Shooting Star!' Grounding (Research on) British Expatriate Belonging." *Area* 38, no. 3: 268–78.

———. 2007. "'It Got Very Debauched, Very Dubai!' Heterosexual Intimacy amongst Single British Expatriates." *Social & Cultural Geography* 8, no. 4: 507–33.

———. 2009. "Geographies of the Heart in Transnational Spaces: Love and the Intimate Lives of British Migrants in Dubai." *Mobilities* 4, no. 3: 427–45.

———. 2011. "Migrant Masculinities and Domestic Space: British Home-Making Practices in Dubai." *Transactions of the Institute of British Geographers* 36, no. 4: 516–29.

———. 2012. "Travelling Together? Work, Intimacy, and Home amongst British Expatriate Couples in Dubai." In *Gender and Family among Transnational Professionals,* ed. A. Coles and A.-M. Fechter, 63–84. London: Routledge.

Walsh, K., H. H. Shen, and K. Willis. 2008. "Heterosexuality and Migration in Asia." *Gender, Place and Culture* 15, no. 6: 575–79.

Williams, F., C. Tobío, and A. Gavanas. 2009. "Migration et garde des enfants à domicile en Europe: Questions de citoyenneté." *Cahiers du genre* 46: 47–76.

Wilson, Ara. 2012. "Intimacy: A Useful Category of Transnational Analysis." In *The Global and the Intimate: Feminism in Our Time,* ed. G. Pratt and V. Rosner, 31–56. New York: Columbia University Press.

Yeoh, B. S. A., S. Huang, and K. Willis. 2000. "Global Cities, Transnational Flows and Gender Dimensions: The View from Singapore." *Tijdschrift voor Economische en Sociale Geografie* 91, no. 2: 147–58.

Yeoh, B. S. A., and L.-M. Khoo. 1998. "Home, Work and Community: Skilled International Migration and Expatriate Women in Singapore." *International Migration* 36, no. 2: 159–86.

Yeoh, B. S. A., and K. Willis. 2005. "Singaporean and British Transmigrants in China and the Cultural Politics of 'Contact Zones.'" *Journal of Ethnic and Migration Studies* 31, no. 2: 269–85.

Index

ableism, 75
Acker, Joan, 9, 212n31, 216n2
advertising, 75–77
Ahmad, Attiya, 100, 105, 212n28, 218n23, 219n1
Ahmed, Sara, 4, 183, 211n10, 211n21, 212n42, 219n25, 220n30, 220n15, 221nn27–28
affects: emotional labor, 71–95, 111–13; happiness, 35–38, 88–89, 183–92, 195, 200–203, 215n53; intimacy, 11; love, 151–59
age, 16–19, 75, 145–48
American (US), 12, 15, 42, 62, 84, 89–93
Arab nationalism, 28–29
Arabs (racialization of), 54–55, 62, 158, 172, 176
Arabic language (as a skill), 69, 82
Arieli, Daniela, 98, 112, 126, 218n8, 218n36, 219n19
authenticity, 148–60, 175, 179, 182. *See also* consumerism, exoticism, materialism

beauty norms, 89–93
Bessis, Sophie, 3
biopolitics, 96–106
Blackness, 85, 162, 190
bodily labor, 71–95
Bonilla-Silva, Eduardo, 53, 216n8
Brand, Magdalena, 151, 213n69, 218n12
branding, 75–77, 94–95, 137, 139–40
Bristol-Rhys, Jane, 181, 191, 213n72, 218n15, 218n20, 218n32, 221n23, 222n34

careers: and race, 58–61, 65–70, 193–200; and gender, 60–61, 90, 96–120. *See also* discrimination, skills
children, 96–138
class socialization, 16–19, 71–79, 126, 142–43, 183–92
colonial history of Dubai, 4–6, 25–35
coloniality of knowledge, 5, 26, 30–35. *See also* skills
color-blind racism, 15, 53
conjugality, 96–120

❋ WORLDING THE MIDDLE EAST

Emily Gottreich and Daniel Zoughbie, editors
Center for Middle East Studies, University of California, Berkeley

This series investigates the "worlding" of the Middle East and the ever-changing, ever-becoming dynamism of the region. It seeks to capture the ways in which the region is reimagined and unmade through flows of world capital, power, and ideas. Spanning the modern period to the present, Worlding the Middle East showcases critical and innovative books that develop new ways of thinking about the region and the wider world.

CPSIA information can be obtained
at www.ICGtesting.com
Printed in the USA
JSHW040552090921
18532JS00004B/5